SWIRLY WORLD

By the same author
Take the Chocolates and Run
Salt Rhythms
Serious Latitudes

SWIRLY WORLD

The Solo Voyages

Andrew Fagan

HarperCollins*Publishers (New Zealand) Limited*

To Seth and Fabian, with thanks to my mother Irene,
without whom this manuscript would still be under the bed.

National Library of New Zealand Cataloguing-in-Publication Data

Fagan, Andrew, 1962-
Swirly World : the solo voyages / Andrew Fagan.
ISBN: 1-86950-402-X (pbk.)
1. Fagan, Andrew, 1962- Journeys. 2. Sailing, Single-handed.
I. Title.
910.9164-dc 21

First published 2001
HarperCollins*Publishers (New Zealand) Limited*
P.O. Box 1, Auckland

Copyright © Andrew Fagan 2001
Andrew Fagan asserts the moral right to be identified as the author of this work.

ISBN 1 86950 402 X

Set in Stempel Schneidler
Designed and typeset by Janine Brougham
Printed by Griffin Press, Australia on 79 gsm Bulky Paperback

The Estuary

The wind has died, no motion now
In the summer's sleepy breath. Silver the sea-grass,
The shells and the driftwood, fixed in the moon's vast crystal.
Think: long after, when the walls of the small house
Have collapsed upon us, each alone,
Far gone the earth's invasion
The slow earth bedding and filling the bone,
This water will still be crawling the estuary,
Fingering its way among the channels, licking the stones;
And floating shells, minute argosies under the giant moon,
Still shorewood glide among the mangroves on the creeping tide.
The noise of gulls comes through the shining darkness
    over the dunes and the sea.
Now the clouded moon is warm in her nest of light.
The world's a shell where distant waves are murmuring
    of a time beyond this time.
Give me the ghost of your hand:
Unreal, unreal the dunes, the sea, the mangroves,
And the moon's white light, unreal, beneath our naked feet,
    the sand.

A.R.D. Fairburn

Contents

	Prologue	9
1	The darkness beyond Devonport	14
2	*Swirly World in Perpetuity*	19
3	On the Old World roads	36
4	Message in a plastic bag	58
5	The wind, the moon and light rain	67
6	Where steeples spike the sky	75
7	King Roadie . . .	79
8	My view of the universe	86
9	Back to the sandbank	89
10	West out of Wellington	95
11	Sailing with a seawolf	115
12	Would anyone be looking?	128
13	Two hours and sponging	148
14	Bleary and belligerent	159
15	Warm beer at dawn	166
16	Evacuation by stool	171
17	The Trance Fluid tour	179
18	Three hours there, how many back?	185
	Glossary of sailor-type terms	204

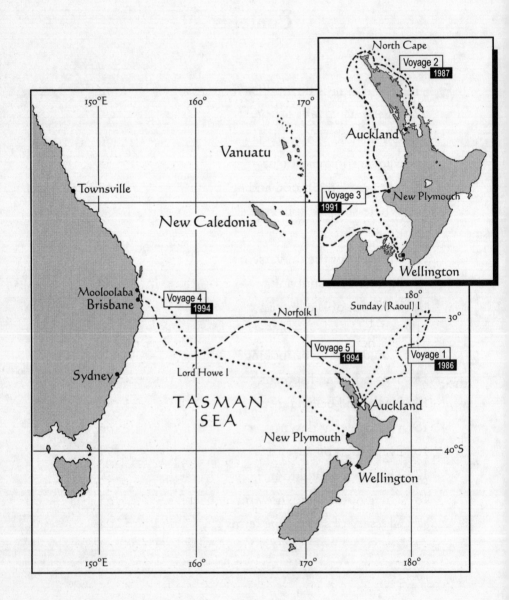

150°E 160° 170°

Vanuatu

• Townsville

New Caledonia

North Cape
Voyage 2
1987

Auckland

Voyage 3   • New Plymouth
1991

Wellington

Mooloolaba   Voyage 4   • Norfolk I   Sunday (Raoul) I   180°   30°
Brisbane   1994

Voyage 5   Voyage 1
1994   1986

• Sydney   Lord Howe I

TASMAN   • Auckland
SEA

New Plymouth

40°S

Wellington

150°E   160°   170°   180°

Prologue

To a certain degree, ignorance was bliss. No knowledge of repeated gale warnings and ominous swell height prophecies . . . but something was coming, and that something had to do with the wind. The swell setting in from the southwest was disturbingly long and large. The 10 knots of west-northwesterly couldn't incite that much motion.

Away east over the curve of the earth, the same light breeze was keeping tree leaves active outside Taranaki bedroom windows. A moonless night, the security of land, the wind a background player. I slept lightly. The wind, my master, was going to be bringing me something in the morning. An experience. An introductory offer to the Roaring Forties . . . a chance to readjust the value system. It was voluntary exile, nowhere in particular, with the barometer steadily plunging. Would I be in for something dangerous, with an audience of sea-ancestors keeping score of where I went wrong, and how often, before finally making their acquaintance? Social disassociation — no land or loved ones, no stimulus or distractions. Only an empty horizon with plenty of salt water, sky and solitary clouds for company . . . alone.

I had conspired for years to get there. Where? Nowhere in particular. Just out there, where the maps indicated no signposts. What was so compelling? It was more what wasn't. There were too many of us. Humans. A plague of them on planet earth, everyone looking for a sense of purpose. I found the obvious solutions — competition, peer groups, procreation, the usual mediums of amusement — all a bit dull really. Maybe I lacked the right vitamins.

I'd put in the years dutifully absorbing the rules and perspectives common to western capitalist education. The economics of staying alive — the economy of competition and hopefully 'satisfaction'. Alternative choices? Pass the exams and get to the starting gate of adult life only to discover the options all look a bit serious . . . proper job dedicated to long-term hours in one place with the prospect of gradual career advancement and pension scheme . . . Repetitive finite experiences week after month after year. All those familiar and often grim faces I'd watched getting older on the Wellington trolley buses had made it clear . . . mortality reality. How best to approach it? Existence as a collection of experiences would do for a start.

I moved to Auckland to live in the back of a blue Bedford truck. No rent or rule book, started collecting experiences . . . To avoid being confined to motor camps, discretion in parking became mandatory. Life on the move — by night sleeping outside suburban hedges, by day growing an affinity for no-man's-land-like public car parks, graveyards, deserted beaches and dead-end roads. When parked with a sea view it became obvious I had to get out there and live on that blue liquid. It looked more autonomous.

The edges of Auckland, with its multiple mud flats, are ideal for shoal-craft living. Many an undetected corner lay waiting to pass the moments between accumulating experiences as a singer/songwriter in a fledgling pop band, the Mockers.

Moving around the country singing songs was similar to joining a travelling circus. You get to see the land, know the towns . . . round and round, moulding frequencies into music to inspire an emotional response. Playing to people enjoying themselves is always encouraging, especially if your own songs are responsible. At the time it was something to look forward to.

I wanted to make a record . . . the vinyl, revolving kind. The songwriters I admired had all toiled in their own minds for years and even lifetimes with little or no acknowledgement. A lack of acceptance was almost a prerequisite for writing emotionally potent songs. At least that was what I told myself while boiling potatoes on my two-burner gas Primus perched on top of band gear that smelt of stale beer, in the back of the Bedford most evenings.

Fortunately it wasn't long before I found a cheap old twin-keeled yacht in a milkman's shed in Kawakawa Bay, southeast of Auckland. 'Here she is, been in here for years, needs a bit of work . . . I haven't had the time . . .' I'd read all the books about solitary boat living on the high seas. Eager I was. Nineteen hundred New Zealand dollars later, it was all mine. All the work and a boat too — *The Prince of Innocence.* The fact I was indisputably at the downmarket end of the yachting spectrum didn't deter me — only authentic enthusiasts live on 18-footers.

Now that I had accommodation to float I felt on the threshold of other worldly adventures. Extremely keen to 'get out there, not sure where . . .' Saline solitary confinement.

Emotional log jams needed dealing to. Fear. A little bit negative. Alone on an ocean drowning. The enormity of non-existence as we know it. Worst case scenario. The biggy. Other ones, like sailing alone in the dark, initially took a bit of getting used to. Easy on the harbour with the help of eternally glowing electric Auckland city, but out round the back of Rangitoto I discovered my sweaty trepidation one night, moving through absolute darkness without a chart to identify safe bays and unsafe rocks, or a decent anchor and warp to stop. For peace of mind it paid to get all the bits that cost the money. Preparation, they call it.

The band gigs were going OK. Sweaty people started dancing to songs they often didn't know. We were doing our best, hoping people would pay attention, gathering together to be collectively known as our audience.

Between shows the musicians were behaving like teenagers on a school trip who'd done away with the authority figures. 'Five dollars a day. We can't afford to stay in motels on this tour . . . it's a ground-breaker.'

With only five dollars in your pocket, food wasn't always the highest priority. Steve Thorpe certainly didn't think so. He was the drummer, originally from Kingston Upon Thames, England. He'd teamed up with two other displaced English immigrant children, Geoff and Neil Hayden (bass and lights).

Down the road from the Caroline Bay motor camp was a wine shop doing flagons of sickly sweet sherry for five dollars. It was agreed. Gordon the keyboard player was having none of it and sat down in the takeaway shop to a delicious-looking burgery thing. I tried not to notice. Steve was hungry too. He made do with a squirt of tomato ketchup fired impressively from the distant container down the back of his throat. Two sachets of free sugar followed, chewed then swallowed, as we looked on, impressed . . . Steve had more important things to do with his money. 'Getting out of it' was something the musicians seemed to have in common.

Our songs started getting played on the radio and our popularity increased. Our musical existence seemed legitimately acknowledged and having an audience that knew the odd song was a novelty.

Income rated poorly. Enough dollars to pump petrol into the truck and get about, but back in Auckland the debts kept accumulating. Amplifiers, lights and sound specialists all cost money, money we weren't really earning. We did our best to ignore it.

Returning after each high profile-low profit tour, the routine was always the same. Unload the black boxes responsible for all the noise; deposit jaded musicians at their various lodgings; clear out the false floor of empty drink cans, mouldy takeaway wrappers, chocolate bar papers, newspapers with torn-out live reviews or ads, and the odd stray item of dirty, forgotten clothing. Cox's Bay or Little Shoal Bay, there it is again, tame mud-flat lands. Waiting for low tide and the barefoot walk back out to the stale scent of damp neglect and life confined to a tiny cabin — kerosene lighting, clothes and books in plastic bags, a hard narrow berth and sleep (or lack of) dictated by the wind and waves. I asked for it.

For a while the bachelor diet was mundane. A part-time job cleaning a plastics factory and a glorious weekly fifteen dollars restricted me to dull bread, sausages, potatoes and honey. I was eventually dismissed, confusion over my spasmodic availability. Or perhaps it was true — I lacked an eye for cleanliness. Not the best in a cleaner.

For many months on the mud flats wisdom teeth figured highly. Two needed to leave my mouth but the band was playing too often to allow the necessary recuperation time. To cope with their growing pains I resorted to little white painkilling pills every few hours for more months than the packet advised. It was unhealthy living, but I felt alive.

After gigs in Auckland I'd return to the sea in the dark hours and often face a high-tide line that required a dinghy ride out to the house. Most times the dinghy floated inaccessibly behind the boat and I would be forced to remove garments and walk out to sobering neck-deep extremes before clambering up, bedraggled and shivery to unlock the hatch. That was the downside of boat living, but the cold wet wade after a night of showing off was still uncomfortable fun. Little Shoal Bay in a southwesterly, lee shore — should I haul up sails and beat for an hour up harbour to the flat calm shelter of Cox's Bay? Depends if you can be bothered . . .

To travel offshore with others for a start made sense, but with the Mockers' frequent band engagements I couldn't fit into anyone else's schedule. Also, I didn't know or hang out with yachties. I hung out with late-night lifestylers. Fizzy grog-swilling, chemical-imbibing social mutineers intent on a nonstop good time as they careered towards oblivion. Something like that. Not me of course — I just drove the van. A team dedicated to the pursuit of pleasure without consequence. 'In The Company of Bored Young Men.'

The scale of tours and expenses increased but profits remained sparse. Now and then a little more pocket money came my way and instantly turned into some nautical life-saving or navigational device. As the seasons went by my list of 'peace of mind' pieces slowly shrank. The wind and sea waited patiently for me.

Chapter 1

The darkness beyond Devonport

The darkness beyond Devonport

I balanced awkwardly on one leg, levering off my sweaty suede boot. They always seemed sweaty, probably because I didn't wear socks. That night they were extra sticky after conducting an evening's entertainment at a nondescript drinking den in one of Auckland's far-flung suburbs.

As I tiptoed across the mud flats, puddles of salt water provided my much-needed footbath. The tide was slowly creeping in, and across the moonlit bay I could see *The Prince of Innocence* lying on her side in the mud. Unfortunately this often happened in Cox's Bay — one of the bilge keels sinking into the mud, leaving me with an uncomfortable few hours until the tide came back in.

Before retiring for the night I perched in the companionway and looked at my surroundings. Silence, except for the subdued gurgling of the incoming tide crawling over thousands of tiny crab holes. It was going to be a clear, cold, Auckland autumn night. The electric lights of water-view windows were all turned off but the stars shone especially bright. The dark skyline silhouette of sleeping Auckland . . .

The dim outlines of boats and shoreline had grown familiar to me over the eighteen months I had lived aboard the 5.6 m *Prince* in both Cox's and Little Shoal Bay. Too familiar. It was, after all, my garden, and the place was endearing, but it also fostered an urge to venture further afield. Keep having a look, see what's out there, this isn't enough, there must be more . . .

Compounding it was a new outline nestled under the trees on

the northern side of the bay. It was a 30-ft junk-rigged bilge keeler that had recently returned from a four-year trip to Canada and the Pacific Islands. From here to there and back again.

Now the boat sat safe on the mud, so far removed from the perils and places it had visited, it was difficult to imagine those oceans being linked to the thin layer of liquid silently crawling up the keels beneath me. Everyone assured me it was.

I awoke around 4 a.m. to the sound of wavelets slapping against the hull. *The Prince of Innocence* was floating upright and pointing into a light westerly breeze coming across the harbour from Te Atatu. I couldn't sleep. My father was dying. Back in Wellington the bad headaches had turned into a brain tumour taking him away to another dimension. The prescribed steroids certainly were . . . but he was still Dad, dying. I dressed for the pre-dawn chill, mouldy PVC yellow wet-weather smock keeping the wind out. Up came the flapping old sailcloth, anchor chain hauled taut and away we fell onto port tack, hard on the wind to clear the southern cliffs of Herne Bay. Destination — the distant shores of exotic Little Shoal Bay (about 2 miles across the harbour). Plying between the bays was a regular thing. Epic endurance — 3-mile odysseys. Huge breaking seas off Fisherman's Wharf. Not.

As Auckland slept that morning, I reached across the harbour with a 10-knot westerly filling out *The Prince of Innocence*'s badly stretched sails. Being a three-keeled keeler with about a 2ft 6in draught, she always went sideways when sailing against the wind, which worked well for developing patience and resolve . . . Sticking it out because you have to. No other choice . . . keep the boat moving . . . don't let the tide get the better of you . . . As I sailed past Watchman's Island off Herne Bay, I peered down, under the boom and the Auckland Harbour Bridge, at the darkness beyond Devonport. There was the gate to sensations the word *adventure* couldn't do justice to. It was a bit disconcerting.

I'd never sailed in the real dark. I had quite a lot to experience, quite a bit to get used to, and hopefully, get over. All I could do was wait and prepare for the day when circumstances would allow me a chance to see if I really wanted to be 'out there alone . . . long way from home.'

I bought a pile of new chain to attach myself to the bottom of some insecure coastline I might encounter, if I ever succeeded in sailing beyond Waiheke Island. Instrumentally there was an afternoon spent up to my neck (and frequently over my head) in the polluted waters of Cox's Bay, struggling to halt *The Prince*'s desire to impale herself on the rocks. A mean westerly winter gale swept the harbour. The puny anchor wouldn't bite. Another learning curve.

I found a second-hand self-steering wind vane. It was a QME design (wind acting on a vane to pull ropes attached to the tiller). This would optimistically be my crew and relieve me of constant hand steering. I'd read all the books. Looked at a lot of pictures. A wind vane self-steering system was up there in priority land. I'd never contemplated extended sailing with anyone other than myself. It never occurred to me to go with others. In my years of centreboard sailing I found gratification feeling a boat working over the waves. The agile balancing act that was second nature to centreboard sailors never failed to enthral me. The solo-voyaging books all pointed to a more potent experience beyond the company of others. I'd have to find out.

In between expeditions about the land singing songs and showing off, I slowly acquired more of those bits and pieces I'd read about. I also debated whether or not *The Prince of Innocence* was up to carrying me out of sight of land. Fortunately, a better alternative revealed itself in the form of *Mylene B*. I thought I had a suitable ocean travelling craft — the same design had circumnavigated the planet.

During this period I was presented with a copy of *South Sea Vagabonds* by Johnny Wray, the true tale of how Wray built his boat during the depression in Auckland in the 1930s and then voyaged about the Pacific and Tasman. He didn't sing, he sailed. It's one of the legendary sailing books and was out of print for years.

On one of my trainee epic voyages to Waiheke (as exotic a name to a Wellingtonian as Tahiti or Waikiki) I was trapped for a few days as a strong southwesterly airflow ravaged the North Island. I'd sailed the boat down to the island, happy to broad reach past Auckland at arm's length on the windy harbour. Three hours and 15 miles later we were there, past Park Point with the promise of a nasty beat back home to the inner harbour if we dared to return too soon.

I wandered around the Putiki Bay foreshore and ended up inspecting an old neglected, very home-built-looking motorsailer. It was moored to a vintage tidal wharf at the bottom of an overgrown section of bush, which extended up the steep hillside to a ridge road. I discovered it was one of Johnny Wray's old boats. He lived there and was then in his seventies. That boat leaning against the wharf was another source of agitation to my adventure glands.

It was his second boat, *Waihape*, which I was told had been rolled over in a cyclone somewhere up above New Zealand. The real thing. Cyclone survivor; upside down then back again, probably someone clinging on, this bit of hull here . . . But there it was — sitting in the mud, a part of the past, paintwork fading fast. Inside a porthole I could see a framed picture of what it looked like when it was first launched.

Amongst the trees was a dilapidated green shed, inside was another half-finished boat Wray hadn't completed building. Old rusted hauling gear, discarded rigging, rotting rudders — everything at the bottom of that overgrown section was the product of years of thought and enterprise. It was all a bit depressing.

I had been told that Wray lived alone in his bach on the bush section, since his wife died some years ago. The time transition took some getting used to. I expected him to be the same man I had come to know through his writing, popping down out of the bush preoccupied with his latest expedition. Not any more. The only constant was the southwesterly wind chasing the clouds above out into the empty Pacific Ocean to the northeast. Nothing out there but the cloud-strewn sky and wind-world waves. A timeless vacuum waiting for me . . . eventually.

That afternoon I walked up and down the ridge pretending to survey the state of the wave-torn bay while I debated whether to go and talk to Wray. He's old and living alone and he'd appreciate someone dropping by to say how much they enjoyed the book, a chat about boats . . . sycophantic years of boring book chitchat, distant past, what can he say anyway? Just being nosy, he'll hate it.

I opened his gate and went down the overgrown path. There was his bach, with neatly stacked firewood on the front porch. The door was open. I could see two other people inside, Bill and Eileen Belcher from up the road (nautically notorious in their own right). I sensed bad timing and had almost turned away when a dog started barking. Sprung, I knocked confidently on the wall (Mormon style).

A weathered man came to greet me — polite, but obviously unsure of my intentions. His face resembled the young man in the book except for the loose, leathered look. He was older. It was him — the one who had done all that sailing. I was star struck. I didn't speak very well. He noticed and it was all over suddenly, I was going back up the path trying to justify my intrusion. The Belchers seemed perplexed by my appearance as well. Sunburn might have masked the way it felt. They could have held up scorecards but awkward silence was enough. Wray muttered his thanks, I bowed out back to the security of the anonymous ridge road.

Out at the point, the waves ran in disarray onto the rocks, driven by the same cycle of winds that had ruled Wray's years. Hard southwesters pushing up over the Tasman, predictable patterns of relentless wind. He'd written about life being lived in compelling sailing circumstances. I decided to sail to his island — Sunday (Raoul) Island, 650 miles from Auckland, where he had regularly sailed. I had my mortality to consider, but that wouldn't last forever. In the ensuing months my father lost his brain tumour battle. Age 58.

The next day the wind came light from the east and the Coromandel Ranges. We ghosted back to Auckland, the boat and I, fiddling with the self-steering gear, dwelling on the passage of time. It was difficult to reconcile Wray's writings with his older self. Onwards moved the moments, and 10 miles later we caught the tide up the harbour, drifting under the big bridge to turn right into Little Shoal Bay.

In the lee of Northcote Point the easterly faltered, and I pulled out my 12-ft lifeboat oars to row *Mylene B* in close to the shore. At high water the anchor and chain was dropped over the side to sit in an undisturbed pile on the bottom while the sea silently departed. The twin keels settled gently on the sand, and an hour later I stepped onto more or less dry land to walk up the hill and along the ridge to the Birkenhead shops.

Chapter 2

Swirly World in Perpetuity

A friend in Little Shoal Bay, Mike Maloney, had a dory in which he must have rowed hundreds of miles each year exploring the inner Auckland Harbour. After one journey up to Herald Island he told me about a small bright green yacht about 18 ft long that looked as if it had been designed and built for single-handed ocean cruising. It was for sale. I'd seen the boat a year earlier from the shore, but never got close enough to check it out.

In Sydney that year, recording an album, I happened upon an unusual folding dinghy. It appealed because it folded up to a normal suitcase size and was ideal for my small-scale boating. With interest rekindled, I went up to Herald Island and paddled out in my frail new polypropylene coracle.

Swirly World in Perpetuity was floating bow down with a large rusty mooring sitting on the foredeck. I hung onto the side and explored. A flush-decked miniature of an ocean-going keeler. Radar reflector at the masthead, twin running poles, twin forestays, two deck-length stainless wires for clipping on the safety harness, a tiny watertight cockpit with several large drains, a servo-tab on the rudder and a standard of woodwork finishing like a moulded fibreglass hull. It was everything you would want in an instant offshore vessel — but with one drawback, the fin keel. Up until then I had lived contentedly on the mud flats, always managing to get a few hours sleep even if a gale was blowing, thanks to the kind retreat of the tide. I enjoyed being able to walk around the boat as it sat on the mud flats, but a fin-keeled vessel needed deep water. And that meant rowing dinghies on choppy nights and the general uneasiness that goes with living on an exposed mooring. Fin keel was a big deal.

But this boat looked special. I could be under the Harbour Bridge and into the unknown in half the time it would take me to get *Mylene B* ready. Its flush-decked design with the one-man cockpit also seemed safer than other 18-footers I'd seen. I rang the number scrawled under the For Sale sign and a very disinterested person said they had nothing to do with it but offered the address of the creator and owner. He was a neighbour doing the boat owner a favour and didn't sound very enthusiastic. I was about to find out why.

I tracked down the address I'd been given for *Swirly World*. In a bland suburban street in Avondale I found an ancient residence masked from view by a row of trees swaying defiantly above the neatly trimmed neighbouring hedges. All the windows were covered with corrugated-iron sheeting, and most of the weatherboarding had discarded its paint in favour of the natural 'rotten wood' look. The place appeared derelict, but a blanket hanging for a front door and several sleepy kittens looked promising. That was about it.

Back in the frontier days while the battles for the North Island raged, I'd have approached that front door with caution. It all looked lived in yet suspiciously deserted. Ambush. I didn't have time to circle round the back, a reporter from *Rip It Up* was waiting in the band van for his interview.

Little did I know I had stumbled upon the Church of Physical Immortality, led by none other than the First World President of the United Planet, Mr Michael Brien. That was how he announced himself once I dared to knock on the front porch.

He made his appearance dramatically from behind the front door blanket, brandishing a stick with a large globe of the world impaled on the end. He had on a bright orange bathrobe with his bare hairy legs sticking out from underneath, with a mass of tangled chains and baubles strung about his neck. His hair and beard were long and grey. The ye old prophet look. Quite authentic, some might say freak. A hair-triggered militiaman might have opened fire but I had to give him the benefit of my doubt, maybe someone he knew built the boat.

He launched straight into a well-rehearsed speech about his self-created church and role as the self-appointed First World President. This man was different.

He was living his life uncompromisingly camped in the heart of suburbia in the house he was born in, from where he preached, by example, a non-conformist philosophy stemming from a distrust of society in general. What's more, he had created *Swirly World in Perpetuity*. You wouldn't have thought so. His asking price was twice what I could afford but half of what the boat was worth. He'd built *Swirly World* twelve years before and lived on her for three years, travelling between North Cape and Tauranga.

I left Avondale impressed, but still unsure about the suitability of *Swirly World* for my perpetually afloat lifestyle. A little later that month, while lounging about in Balclutha, I wrote to him offering all I could afford for *Swirly World*. His reply would decide whether I should persevere with *Mylene B* or be forced to discover the realities of owning a fin-keeled boat. Months went by and it was obvious he had refused my offer, so I forgot it. After an extensive tour around the country, the band returned to Auckland and lay low for a bit. We were tired. Too many late nights in a row.

The first gig after catching up on sleep was out at the Pukekohe Town Hall. A humid late summer's night, suitably subtropical, with a reasonably healthy crowd. We were finally sort of popular. To the side of the stage were some large loading doors, opening out into the cooler night outside. After we finished I got Sandy, our 'sometimes put it right if it goes wrong' roadie, to open the doors before we rushed back on to do an encore as quickly as possible in case the audience, left to their own devices, stopped clapping and wandered off (it does happen).

While doing the last song I kept glancing through the doors, enjoying the contrast between the sweaty humans in front of me and the still darkness beyond the side of the stage. Halfway through the song, I glanced across to be confronted with a vision of the First World President of the United Planet jiggling about in the cargo bay. He'd got in and he wasn't going to go away. I later learnt Mike

Brien wasn't into communication via letter writing. He preferred to eyeball his intentions (he later called it hypnotising) and I didn't feel qualified to argue. Not with the President. The next day he had me out with him in a borrowed dinghy for a closer inspection of *Swirly World in Perpetuity*. Little doubt was left. The boat would be relevant to my future sailing.

We settled on a price, plus a little more once I made my first hundred thousand dollars (I appreciated his confidence, as I still haven't). *Swirly World in Perpetuity* became my responsibility. I would look after her. I would inherit the creation he had grown tired of.

The weekend I chose to sail her down the harbour from Herald Island to a deep-water mooring in Little Shoal Bay coincided with a gig the band played at Whenuapai Air Force Base, about a mile from where the boat was moored. I slept on board that night, and the following afternoon I lowered myself into the coracle and paddled down with the outgoing tide to a clay bank just under the Upper Harbour Bridge. I folded up the dinghy to its suitcase size and hid it in the trees then moved up the bush path just a few hundred yards to where the stage had been erected. Most convenient.

That evening we played while the sun went down and a large amount of semi-barbecued sausages came up out of booze-sloshing Air Force bellies. They wanted to hear the songs we'd had played on the radio and TV. 'Cleopatra', 'Swear It's True', 'Forever Tuesday Morning', 'One Black Friday'. The only ones they knew. The rest they didn't really know at all.

It started well. The whole gathering in high spirits, as you would expect, our Armed Forces in between battles. After a short time the heavily subsidised grog seemed to be having an adverse affect. Perhaps some of them had noticed my black nail polish. I was doing my version of Polynesian dancing, all hips and innuendo. The females never had a problem with it, blokes were always suitably uncomfortable. Missiles started landing sporadically on stage. Stones and things . . . they were trying to soften us up with artillery fire.

The bright stage lights and a few free brown bottles did nothing for direction finding on my way back to the hidden dinghy. Half an hour was spent blindly fumbling through the undergrowth. It was my escape route. Some of the audience had ended up not really liking me. It might have been mutual but I didn't have the opportunity to find out. I paused frequently on my way to the water's edge, making sure no disgruntled Air Force personnel were trying to track me down . . . Many scratches later, I happened upon my folded transport. Unpacked, I embarked on the best ride home I'd had, sedately paddling up the dark estuary with the incoming tide. I was safe, no rapids ahead, no rubber dinghies being launched in pursuit, another minor showbiz night done. *Swirly World in Perpetuity* was just up there, all still and quiet on the last of the flood tide. All neglected, dormant, waiting . . .

The next day I hanked on the sails to take her down the harbour. Unlike previous boats, she had an inboard engine with a salt water-cooled exhaust system. Other experiences with outboards had resulted in the seizing of the Seagull on *The Prince of Innocence*, leaving me to fit two 8-ft oars to row facing forward from the cockpit. (It took an hour to row with the tide from Cox's Bay to Little Shoal Bay.) I'd left *Mylene B*'s outboard untouched in a garage and carried on with my reliable rowing where required. I decided to give *Swirly World*'s engine the benefit of the doubt, and having followed the instructions, left it idling as I set us adrift on the ebbing tide.

Mike Brien was supposed to meet me that morning and show me how the systems worked. He never showed. I half expected it. I found out later he'd blown the money I gave him on speedy drugs and helicopter rides in the Coromandel. 'Flying! I'm getting a microlight . . . flying's the way to be now . . .'

The estuary was too sheltered to allow us to sail with any ease down through the moored yachts, so I gave the inboard engine a rev up and we motored slowly past the other craft. Black smoke began billowing out the exhaust pipe. Not a good start. Not knowing what was wrong, I carried on until a strange whirring sound followed by black smoke billowing out of the companionway agitated me. Beyond the obstacle course of moored yachts, I rushed below and switched off the engine. Unbeknownst to me I had failed to switch on the water pump that sent salt water rushing through to cool the exhaust system. The President should have shown me.

The rubber hose at the stern had delaminated from the heat and blocked the flow of exhaust fumes, causing them to escape from a hole which had just been blown in a weak rusted part of the exhaust pipe somewhere inside. As the tide was speeding down through the narrow upper reaches, I pulled up the sails to gain some control to pass under, not into, the Upper Harbour Bridge.

The breeze was light and fickle, a northwesterly, all but stifled by the high land about us. It was then that two years of marine growth on the uncleaned hull really made itself known. She heeled over, responding sluggishly, clearing the last of the off-lying shoal, nail-biting stuff, slow, retarded in steerage, all that seaweed stuck underneath . . . At last we bore away into open water and a constant wind. We made it. Later, against the poles in Little Shoal Bay, I scraped a thick beard of two-inch mussels from the bottom.

Reaching down the inner harbour with a clear 15-knot northwesterly, it might have been sluggish by *Swirly World* standards but we were sailing. Even with the underwater growth, Mike Brien had obviously created a yacht with reasonable sailing qualities. No more going sideways, at least not quite so much.

Within six months of finding *Swirly World* nearly everything relevant to crossing the open sea with relative peace of mind had been accumulated. RFD Life Rafts in Wellington made up two large buoyancy bags with instant CO_2 inflation to fill the interior of *Swirly World* and keep her afloat, should we be so unfortunate as to encounter a submerged container, or whatever else might be lurking out there to puncture my little plywood cocoon. Combined with a US Airforce two-man life raft, an EPIRB and an old DSB radio that transmitted on the emergency frequency, the backup systems were primitively complete. It was all I could afford so preparations had to be considered complete. I couldn't wait forever.

There was only one real obstacle between me and my pursuit of uncertainty — the New Zealand Yachting Federation. They had taken it upon themselves to come up with a set of rules governing every New Zealand registered vessel which intended to go further than 60 miles offshore. Once their rules have been complied with, you receive a Category One certificate. Without this certificate no one will be given a customs' clearance to leave New Zealand waters, and without clearance papers very few countries will accept you. It's a well-devised system, designed with the honourable intention of stopping unprepared or wholly ignorant beings from rushing off in search of the Pacific paradise they saw on a recent television advert. As with most rules applied with the blanket approach, they make no allowance for the individual and consequently some suffer. All their whistles and plastic buckets didn't worry me, I viewed their rules as useful suggestions, but I had compensated for the life raft they stipulated as necessary with my buoyancy bags (very practical on a boat half the average size) and my lesser, alternative, life raft. Predictably, such a variation from their rules was unacceptable.

'Sorry there's no provision for exceptions . . . you've got to have all the safety items in the handbook. Anyway you can afford them . . . you're a rock star!' A rock star with insufficient remuneration. Fame without fortune . . . intolerable.

One rule that discreetly appeared in their 1986 update stated that all cruising yachts must have an inboard engine. At first I couldn't believe it. Of all the greatest voyagers — Joshua Slocum, Alain Gerbault, not to mention the initial explorers, none of them would have been allowed to embark on their travels had they been New Zealanders starting from New Zealand in 1986. How was this rule going to affect the modern voyagers who preferred to carry an outboard engine for windless emergencies, stowing it out of salt water's way when relying on their 'usual' motive power?

The hypocrisy sounded loud and clear when one year Margaret Shields (then Minister of Customs) was out in her best frock to welcome the engineless *Hawaiiki Nui* canoe to New Zealand after its voyage re-enacting an original migratory trip down from the islands. If *Hawaiiki Nui* had been a New Zealand registered vessel trying to leave New Zealand they wouldn't have had a chance. The only legal way around the rules is by owning a vessel that is other than New Zealand registered.

At the beginning of 1986 my friend Karyn Hay moved up from Wellington. I'd started meeting a few radio and television presenters. The usual showbiz self-consumed conversation dominators . . . 'I got where I am today by everyone paying attention to me.' Hay was a bit different. More substantial yet thoroughly insubstantial physically speaking — a bit thin for some reason but very well read.

After three years of living alone on the mud flats I was ready to move ashore. Karyn did three months in Little Shoal Bay sleeping around the mast post on the vinyl squabs. It was a bit awkward.

In the luxury of a basement on land, I amassed and organised all the gear I had acquired over the past years. This would be my mission control. I was almost ready to sail away. Not being sure when this would be, I went about doing jobs like installing the DSB radio complete with an alternate power supply, fitting the inflatable buoyancy bags, making up food parcels and generally being cautious about everything to do with my unknown enterprise. Sometimes it made me uneasy. All that self-inflicted blatant uncertainty coming up.

I had never previously been alone for more than about 12 hours since I spent the night around the Wellington coast at Long Beach, when I was twelve. How long alone do most of us ever really do? My own company, or rather the lack of anyone else's for an extended period, was an unknown. Going where there was no land to be seen? I had never been out of sight of land before but others had, so it couldn't be that bad. What sort of seas would I encounter? And how would I react to their perhaps unnerving proximity? Would I be able to find Sunday Island (which was only about 6 miles wide)? The nearest land to the north was Tonga, some 700 miles on. An island not to be missed.

I studied volumes on celestial navigation and eventually worked out the long way of finding my position. Real sailor stuff. I bought a small calculator that stored the tedious lists of tables and did the salient sums in a few seconds.

I made the most of a paid trip to Blenheim, reading a few poems from my first slim volume, *Take The Chocolates And Run*; and compering an afternoon's music. Peking Man and the Dance Exponents were playing. I had an ulterior motive for being there. My friend Roch had a sextant for sale. I had always coveted Roch's sextant. All plastic, robust, nautical . . .

Roch had lived on his 24-ft keeler in Evans Bay in Wellington during the early eighties. I'd found it compelling parked up on occasional wet and windy nights, on the reclaimed gravel, looking out at the light in his little house moving to the sporadic gusts that came racing down from the hills into his sheltered corner of the bay. He was then preparing for my kind of expedition. Salt-water solitary confinement. He'd read the same books . . . Eventually, he relocated his base to Nelson, then sailed solo up the east coast of the North Island, taking in most of the ports, Napier, Gisborne, Tauranga, on the way. It was a big trip for Roch. Changed him. On arrival in Auckland he declared his thirst had been quenched, sold his boat and went to Taradale to train as a priest. He'd been hammered off Mahia Peninsula, big seas, salt-water seriousness . . .

I visited him once in summer at the monastery and spent a Sunday afternoon discussing the world beside their open-air swimming pool.

'Do you hold any beliefs yourself, Andrew?'

Three tall bottles of beer and a rich Sunday lunch later I did have a few beliefs. I'd suspected it might get awkward. I was ready. 'The Gnostic gospels, the ones found near Nag Hammadi in Egypt in 1949 — the gospel of Thomas, Valentinus, all that stuff about suffering the depths of torment before you gain *gnosis* (self-knowledge). Understanding beyond the control or decree of other hierarchies.'

'But that's subjective, beyond universal application, no governing authority.'

'It doesn't make it less relevant.'

'What about Christ?' I knew they'd cut to the big one.

'Is that beer down there?'

They all agreed it was the best place for it. On the bottom, down the deep end of the pool. 'Do you want another one, Andy? What's Karyn Hay like?'

I hadn't told many people about my trip. The extra pressure of other people's expectations hanging over me would be an unwelcome complication to my already delicate psyche. I couldn't be dealing with an audience; I'd have to do this it in private.

Collin Jolly lived on Great Barrier Island, but spent time in Little Shoal Bay and had witnessed my messing about. I'm sure he thought I was never going to get beyond the Harbour Bridge. 'Auckland's rubbish compared to the Barrier. I'm in Tryphena. Peach trees, own honey, the wasps are a bit of a problem, potatoes next season, passionfruit vines . . .' He exhorted me to sail over to the Barrier but I couldn't tell him I hoped to go a bit further afield. I wasn't sure I would. I had been set on not taking *Swirly World* beyond Devonport until I was prepared to sail away from New Zealand. Why set yourself a difficult objective when you could be enjoying without anxiety? Perhaps pleasure isn't enough.

The week before leaving, the compass had to be swung at the compass rose off Parnell. I arranged to pick up the qualified adjuster from the Admiralty Steps at the bottom of Queen Street. On the phone he tried to put me off by insinuating that a 5.6 m boat, in his mind a trailer-sailer, wouldn't need his expert attention. He was the closest I had to come to revealing my true intentions.

Without any wind, we motored up the harbour to collect our passenger. He was waiting with little black briefcase in hand — shoes polished and thin black tie tucked neatly into his jersey. As he climbed down onto the side of the deck, *Swirly World* lurched over, almost sending him under the smelly low-tide wharf. He clambered back to the cockpit and we silently motored out past the huge ships towering above us. On the way out he pointed to the other massive ships he'd swung; *Swirly World* was his smallest job. 'Where did you say you're going?'

'Just up the coast . . .'

At last I felt as ready as I was ever likely to be, given deadlines and budget. I promised to be back by 1 July at the latest, in time for a poetry tour the Student's Arts Council was organising. The spoken word. My spoken words. My written-down words to be spoken by me. Hone Tuwhare next, Api Taylor. They'd done it more than me. I might need to practise. I'd do it at sea, hopefully. Allowing an excessive twenty days each way in case the winds chose to be a problem, now it was time to go out there and see what could happen.

As an intimidating front bringing northeasterly winds and rain swept through Auckland, I rowed out and piled water bottles and stores aboard *Swirly World*. She has a stainless-steel water tank built in under the forward bunks that holds twelve gallons, but I took another ten gallons in old milkshake syrup containers that Karyn's mother, Shirley, had given me. I never could get rid of the lingering flavours and later found myself sipping spearmint water, lime water and unsavoury chocolate-flavoured water.

The front went through that night and the next day was flat calm. That afternoon I went for a walk through the Auckland Domain that backed on to where we lived in a damp Parnell gulley. I sat up on the steps of the museum and stared out at the horizon to the right of Little Barrier Island. A wind-determined adventure, volunteering to feel vulnerable, insecure because you're bothering to try. All my worry sat there on the steps with me. In a direct line from where I was looking northeast, beyond Little Barrier, lay Sunday Island, 650 miles away. Tomorrow I would sail over that horizon, the curve of our earth and see how far I could get. I could always turn back if need be. That sounded reassuring but I still felt as though I was possibly sentencing myself to an early exit.

That evening shortly after the autumn sun had sunk down over Helensville, I pushed the folding dinghy into the shallows of Little Shoal Bay. A few friends had come down to slip about on the clay bank and see me off. Peter Funnell, who had helped me with several projects that had been beyond my limited tool kit and talents, was having an annoying time trying to get his daughter's camera to work. I had to leave them to it. I paddled out over the flat dark sea and could still hear their farewells, punctuated by Peter's frustrations, long after the darkness had taken them.

Out amongst the moorings, *Swirly World* floated low in the water. She had a lot inside. I clambered on deck and pulled the dinghy up after me. Not wanting it to fall victim to some waiting wave, I folded it into its bag and tied it onto the foredeck. After the preparation of the past few days, I was ready to lie down and sleep until morning. The plan was to leave the harbour in the night so as to get out past the end of Great Barrier and the Mokohinaus in daylight the next day.

Unfortunately, I had no time for sleep and had to spend the next 5 hours tediously stowing everything properly to avoid chaos later on. I'd done it now. This was it. I had to do it because I'd always wanted to. But now I was tired and not so convinced about my own conviction.

At midnight the wind suddenly came up, blowing strongly from the west. I don't feel like this. Sleeping would be nice, goodnight. It had been a long day. I climbed up onto the deck and got the sails ready for action. Rain squalls started coming across the harbour to add to the general pleasantness of the night.

Two reefs in the main and the No.1 jib hanked on, then back down below to write the first entry in the unblemished logbook. A beginning. Heavy gusts swept down the harbour making *Swirly World* pitch and heave awkwardly on her mooring chain.

Sitting there, fatigued, in new-smelling wet-weather gear, with the safety harness uncomfortably bunching up the fabric round my shoulders, I almost gave in to the desire to take sanctuary in the sleeping bag. Tuck obliviously away from my own intentions. Outside, Auckland snored. Inside I felt acutely alone with my uncomfortable ambition. I forced myself on deck to pull up the sails. Goodbye, Auckland.

I finally sailed *Swirly World* down the harbour and out into the darkness beyond Devonport. We beat up the coast off Takapuna through dark gusting rain squalls then bore away past Rangitoto on course for the water between the two Barrier Islands. I set the self-steering and crouched in the tiny cockpit, watching out to make sure we cleared the moored ships off Whangaparaoa. As we moved slowly away from the Takapuna coast, a short sea started building, and I began to feel unsettled. Queasy even.

The tide had set us closer to Tiri Island than expected, and out in front was a white flashing light. According to my old chart it shouldn't have been there. Soon the Coromandel Ranges were back-lit with dawn, and I saw the man-made light was closer than before. It was Shearer Rock off Tiri and wasn't lit on my outdated chart. I over-reacted putting about, and we beat up away from it, in case any new rocks had popped up that my chart was missing. Weighted down, *Swirly World* ploughed wonderfully into the steep short waves with no hint of that old sideways bilge-keeler feeling. We bore away again, and I pulled down the mainsail, replacing it with the almost-new, poled-out twin running sails. The night was suddenly over, and we, *Swirly World* and I, had finally escaped from Auckland Harbour.

It was shaping into a good day, clouds dispersing and the wind backing to the southwest, steadying at around 20 knots. *Swirly World* surfed down the little waves, self-steering under control, the twins pulling us gallantly away from Auckland. This was it. My much preconceived escape. Thunderbirds were go. Maintaining the resolve to point in the right direction, even though I was feeling quite ill, I did appreciate the detail of it all.

On went the acupuncture wristbands, an Avomine pill, then sitting in the sun on the folding dinghy between the twins. I hoped it was more nerves than genuine motion sickness. A court of inquiry would have ruled a bit of both.

The miles and moments moved on and by late afternoon we were becalmed between the two Barrier Islands and being visited by some interested whales. I turned the radio up loud and tried to get out in the warm sun. Gradually, a light easterly got up, and, with the wind our master, *Swirly World* progressed out past the northern tip of Great Barrier Island. The sea was flat and ahead of us lay a clear, uninterrupted horizon. The rest of the watery planet . . . waiting.

The evening sky had slowly clouded over with the classic mare's-tail look that warned of a coming gale, but as the local AM radio made no mention of it, and the barometer didn't appear to be falling, we carried on out under full mainsail and genoa. I set our course for Sunday Island, north-northeast, emulating Johnny Wray and the *Ngataki* from the 1930s.

If I'd been in possession of an SSB (single sideband) radio or VHF and monitored the marine forecasts I would have heard of the disturbed frontal activity associated with a late tropical depression far to the north. Most would have prudently retreated, but instead I sailed on, exploring my determination with gross uncertainty.

Alone in my unknown. A large fishing boat came past returning to the gulf and in the fading light behind us a trimaran with sails hanging lifelessly motored for the shelter of Great Barrier. It seemed in a hurry, which made me worry. A little bit alone. Dun dun dun. That churning 'time to go home' feeling. Behind us lay security and companionship, ahead of us lay an unwritten future with how many perils?

Great Barrier became a dim, jagged outline in the dark, and the Mokohinau light swept reassuringly as *Swirly World* sailed slowly away from land. I hung out my small hurricane lantern in the cockpit, under the sheltered Perspex dodger, an almost futile symbolic gesture to all the books I'd read where oil lanterns hung for an ancient romantic seafaring world to see. I set the self-steering and retired below to write in the security blanket called logbook and forage pessimistically for rest.

I set the egg-timer alarm for half an hour, then lay down in the sleeping bag. *Swirly World* sailed blindly over the flat sea as I lay listening to the wavelets slapping against the hull. Some loose bits and pieces bumped about, and the halyards rattled around inside the aluminium mast. Certainly plenty of noise. Mainly aggravating unrhythmic sounds. Actually too much noise.

I couldn't sleep. From readings it seemed that when the body demanded rest, such irritating sounds would not disturb it. I was looking forward to exhaustion, because it sounded like there wouldn't be much sleep until then. I thought about the mare's-tails in the sky. Perhaps I should go back and wait in one of the sheltered coves on the Barrier until I was certain there was nothing mean brewing? I'd sleep like a human there. The weather charts religiously examined prior to leaving had made no indication of a secondary depression in the Tasman. Returning to a safe anchorage seemed to represent defeat. If we were in for a big blow and retreated, we may never have the resolve to head north again. We being me and the boat. Me specifically. I decided to continue out away from the coast and take what was possibly coming. I could always aim back for Little Shoal Bay if it wasn't my scene. One should never discount the possibility of retreat.

All night the wind increased and backed to the northeast, bringing *Swirly World* hard on the wind and heading north. The comforting loom of the Mokohinau light disappeared in the early hours, and I knew then we were out of sight of land. It had sunk in the dark, somewhere over the unseen western horizon, gone.

The motion became jerkier as *Swirly World* rose and dipped to the growing waves; I began to smell the distinctive aroma of petrol. Given the delicate state of my stomach, it came unappreciated. I didn't like that smell at all. The 'try to make him sick' competition. With the new uncomfortable motion, the tank was leaking petrol from an inaccessible breather pipe onto the engine. The answer was to drain the tank sufficiently to stop the petrol slopping up onto the breather pipe connection. An extra gallon of fuel had been stowed away for a windless emergency. I detached the fuel line from the carburettor and started filling a plastic container. It took longer than I would have preferred to drain out the couple of gallons. By then *Swirly World* was bucking unpleasantly and, feeling wretched, I wrote up the log then lay down for half an hour of fitful dozing.

I wrote in the log at best every hour, noting the magnetic compass course, miles run by the speedo, the state of the wind, sea and sky, and the barometer reading. It was mentally pacifying keeping a record of where I thought we were and what sort of gradual weather changes were taking place.

The details of overlooked sailing systems took high priority. The twin forestays allowed me to have one sail set pulling us along, while the other smaller or larger sail (depending on what the wind was likely to do) could be hanked on waiting to go. I pulled the No.1 jib down and replaced it with the smaller No.2 jib. As I clung on, fiddling with the sail hanks, *Swirly World* would drop into a trough, sending water up my wet weather smock. She would then rear up on to a crest, giving me a glimpse of the empty sea around us. I was reminded of Alain Gerbault's description of the same wet routine he experienced in the 1920s. We were almost time travelling. All those dull afternoons I'd spent on tour, in nondescript hotels and motels, waiting for sound check — thinking boat land, visualising such isolated toilings. I was faced with the reality of struggling with wet sails beyond any sanctuary, and it wasn't too bad.

A small amount of water had begun pooling on the leeward side of the cabin, up above the sink and stove. I discovered it was fresh water and every time *Swirly World* dropped off a wave, the water was being forced up from the main tank, through the pump and into the cabin. I blocked it up with a shaven plug and some binding tape, but not before a large amount of errantly exposed matches were soaked.

All that day the wind slowly backed and increased to around 35 knots, so I let *Swirly World* jog slowly forward under the No.2 jib. After the continual motion and the odd seasick pill, I was in a fairly soporific state and unsure of our DR (dead reckoned position). As the wind was blowing from the general direction I wanted to go, I had let *Swirly World* sail more or less in an arc curving out from Great Barrier, up past the Mokohinaus, and back in towards Cape Brett.

All day, off and on, I peered at the lumpy horizon around us for any sign of land, and at 3 p.m. as a rain squall cleared, I saw an island about 20 miles away. It seemed a little premature for Sunday Island, so I pulled out my RDF (radio direction finder) and got a bearing on Whangarei directly through the island. It was the Poor Knights and we were north of them.

In the past few hours the wind had shifted to the northwest, completing our course back towards the coast, so I put us about and we started heading out to sea, bucking into very steep and confused waves. Very steep in my spectrum of experience. New to me but wait and see . . . Now and then a flying crest would crash down on *Swirly World*, sending water spurting in around the forward hatch, creating a scene like something from the old submarine TV programme *Voyage to the Bottom of the Sea*. I hoped it wouldn't be. In such relatively shallow water (less than 200 metres) *Swirly World* was likely to get flung around more than in the deeper ocean. I sat bracing myself in the sheltered companionway, thankful for the permanent Perspex dodger Mike Brien had fitted over the main hatch area. It was like being at the movies — viewing the jumble of disorganised waves, yet free from the flying spray. It gave me confidence in the boat's ability to dance about on top of that agitated scene. Lifting and flinging, falling off waves then back up again. There was a lot of movement going on.

As it was getting dark that second night, I was suddenly shocked by the deafening sound of thunder directly overhead. I hastily pulled out my puny looking lightning conductor (a few yards of battery cable bolted to a roll of copper), clipped it to the backstay, and dropped it over the side. I peered over the windward canvas dodger to see an evil-looking rain squall bearing down on us. As I clung on, thinking about dragging out my tiny storm jib to replace the No.2 jib, a blast of wind flattened *Swirly World*, leaving the sheeted-in jib to shiver uselessly in the lee of the then vertical deck. The crests of the waves around us were whipped off in an instant and flung over the surface of the sea. I crawled inside and slammed the hatch shut.

Swirly World slid sideways on her side over the flattened seas, while lightning flashed about with malignant intent. So thought all of us. The squall moved on, and *Swirly World* went back to steering herself and we headed away from the land, out to sea. The jib was still in one piece only because *Swirly World* was light enough to lie over on her side and give in to the wind.

All night we played submarines, ploughing slowly away from the Northland coast, while I hid in my damp, dark cubbyhole. Tops of waves would flop down on the deck, submerging us in solid water. There was no momentum or power to the sea tops, just a lot of liquid falling and squirting its way inside onto me through air vents not meant for water.

I learned via the AM radio that our unexpected blow was the by-product of an out-of-season cyclone raging up in New Caledonia. The mention of the word 'cyclone' at that time of the year gave rise to my second acute churning, yearning, 'time to go home' feeling. According to my routing chart (which shows what blows when and where), the only other cyclones recorded in the month of May throughout the whole of the Pacific had always travelled down through the waters where we happened to be. This one died well north of us. Very good.

Chapter 3

On the Old World roads

On the Old World roads

The next morning we were beyond the 1000-fathom line, and the seas were different. It was as if we had entered a new world. A big rolling swell came down from the northwest, the advance party campaigners of the cyclone to come, possibly. *Swirly World* rode confidently along, effortlessly lifting up then sliding down the liquid hills. The wind had moderated to 20 knots, and as we ploughed along on a tight reach, so much movement.

I hadn't been eating much, the odd apple marinated in salt water, crackers and cheese, handfuls of scroggin (peanuts, raisins, chopped chocolate). I still disliked the thought of chewing food, but I'd read it was best to force down something. I engaged in a long struggle with the gimballed kerosene stove, during which black smoke poured forth to fill the closed-up cabin, covering everything in a thin film of foul soot. Whenever I pumped some pressure into the stove, kerosene would escape from a worn gasket on the barrel, so I rummaged through Mike Brien's excellent bag of ancient bits and pieces and found a replacement gasket. I had another cheap kerosene stove I'd bought before I left but I didn't have to butcher it for spares.

Having narrowly avoided asphyxiation, I boiled up some dehydrated vegetables and heated a can of bully beef, only to discover my desire for the scent of food wasn't that great, and I definitely hated heated bully beef. Disgusting. Which book was that from? With my only preparation based on reading the precedents, it was going to take some time to develop my own knowledge and understanding of what worked for me and what didn't. Personal experience. Gnosis . . .

In the middle of the night I felt chilled for the first time, even though I was deep inside a thick sleeping bag. I poked my head up through the hatch to check the compass course, shining my pocket torch at the gimballed bowl. It was a grid-type compass, which had two large arrows. When they were lined up, you were on the desired course. They were pointing away in two different directions, indicating that the wind had shifted while I was dozing. For a few moments I hadn't a clue where we were heading. The wind was blowing strong and cold from somewhere, and *Swirly World* was racing along. Even though we were on the 'Old World roads', it wasn't as if we were in danger of running into a tree, yet I felt we had to urgently get back on course to regain the fragile sense of normality that came with knowing which way the wind blew, and where our intended destination lay. For those few minutes I felt utterly lost. By swivelling the movable arrow on the compass bowl to match the magnetic arrow, I found out where we were heading, and from there, the wind's direction. It was blowing from the southwest — directly from Auckland. For the first time we had an offshore breeze, and it felt as though a gate had been slammed shut behind us. Up until then we could have run back to Auckland with a favourable wind, but with a southwesterly it would take twice as long to beat back the distance travelled. We were finally committed to our offshore destination.

I turned *Swirly World* back towards Sunday Island, got the sails and self-steering balanced, then went back to bed, leaving her to run with the wind and leftover cross-sea, doing about 3 to 4 knots under the No.2 jib. It may have been a bit cowardly to be sailing under such a small headsail, but I found this speed at night to be about all I could initially handle, lying in my bunk listening to the water rushing past as we sailed blindly through the dark. It also saved extra sail-changing work if the wind decided to increase. It's called cruising.

At dawn, I set the poled-out twin headsails and let *Swirly World* surf down the big following seas with a cold 25-knot southwesterly behind us. It was time to interact with my sextant, so that morning, lunchtime and afternoon I balanced in the cockpit, clutching the instrument, bringing the sun I could see in the mirror down onto the distant horizon. Once done, I'd glance at the stopwatch nestled in my bunched up sleeping bag, and note down the time and the sextant readings. Each time I would take several sights at once to compare intercepts, and much to my ridiculous surprise, I found the sun to be rising according to my group of sights in the morning, and descending in the afternoon, just as it should have been. The sunsights put us several miles further on than my DR, and this became usual, due to the current.

Clutching the sextant, braced in the cockpit with *Swirly World* surfing down the large waves at up to 8 knots and the twins pulling gloriously against the clearing sky, I felt I had arrived. The cloak of vulnerability that had weighed upon me during the first few days had lifted and I was finally fully participating in that which I had so often read about.

Every evening I would light my cheap hurricane lantern and hang it in the cockpit. An insipid light show for anyone who happened to be looking. Its pale yellow glow was comforting on unpleasant nights and when it blew out, it was a priority to restore its presence. Naïve faith in letting other vessels know we were there, if they were looking.

My sailing routine was constant throughout the 24 hours of each day. I would sleep for an hour or so, as best one can in such circumstances where one's sixth sense is alert and ready to respond to the wind's ever-fluctuating demands. My egg-timer alarm would wake me to check out for ships and check the compass course, sumlog (speedometer) reading, wind strength, and to write up the log. I might then chew at something, only making one real meal in the last light hours of each evening. Tins of things and pressure-cooked root vegetables.

I read while lying in the bag, or listened to the radio when I could pick up the stations (usually at night). The radio took on new meaning, representing a link with life lived in relative security compared to my self-imposed exile. I could never forget there wasn't a lot around except sea and sky, which seemed to serve as a stage for the dramatic and ever-changing cloud formations.

Loneliness dissolved into a subconscious preoccupation with attentive sailing and a stoic matter-of-fact approach. In this environment even the most dull and uninspiring radio conversation could
be listened to with renewed interest. 'The all-new Coast FM, always a better music mix . . .' Not usually. DJs all shapes and sizes,
voice-modulated disguises. I knew a few in Auckland. Well-heeled
hosts, St Mary's Bay grandeur, a private audience of real estate agents,
car salesmen and others slightly star struck, acutely aware of the
marketplace value of celebrity. A lot of ageing wastrels about. 'Do
you want a smoke? I've got some primo heads at the moment.'

At night you wake up and grope for the small torch tucked down
between the squab and the hull and do routine checks regardless of
weather conditions. It was life lying down most of the time, except
when the wind summoned you to pull on the usually damp, clammy jerseys, wet-weather gear and safety harness, and alter *Swirly
World*'s sail plan. Internal evacuations were done in a small bucket
wherever was convenient, depending on the spill factor incited by
rough seas. A mobile primitive facility with a minimum of fuss.
Faeces and urine, there's a lot of it about.

A week after leaving Auckland we were becalmed some 500 miles
away from Great Barrier Island, and about 100 miles west of
L'Esperance Rock, which makes up the southernmost point of the
Kermadec group (Sunday Island being the most northern). We'd
sailed 500 miles from Little Shoal Bay. I wanted to stay well clear of
the other islands (Curtis and Macauley) and aim for Sunday Island
by curving in from the west. Having as much sea room as possible
became a paranoiac concern. You're tired and overreacting, go to
sleep while you're becalmed.

The afternoon brought mare's-tails in the sky from over the western horizon. It looked as if we were in for another gale. I spent the
evening cutting gaskets for the forehatch and anchor chain locker
out of plastic bags, an attempt to halt the usual heavy-weather deluge, then reduced sail for the night. Sure enough, a headwind built
up overnight so the next morning we were lying ahull with the
waves buffeting us back to Auckland.

'Lying ahull' they called it. I just couldn't get *Swirly World* to lie pointing up into the seas even with the storm jib backed, trysail up or a storm jib on the backstay, so I pulled them all down and let her drift, taking the brunt of 'waveworld' on her quarter. They were quite steep, and every now and then a breaking bit would crash down on the topsides, sending us sideways, much to the discomfort of the sole occupant.

Down indoors I was feeling well but very uncomfortable. Seasickness was a distant memory. Not to waste time, I went about making a whole packet's worth of pancakes. Elvis would have been pleased. It turned out to be four extra-thick ones festooned with nuts and raisins and liberally doused with brown sugar. I finished them off then repositioned my sleeping bag on the leeward side of the forward berths. Fortunately the company of a bucket wasn't required. I usually lay in the quarterberth across from the stove and sink, with the lee cloth rigged up to stop me falling out. This time the motion without sails was so violent, it was unbearable there.

The plastic bag gaskets stopped a lot of water coming inside, but now and then an extra sloppy bit would crash down, silencing my submerged world, and sending a jet of water in through the locked main hatch. It was wet ocean sailing for the uninitiated and I liked it. The keel wasn't going to fall off so the angle of heel, while uncomfortable, was not life threatening, far from it. Just tiring. The continual bracing of one's body to avoid being lurched involuntarily about. Just lock into a wet corner and endure . . . It won't last forever. The wind will let you go when it's finished . . .

I frequently checked to see if the wind had shifted by viewing the handbearing compass mounted on the forward bulkhead, but for 12 hours we kept drifting slowly back towards Auckland. As I lay there jammed in between bags of food and the wet leeward wall, I imagined what *Swirly World* looked like, there in the middle of nowhere, all shut up, devoid of sails, drifting buoyantly along on top of the foaming seas. Like a dormant cruiser that had broken her mooring months ago and drifted out into the ocean. The difference was, I was inside. Sometimes she would lurch over on her side, deck vertical, but the large heavy keel always brought us back up the right way. Plough on through the dark, it's the only way.

At midnight, my handbearing compass showed a new heading,

so I struggled out to get us on our way, aiming towards Sunday Island. The wind had backed to the northwest and moderated a bit, so up came the No.2 jib and *Swirly World* steered herself once more on course for the island. That night we really played underwater sports, often slamming to a silent halt, as stray cross-seas dropped down on the deck. The rough conditions were genuinely exciting, as there wasn't enough force in the wind or waves to threaten our watertight integrity. The motion would be shockingly uncomfortable to many people, but you get used to it.

After broad reaching for 24 hours with a 20-knot westerly on the port quarter, a full moon lit the surface of the sea. I spent most of my time peering under the boom towards the east, where I expected Curtis Island to be lurking, some 60 miles away.

One thing I had never given a great deal of thought to before was the distance land could be seen from. Frequently, when the dawn clouds were silhouetted on the eastern horizon, I imagined the very certain shape of an island, even when I was 200 miles away. Overly enthusiastic. A quick consultation of *South Sea Vagabonds* put me right — I shouldn't start looking until I was at least 40 miles away from Sunday Island. I didn't spy Curtis Island that night, but we were closer and well adjusted to a life lacking sleep. Catnapping equals more moments for your lifetime. It also made you feel a little unusual. Similar to what they call being on drugs. The F drug. Fatigue. You haven't had much sleep and you're not likely to. Perception changes, you're emotionally volatile. With experience you can understand what's happening, use it to your best advantage, even enjoy it. Without 'proper sleep' life seems often more pertinent. Spontaneous.

I'd been looking out for birds, which were supposed to be telltale signs of the proximity of land, but there was nothing much about. Only one that had been trailing us day and night. He was quite alone, and often tried to perch on the red polystyrene buoy we towed behind us on a long grab line, in case I fell overboard. Grab onto it and haul yourself back to the boat, it's your last and only chance. He was no doubt a hardened fishing-boat scavenger bird but I thought more of it. Birds and flying souls, it all made sense at sea. The Theosophical Society seemed to agree. Disembodied entities, activated shells, consciousness in frequencies imperceptible to humans. In the wrong frame of mind all a bit disturbing, out at sea alone on the F drug . . . who can be sure?

At 9 a.m. on our tenth day out, I got a position line from a sunsight that placed us 45 miles away from Sunday Island, but as one needs three position lines to find out your exact position, we could have realistically been hundreds of miles northwest or southwest of where we wanted to be.

I set the twins to make the most of the dying southwesterly, then retired below for an hour's rest, which turned into a debate about what to do if we couldn't find the island by nightfall. When I came up at 10 a.m. and clung on to the twins to peer forward, I saw a smudge more certain than my previous imaginings. We'd found it.

Forty miles away and dead ahead lay Sunday Island. Unrestrained jubilation. The navigation had worked. Given my lack of practical experience, I marvelled at it. The day was shaping up perfectly with the southwesterly holding out at around 10 to 15 knots.

A celebratory meal of potatoes and three-quarters of a tin of cold bully beef. I put the last greasy remains (still in its tin) up in the cockpit to use as bait when we arrived. While studiously hand steering, the wind suddenly shifted and started blowing from the southeast, making it a reach to Sunday Island. I removed the twins, put up the No.2 jib with the reefed main, and we got going on a tight reach. The wind picked up, and soon low dark clouds came racing over the horizon. It was going to be difficult to get anchored before the early darkness. Sunday Island had no lighthouses or lit beacons. I didn't relish the idea of tacking back and forth waiting for the sun before we could go close in and anchor. Impatience became a very familiar theme.

Rain squalls soon started bearing down, blocking out the island, which had been growing more defined by the hour. *Swirly World* was leaping along over a steep confused sea at a steady 6 knots. I was pushing her too much with the single reefed main and No.2 jib. Anxious to reach the shelter of Hutchinson's Bluff, boat speed was the order of the day.

Sometimes the island was partially revealed between rain squalls, looking decidedly sinister with its surrounding stormy shroud. The wind was now up to about 40 knots in the squalls, so I had to let the self-steering take over while I clawed the mainsail down to put another reef in. Clinging on to the mast, tying that reef in, as *Swirly World* leapt from crest to trough, proved to be the hardest time I'd had on deck. I crawled back to the cockpit and took over steering. I was hungry again so made do with the salt-watered remains of the bully beef. Anything chewable would do. It wasn't too offensive, given my rough and tumble circumstances. I needed the fuel. Bare essential living.

It was there that I felt more threatened by the wind and seas than before. Perhaps it was the proximity of the relative shelter heightening my own vulnerability, but it felt strange how the weather had quickly degenerated and come in from the southeast.

In the rain squalls the loner seabird with its identifiable markings hovered under our lee close by. It would circle *Swirly World*, flapping hard to windward, then glide back down and around, behind the heeled-over mainsail, disappearing to leeward, never far away. No doubt about it then. It was keeping an eye on us. Exactly whose eye, I wasn't sure.

In twilight, we came into the shelter of Hutchinson's Bluff where the sea was reduced to a confused swell. It was colder, so I went below to pull on layers of woollen warmth for the final miles of outdoor mission. The chart showed the sheltered northwestern side of the island to be free of off-lying dangers so we would be able to creep in close to anchor.

There's a Met station on the island, and I wanted to contact them to tell those at home I was still a human. Armed with a bag of scroggin, I began steering for the point I had identified as part of Bell's Flat. The wind was treacherous in the shadow of the island; heavy gusts came rushing invisibly down from the high land to flatten *Swirly World*. When she wasn't stalling on her side, she was wallowing hopelessly under-canvassed in the lulls. Eventually we worked into clearer air (or were blown out into it) and made progress towards the point.

A bright light that belonged to the Met station came into view. An unexpected bonus, the electricity generator. As we drew closer, a well-lit building could be seen and the problem became judging how close we could get to the shore before anchoring. I put the wind vane back into action and went forward to pull the anchor chain into the forepeak locker for immediate handling. When we were close enough to hear the swell heavily breaking on the shore, I let the sheets go and scrambled forward to throw the Danforth anchor over the side. The sails thundered free in the gale-force gusts, and I fed out the full 45 fathoms of chain (I later learnt to pull the sails down beforehand). A trail of phosphorescence marked the chain's passage down through the dark sea. I leaned back and re-leased the halyards, letting the sails come down in a bundle around me. Slumped down on the billowing headsail, *Swirly World* rode sideways with the wind, letting her chain drag out until the anchor took the strain. I could feel the vibrations rumbling over the gravel on the sea bed below and just when I thought *Swirly World* was going to drag her anchor across to Norfolk Island, it dug in, and we turned to face the offshore wind. We'd arrived.

I stayed slumped on the deck, staring out across at the warm lights ashore and inhaled the scent of damp foliage coming across the water. Smelling at it in a primate way. Especially special. How could I ever take that for granted? Eventually I tidied up the sails, lit the lantern as an anchor light and retired below. Thankfully, after the constant ploughing and plunging about of the last ten days and 10 hours, *Swirly World* felt dead in the water. I wrote up the logbook and then had a go at calling the Met station on my radio. I hadn't got a licence to transmit and I'd never tried using it in Auckland to see if it worked. Yes, negligence. I had been assured it did, and I had installed a proper DSB aerial so that the lights and dials looked as if they worked. Being a DSB it only transmitted on one channel — 2182, the emergency frequency. I didn't think I'd be causing too much of a stir up there, if indeed anyone would hear me, so I re-peated into the handpiece, 'This is *Swirly World*, *Swirly World* calling Sunday Island Met station, come in please.' No reply. I crawled into the bag and left *Swirly World* to look after herself until the next morn-ing. I was pleased the chain I had bought to attach myself to the bottom of some insecure coastline was doing exactly that, even though its rumblings on the gravel sea bed 12 fathoms down sounded disconcerting. Outside it was the rhythmic sound of the sea on the land, the pounding surf letting me know we were very near Sunday Island tonight.

As soon as the sun had pushed the darkness from our new surroundings, I clambered up to see what I could see. It was an island all right, no cartographic conspiracy. A rugged-looking bit of land. I saw immediately that in calculating our distance off, I'd been deluded in the dark. We were anchored about a mile off, at a spot where ships usually anchored. More than enough sea room. Embarrassingly so. Dense subtropical foliage covered all the peaks and slopes apart from Bell's Flat, which was covered in grass, kept short by grazing cattle. The building I had noticed by night looked deserted. The wind still blew in lesser gusts offshore, but the rain had gone and the sun shone between the racing clouds.

At 9 a.m. I tried the Met station again and got a loud garbled reply. The radio worked. After a conversation in which I couldn't understand a word, the voice suddenly became intelligible. He'd been transmitting with more power (or something like that), thinking I had an SSB instead of my antiquated, almost redundant DSB. Having never used a radiophone before proved to be another source of elation.

The first thing the voice said before I introduced myself was, 'Are you Mr Fagan?' I immediately assumed an unnecessary search had been undertaken to find me, and was almost right. One of the Sunday papers heard about my trip and ran a sensational-type story. They had rung the island to find out if I'd arrived.

The radio operator gave me a weather forecast and told me to anchor in closer up at Fishing Rock, where most of the visitors came ashore. They would be out in their inflatable. There were five people living on the island: the ranger, Alan Johnson, the radio operator, an engineer for mechanical breakdowns, and two Met men. The radio operator said he would send a message back home for me.

To get to Fishing Rock I had to first retrieve the 45 fathoms of chain, which, given its accumulated weight, proved to be difficult. I finally hauled it all in and motored up to Fishing Rock, anchoring with the rock-strewn bottom clearly visible. With the wind gusting around the point, and the swell jerking the chain about, it took me several attempts to get the anchor to hold, and even then it seemed risky, given the menacing aspect of the nearby cliffs. Fishing Rock was a landmark referred to by Wray, he'd landed stores there for a Robinson Crusoe adventure he once assisted. He'd also landed himself there a few times. I sat up on deck absorbing every detail of a new environment as we waited for our visitors.

Eventually two people dressed in wetsuits came down the narrow cliff path. One started up a generator while the other disappeared up into the bushes. Slowly, on a flying fox, a large inflatable with an outboard on the back came down from the cliffs and was swung out over the water, then dropped onto the swell surging around the rocks. One man jumped in to guide it off its floating cradle, then another person appeared and all three leapt in and sped out to *Swirly World*. Three grinning faces clambered onto the back of *Swirly World* and perched in the cockpit, leaving her floating at an unhealthy angle.

'Mr Fagan. How are ya? I'm Alan, the Island's Ranger; we've been expecting you for a few days now. A newspaper journalist's been ringing up.' They took some photos and peered inside at my tiny world, unanimously agreeing it was a bit claustrophobic for their tastes. 'You're dead keen, I'll give you that.'

They took me ashore where we sat in the warm sun on the motionless rocks and chatted for an hour. I'd had a lot of vivid dreams and this was like another one. 'I saw you play in Greymouth, good night, we were off our faces . . .' Greymouth had figured memorable for the Mockers. One time, Tim the keyboard player, heavy with fatigue and listing to port, had suddenly fainted and fallen from his elevated keyboard riser. The show dramatically stopped and we all stood around his prostrate body, aghast at the sight of eyeballs rolled back in his head, nothing else going on. Tim lived but the show had to be stopped. On the return voyage to Greymouth we encountered female teenagers thrusting rude signs above their heads, 'Brett you ******* spunk' and 'I want to suck you off.'

I kept a close watch on *Swirly World* as she floated there alone, looking tiny and fragile with nothing but an empty horizon stretching out behind her. They invited me up for a meal and associated convivial grog in their building along the shore. It wouldn't do to leave the boat unsupervised. She was the fourth yacht to arrive that year, and the smallest they'd ever seen. The second gale I had encountered on the way there had apparently taken its toll on the Tauranga to Brisbane race with several yachts sustaining damage, a few dropping out into the Bay of Islands early on.

Sunday Island is famous for its oranges. Wray and his crews had gorged themselves frequently, and at one time he made a trip to collect as many as possible to take them back to Auckland to sell (they ate them all on the way home). I'd been looking forward to the same treat, but they were quick to inform me I was a month too early.

The island's history is predictably varied. In the last century a vessel full of leprosy sufferers denied landing elsewhere in the Pacific finally put into uninhabited Denham Bay and most of the passengers went ashore. The crew left their live cargo there and most of them died.

Later on, the Bell family laboured for many years to create a homestead (now Bell's Flat), which was then taken from them when the New Zealand Government annexed the island, callously breaking the spirit of Bell, the original frontiersman. There were also several shipwreck tragedies, one only two years earlier when a solo sailor had anchored offshore where I had spent the night, only to be drowned when the wind shifted, sending his boat onto the rocks. A few months after my visit, a Japanese fishing boat dragged its anchor in Denham Bay, and remains a stranded shell on the beach to this day. After their morbid tale-telling session, which included a few spine-chilling 'bad-vibe' stories, I was quite keen on keeping *Swirly World* in my sights. She was my ticket home, and it was clear that with only their small inflatable, rescue missions were not to be relied upon. With a forecast for a northwesterly change, which would have made our anchorage exposed, I was keen on finding somewhere else to spend the night. According to them, the blow yesterday had made for a rough sea on the other side of the island, and even though the wind was dropping, those bays would have been untenable due to the leftover waves.

Soon the talk drifted around to what was for dinner that night. I was again invited up, but without an anchor watch I couldn't leave my tiny transport to be teased by the hoards of disgruntled entities that surely roamed the coastline. In my seclusion I had become acutely sensitive to the concept of supernatural other frequency, disembodied interest in *Swirly World*'s activities.

As they discussed the steaks that needed removing from the freezer, I visualised lifting *Swirly World* out of the water by the crane used for landing their stores, but it wasn't quite big enough. It was demoralising listening to their domestic discourse, as the only similar situation for me lay far away over hundreds of miles of uncertainty. Oh, for a sheltered anchorage. I could have lingered indefinitely then, though I still had the poetry tour deadline. With another couple of months up my sleeve I could have continued north, we were already halfway to Tonga, and would have soon run into the southeast Tradewinds.

I decided to leave for Auckland that evening. For someone alone, Sunday Island isn't the ideal place, but I had known that before I left. My goal had been to find the island and my way back to Auckland. I was halfway there. Alan Johnson took me out to *Swirly World* then sped back to the rocks. They had an appealing existence there on the island, their various duties occupying a certain amount of their time, with the rest given over to their own private pursuits, whatever they may have been.

I watched them remove the inflatable from the water and send it back through the air to the cliff top. I had a celebratory bottle of wine all ready to open, but on second thoughts, I decided to wait until we reached Little Shoal Bay again. I pulled up the anchor and let *Swirly World* sail slowly away from the coast under the No.1 jib. The sun was setting in the west and off our port quarter I could see two figures making their way home along the narrow cliff path.

As we crawled along in the wind shadow of Hutchinson's Bluff I noticed that even though I was trying to steer *Swirly World* at virtually right angles to the cliffs, a strong current was setting us back in. With the isolated gusts we painstakingly worked out past the unattractive cliffs and into the clearer air blowing across Denham Bay. The current set us over a shoal patch, where the seas tumbled with seemingly hostile intent. *Swirly World* bounced about, rearing up high above the contorting gullies, then fell rapidly, to be swallowed by assorted broken crests. After ten drenching minutes tossing about, we were released to reach southwest over large leftover seas with a dying 15-knot southeasterly. Heading back the way we had come . . . hopefully.

In the dim twilight I stared back at the amphitheatre of high ground surrounding Denham Bay. It looked like an unspoilt spectator, silently observing the inconsequential enterprises of generations of dreamers and derelicts alike. Gradually it faded to a dark outline, then disappeared into night. My heavily symbolic subtropical island dissolved.

There followed several days of light winds, which kept *Swirly World* ghosting along under grey, sullen skies. The seascape seemed to be divided into various zones of slow-moving rain banks, lingering all day and making for intricate sunsets. The bird continued to circle and follow us south. It wouldn't go away. This was a timeless vacuum where days and nights fused into one indistinct continuum. Being by then well adjusted to a life alone in *Swirly World*, I became obsessed with making the most of the shifting breezes; hand steering over long lazy swells, with maximum use of our resource — the wind. The quest for fully efficient sailing, primitively occupied and somehow complete.

I had suspected that a voyage would purge me of this sailing sickness, desire quelled, but it was only serving to encourage me. Acutely tuned to the demands of just having to do it. If you don't do it then you're not going to get there. Tired, it's easy to be pessimistic. Camped on the mud flats with subsistence perspectives, I'd managed to dislodge any value system I'd had by interacting in upmarket and downmarket lives around me. Whatever the social function, the real action was always going on backstage. Individually striving to improve comfort zones or at least maintain the current ones with some adventure thrown in. From all the news and amusements available it seems we can then get on with the real business of life behind the scenes — having emotional problems. A population divided by peer groups and cultures, but united in concealed emotional unsteadiness. Not quite happy enough, unhappy in our private ways. Life in a capitalist democracy discreetly manifesting the perpetual consumer audience, or just where the species is emotionally up to?

My cynicism was leaking out all over the place.

The forecasted gale never arrived. Instead a fresh southwesterly came up hard on the nose and *Swirly World* started slogging into the head seas under a double-reefed main and No.1 jib. The closest we could point to Auckland was Whakatane or North Cape. Not very close at all. With such a contrary wind it would take a while. I started getting worried about the poetry tour. Would we get back in time? Would I be up to reading my poems to people I didn't know? There had been a day in Pukerua Bay . . . the New Zealand Arts Council flew us down for publicity shots for the tour. I was a poet on the plane. I liked it a lot. Flying was easier than sailing, someone did it for you, and they gave you sweets. Hone Tuwhare, Api Taylor, Cilla McQueen and an opportunity to be taken seriously. A review in the student paper *Salient* hadn't taken my first slim volume, *Take The Chocolates And Run*, very seriously. The kind of personal affront that would have had us out with our seconds and swords at dawn on the beach two hundred years ago if I'd had my way. I never got my way, and apparently my tormentor was appointed the poetry tour publicist. There he was in the room. I can't remember what was said. My fellow poets also seemed a bit uncomfortable, though not for the same reason. It appeared they wanted to get off their faces. Who was I to stop them . . .

For seven days we beat south and west while yearning for a fair wind. The adverse current was also knocking 10 to 15 miles off my DR every 24 hours, a bit depressing. Pull up. Emotional fortitude. One night, around 2 a.m. my terrible craving for chocolate brought me to the lowly act of raking through my bags of scroggin to sift out the tiny nuggets of satisfying sweetness. I had to have the stuff. All my life I'd fed that addiction. Sugar. It's legal and encouraged everywhere. Irresponsible. I'd always been a chocolate addict, a habit that even led me to persuading young fans to send boxes of chocolate raisins, which I then consumed in frenzied gluttony in my cabin. Now I was truly deprived — tormented by the memory of that supreme indulgence. My appetite for everything had increased, and a new favourite was porridge. It tasted strange, but by sprinkling on plenty of brown sugar it became palatable. The last time I'd had porridge was when I was about six years old, and I'd forgotten the taste. Little did I know until later (when trying to force it unsuccess-fully on friends) that my oats had gone off and the porridge was sour. Not too bad though, you get used to it.

After one week's worth of headwinds, we were left becalmed about 200 miles northeast of Great Barrier Island. For 24 windless hours *Swirly World* rolled on the glassy swells, slowly drifting back towards Sunday Island. The halyards slapped incessantly against the mast and the tiller jarred viciously against the transom. This happened whenever the self-steering was left to cope with the light zephyrs that always seemed to vanish as soon as I'd retired below. My hair-pulling habit reached its all-time worst that day, and a bot-tle of dishwashing liquid discharged its contents all over the cock-pit, and made for treacherous clamberings and foul-tasting genoa sheets (I usually gripped them in my teeth when trimming sails). Tedious and unsatisfactory, marooned without the wind. Test of resolve.

When the wind finally found us, it came from the north, allow-ing me to set a course direct for the Mokohinaus, not that I could see them. I pulled out the large genoa and contentedly watched our progress over the dark, wind-rippled sea. That afternoon I'd listened, absorbed in the peculiar sound of the sea as the wind teased the glassy calm surface into noisy, tumbling, tiny wavelets. The sumlog had decided to deceive me during this calm and the familiar whir-ring sound of rotating cable denoting progress was absent. I pulled down the sails, and lowered myself over the side to check out the impeller that rotated under the hull. I had goggles strapped uncom-fortably across my forehead for a quick inspection, but on reaching water level I opted for a short wiggle of my toes around the rotator, then a quick exit back to the safety of the cockpit. There was some-thing unsavoury about dangling around in 2000 fathoms of water. I didn't like it at all. The impeller was clear of obstructions, so the cable had broken.

Since we were now getting close to the coast and needed to have a reasonably accurate estimate of when to look out for obstacles, I laboured long the next day to get good sunsights, to start my guess-timates of how many miles we were running. Just to add another minor complication, Radio New Zealand forecast strong to gale-force northerlies for the Northland coast. That happened to be the bit I was aiming for. On our eleventh day out from Sunday Island, we were running towards the uninterrupted southwest horizon under the No.1 jib, with the wind vane steering us along at 5 knots. There was a 25-knot northerly blowing, while behind some ominous rain squalls blocked out the horizon. In the afternoon I tried to get an RDF bearing on the Mokohinaus. As *Swirly World* slewed down the waves and lurched in the troughs, I stood in the cockpit, braced, clutching the RDF with the earphone set on. Just as I'd always wanted to. Tuned to the correct frequency, I moved the set around listening for the null (where Morse signal was inaudible), this meant the set was pointing at the signal's source. Sure enough, the RDF indicated the Mokohinaus lay dead ahead, some 60 miles away by my reckoning. Using the sextant had brought us over the empty ocean to our destination. Later I picked up a Whangarei FM station, which also acted as a rough bearing. We should find the Mokohinau light around midnight, providing visibility didn't deteriorate. I thought about slowing down for the night before running into a lee shore, and would have, if I'd been without the RDF bearing. But after seven days of headwinds and foreseeing the inevitable backing of the wind to the contrary west, or southwest, in your face, we had to make the most of it.

During the evening *Swirly World* did her best to steer us on course, the rain squalls rushing past towards the unseen coastline ahead; waves growing steeper over the shelving sea bed. I was naturally enthused for action. Sitting on the companionway steps, hatchboards in place behind, poking my face out into the wet, unappealing darkness. Land would make a refreshing change of view.

I peered ahead for the faintest sign of light. Mid-evening, when the squalls cleared and visibility improved, I retired below for a bit of revision, in case we happened to come across any lights that wanted to confuse me, or any other pieces of New Zealand that might be nearer than I expected. At 11 p.m. I took my eyes outside again and saw the distinct low-sweeping loom of the Moko light off our port bow. We were back in coastal waters.

Dawn revealed the Hen and Chickens, shrouded in light rain, off our starboard quarter. Land of the 'New Zeal' kind. The wind had shifted to the northwest in the night, bringing heavy rain. I'd stayed in the cockpit hand steering and feeling a bit seasick for the first time since leaving. The shorter, steeper movement of the inshore seas was to blame, and I'd been naturally apprehensive about the wind.

In the early morning light, I sat tired as usual, directing *Swirly World* down the steep leftover waves, good sailing, reaching on course for the clear water between Little Barrier and Leigh. With the wind settling constant at 20 knots, I changed headsails and let out the reefs. I set the self-steering and went below to get some rest before closing in on Leigh. I set my egg-timer alarm for half an hour, climbed into the bag, fixed up the lee cloth and curled up to sail that private sea. Five minutes later, the tiller started banging against the transom and the sails flapped lifelessly. I dragged myself up to see what had gone wrong. The wind had left us. All day we lay becalmed, rolling about on the leftover swells in between Little Barrier and the Hen and Chickens. No doubt about it, the land was good to look at.

With the shelter of the coast the bird that had tailed us had gone. Left in last night's gale without saying goodbye.

The wind returned that evening, sending *Swirly World* slowly past the twinkling lights of Leigh. It was frosty cold and by midnight we were becalmed again, so I hung up my lantern and went inside for a quick half-hour's rest. I slipped into an exhausted sleep that lasted 3 hours but awoke as soon as the wind came up again, leaping out in panic to find, with much relief, that we were still mid-channel. I was OD'ing on the F drug. Losing control of consciousness is not recommended when near the edge of the land.

At dawn on the thirteenth day since Sunday Island, we were ghosting along past Kawau Island. A forecasted northwesterly raised my hopes about making Auckland that afternoon, blowing bush fragrances out across the water. The supreme odour of natural Northland bush again. I'd never noticed it smelling that marvellous before. As *Swirly World* steered herself over the flat sea, I made my last helping of sour porridge. Very nice. Once we were through Tiri Passage the wind unexpectedly backed through to the southwest and we were forced to beat towards the familiar landmarks of Rakino

Island, Rangitoto and the East Coast Bays. The sky was perfectly clear and the wind blew cold from Auckland, at 10 to 15 knots. Looking across at Rangitoto, it felt as though we'd just been out for a leisurely weekday sail to Kawau and back. I stripped off the plastic bag gaskets from the forehatch and anchor locker, and let the fresh air circulate through the open vents; no more 'submarine' seas back in the harbour. At dusk we arrived off North Head with the last of the southwesterly. Up ahead of us was a yacht I'd seen earlier in the day. As we closed in, I saw it had a QME self-steering vane on the stern, like the one I'd bought for *Mylene B*. I soon realised it was the well-equipped *Caprice* I'd thought of buying in Whangarei, some seven months before. In the fading light, we sailed up under her lee and I greeted her skipper, Richard Raea. Coincidentally he had left Tutukaka on the last of the northeasterly, having earlier in the month abandoned a trip to Sunday Island. Two hundred miles out to sea he turned back. 'A lot of trouble with this self-steering gear and a hatchboard went over the side, had to make one out of a ply bunkboard, not much fun.' His self-steering was the same as the one I'd had on the previous boats. As *Swirly World* sailed along beside her, it was as if I was looking at an image of myself, had I decided to go in *Mylene B*; or had I bought that same boat. It felt a bit peculiar, especially as I was coming into the dying moments of the 'got to stay awake' game. Everything was a little bit larger than life.

I sheeted in the lifeless mainsail, and we slowly pulled away up the harbour with the tide. I crouched in the cockpit in tune with the feel of *Swirly World*, simply, sensitively, sailing. After the past moonless nights, the intense lights of the floodlit container terminal shone intensely overbearing and brilliant. A lack of sleep was impairing perception in a way I'd never experienced before. Although I could concentrate on the task of keeping watch, it seemed my senses were impaired. Twice a ferry appeared close by, as if out of nowhere. As we ghosted past the breakwater off Westhaven, the wind finally disappeared and it looked as though it had gone for good. It was shaping up to be another still, frosty night, the tail end of autumn. I started up the engine and we motored under the Harbour Bridge, back to the Little Shoal Bay mooring, where finally after the miles of constant motion *Swirly World* lay absolutely still. Across the water the bay lay calm and silent. We'd come in direct from the darkness beyond, and it made for seeing Little Shoal Bay in a more fabulous way. I removed the sails and went below to write up the logbook. After 1400 miles sailing we were back.

I had something to talk to Johnny Wray about. I struggled with the folding coracle, prising it open at the back, only to have the front slam shut and send me toppling about the foredeck. Eventually I tamed it, dropping it onto the water, and clambered down with the kitbag and still unopened bottle of wine.

I paddled past *Mylene B,* over the misty surface towards the motel lights ashore. In the car park mums and dads waited patiently for the Wednesday night Sea Scout meeting to finish. I stepped ashore, folded up my dinghy and started to walk to the phone box. After twenty-three days of constant motion over an undulating ocean, I staggered about with my wine bottle in one hand, and my kitbag in the other. There was no point trying to appease the unimpressed parents.

I phoned home and found the poetry tour had been cancelled due to one of the performers pulling out. Karyn was at an awards show in Wellington. I had mixed feelings. I took a taxi ride back home to Ngahere Terrace, and finally opened the bottle of wine.

In the middle of the night, I awoke in a sudden disoriented panic and lunged out to feel the side of *Swirly World.* There was nothing there but blackness. I felt around for my flashlight to check the compass course; nothing familiar, too much space around me, where's the side of the boat?

The next day I found out that while I was away, Johnny Wray had died.

Slowly, my appreciation for land living was contaminated by the reality of our musical affairs. You can't arrive in a small town every couple of months and consistently expect to command a large audience. There's a universal tendency to lose interest after a while. Our publicity peaked after a handful of 'hit' singles but stoically (for want of something else to do) we kept returning on an overexposed, too-frequent cycle to all those little towns that had been so good to us.

They'd eventually lost a fair amount of interest and we had to face the overbearing reality that in the high turnover, rapid-use media, the use-by dates stamped on our foreheads had apparently expired. We were skiing on the downhill slopes of a well-worn trail. Part-time jobs loomed their ugly heads again, character-building episodes. We swore dedication to another album to exert our musical selves. Reluctantly it was agreed to curtail further live outings until we glimpsed the future possibility of larger audiences. A tactical withdrawal.

Reinvention, a well-precedented thing. You peak, everyone knows about you, then it's someone else's turn. The commentators become the constant voices, the artists rocketing off to well-meaning, self-funded obscurity.

'Big in NZ? Then what?'

'It's a difficult one. Unless some other part of the globe embraces you, you're done for.'

'Thanks, I'll remember that.'

'It's nothing personal, marketplace context, written in the eternal book of economics, good luck.'

We stopped playing for a few months. No one wanted to stop. Overexposed, tubed. The drummer, bass player and his brother the lighting pirate, started working on busy nights in a wine bar backstage off Queen St. Once again *Swirly World* grew weeds on her bottom, occasionally going around the inner harbour to charge the battery and keep the engine in working order. I refused to let her go by herself.

Drumming burns up lots of energy. Steve wasn't really into cooking. He'd rather be a rock star, he'd had a taste of it. Full time, well funded next time, not part-time New Zealand style. 'That's the trouble with here Fagan, there's not enough people, it's tubed.'

He was as bored as we all were with going round beautiful, scenic New Zealand, tour after scraping-by tour. Seen it all before, familiarity truly breeding our contempt. We talked of the States. Steve was convinced he wouldn't get in — adolescent pot convictions. We got a winter Chateau ski gig and played for the first time in a few months.

Playing felt new again and we enjoyed it. Someone threw a glass, but I vaguely remember having provoked them. The next morning Steve was in the Sunday paper. Six months earlier at the Windsor in Parnell a policeman had asked for ID to prove his age. Steve was undersized compared to most, but not underage. The policeman didn't like his indignant attitude and he was arrested. The article compared him to Keith Moon, calling him the 'Wild Man of NZ Rock.' Life of the everlasting party. Steve was having none of it. Within a week he was dead. Found in a car up past the East Coast Bays. Left the party unannounced.

Chapter 4

Message in a plastic bag

At dawn on the eleventh day of 1987, I paddled out to *Swirly World*.
Up came full main and genoa, and off the mooring to beat up the
harbour, into wind and sun slowly rising from the east. As we rounded North Head, I could see the first of the P Class sails being hoisted
over at Tamaki Yacht Club. It was one of the closing days of the
P Class nationals, and there would have been a few people there
more anxious than me that morning.

I'd done it as well. Dunedin 1978, the Tauranga Cup. A big year
for my racing career. Russell Coutts was sailing his last season in
P Class yachts (7-ft solo trainer boats hotted up to violin-case finish-
es, custom alloy spars, the thinnest of sails).

Coutts was a legend in his own adolescence. I'd heard about him
in Wellington. He was from Dunedin. He had long hair, wore a
wetsuit long on his thighs, and was favoured to win on his home
turf. We never saw much of him. He seemed to get chauffeured
about by his father and associates in presidential style, sweeping
into the Vauxhall Club car park from Ravensbourne in a big long
car.

I'd got the measure of him in light airs earlier in the year when he
sailed in Evans Bay on his way back from an Auckland regatta. Rigging our boats one Saturday morning we were stunned to see 'Team
Coutts' pull in to rig his P Class. He even changed in our club changing room where the urinals smelt fiercely of urine . . . A light southerly, the last breath of a gale had the bay at its best for me. I was a

lot lighter, he had more hair on his legs than me. I had more boat speed, picked the right shifts, knew where they would be. All the way up the final beat keeping a loose cover, no flyers, sticking to the rhumb line, the luxury of better boat speed. It was good for my local reputation to beat him. Good for my summer club championship points as well.

I'd decided to have a go at sailing *Swirly World* down to Wellington to leave her there while we went to the Northern Hemisphere to see what it was like. I'd read of all the 'hell-trips' associated with the Wairarapa Coast and Cape Palliser — boats failing to beat up to Wellington against the northwesterlies, southerly busters destroying racing fleets. It could be a severe stretch of sea, I'd often witnessed the wind's fury in Wellington. I decided to go the extra 200 miles up around Cape Reinga, and then 500 miles down the west coast. We could then, if need be, run in on the westerlies to sanctuary somewhere in the Marlborough Sounds. It sounded easy to say.

The previous week had been spent tracking the paths of various cyclones; the tail end of one having blown most of the tents off the Northland Coast a few days earlier. I also visited the Met office to get an educated prediction on when would be the best time to charge north for 200 miles. Unfortunately, there wasn't a 'foreseeable' southwesterly anywhere in the near future, and the proposed charge north looked destined to be a dawdle. And so it was to be. A light northeasterly headwind we picked up off Rangitoto forced us to beat slowly up past Whangaparaoa and Kawau, leaving us becalmed off Leigh for the night.

I put out the lantern and retired for a rest as *Swirly World* slowly sailed over the flat sea towards the distant glow of Whangarei. I popped up a little later, to find that the breeze was blowing directly from Whangarei and, combined with the tide, had set us towards the long uninterrupted surf beach beyond Leigh. The Cape Rodney light blinked a little too close for my liking, and the sound of the surf had become distinctly louder, so I put us about and hand steered gradually away from the shore until daylight.

All that morning we were becalmed, picking up a light headwind in the afternoon, which again left us motionless the following morning off the Poor Knights. The excellent weather, bringing lots of sunshine and thirty-plus temperatures to Northland, did nothing for progress north, and it was made more unbearable by the 'Dacroned Armada' sailing downhill past us back to Auckland, after their summer holidays. One catamaran, with copious suntanned pillars of gender-pronounced perfection, came close by and asked where I was going. They were quick to point out that Wellington was in the other direction, so I resolved not to be truthful with others, should I have the misfortune to encounter them. Sailing to Wellington was not a humorous proposition for me.

In order to find a bit of relief from the constantly adverse headwinds and yachting traffic, we headed out from the lee of Cape Brett for 12 hours, until the land was no longer visible, then went about to point hopefully as close to North Cape as we could. At this stage, the temptation to return to Auckland was great, as it would have been easy to turn and run back down the coast. I longed for that gate to be slammed behind us by a brisk following breeze. North Cape represented the starting line of my trip to Wellington and all the drifting about in those well-frequented Northland waters tended to compound my many reservations about entering the Tasman.

Certain stretches of sea are viewed as almost out of bounds to modern-day sailors, when only a hundred years ago, sealers and whalers were lingering in those same waters, in sailing craft less equipped and less seaworthy than a lot of those about today. Not necessarily less seaworthy, but certainly less manoeuvrable. Not that it stopped them. Wanganui, Patea, Wairoa, Greymouth, Manukau — in over the bar, taking the close, engine-less inshore chances our modern sailing minds are not conditioned for.

Twenty-four hours later we were about 5 miles off Matai Bay on the Karikari Peninsula (35 miles short of North Cape) and after a forecast promising more headwinds, I gave up in disgust and dropped into Matai Bay. I intended to wait for a possible southwest change the following day, and try my luck in getting a replacement battery for the RDF, which had deceived me and died after its battery had been overcharged in Auckland.

At 7 a.m. we drifted in past the early-morning holiday fishermen, and anchored close to the nostril-stirring shore. After four nights and days of attentive sailing against light headwinds, we'd only managed 170 miles, and that was in the direction of Norfolk, not Wellington. I pulled out the coracle, wrapped the RDF in a plastic bag in case we got swamped in the surf, and paddled into the sheltered end of the beach. Birds and cicadas greeted me with the tones of a Northland summer paradise. After some tricky leaping about to avoid a drenching, I folded the dinghy and hid it in the bushes. It was going to be another scorching day. I barefooted it along the empty beach, feeling fortunate for the fine, unthreatening moments. Out in the sheltered bay beneath a cloudless blue sky, *Swirly World* rolled a little, sturdy and inspiring.

I hitched a ride to Kaitaia with some bored young men. The driver seemed intent on making those 20-odd miles the most dangerous part of my journey. He was showing off. I didn't want to be a part of his audience, captive till the car accident. Suburban Auckland rally-driving on holiday.

Eventually Kaitaia hove into view and they let the hitchhiker go. I was grateful. A very knowledgeable electronics man diagnosed my RDF as suffering from overcharging, and while he fitted a substitute power source, I sat in a cheap restaurant stuffing fish and chips into my body. I hadn't really been eating anything in the heat, and most of the food I had with me was left over from the Sunday Island trip, not very appetising. I was tired, and the pressure of the distance to run brought on a wave of pessimism that led me to thinking about returning to Auckland to sell *Swirly World*! In some ways it was more pressure going to Wellington. Convincing myself it was the only place to leave the boat was denying myself the alternative of returning. No retreat.

After a real night's sleep, confidence of a sort was restored. I tuned into the weather forecasts to find out if we were going to get the right breeze for sneaking around the top of the North Island. The next day was going to be the one, so I spent 12 sunbaked hours roaming the peninsula and ridges round the bay, staring down at the tiny green boat. At one spot a large platform had been built, more like a bed than a bench, and from it I could see the whole of Karikari Beach stretching out below, and the east coast stretching up to the distant hazy outline of North Cape. I lay there watching the paths of gusts endlessly crossing Rangaunu Bay, and faced with such a natural timeless context, attempted to bury a message in a bottle. Unfortunately I didn't have a bottle so I made do with a sealed plastic bag. In it I put a dollar note and the message, 'Waiting for the wind to round North Cape en route to Wellington.' I buried it in hard sand; to remain a future reminder of former uncertainty, should I be led back in other circumstances.

The adverse wind left overnight, and the next day was character-istically calm with the promise of an increasing northwesterly that afternoon. To reduce the amount of beating to do when the wind arrived, I let the engine chug us noisily across 30-odd miles of Great Exhibition Bay.

Off the entrance to Parengarenga Harbour, a refreshing light breeze arrived to dry my sweaty body. The sun had become a nuisance, inflicting on me an over-baked face, with an uncomfortable cluster of wickedly oozing cold sores on my lower lip. Herpes. Jumped me from a kiss when I wore a five-year-old's face, it's hanging in for the ride . . .

With no sign of life anywhere around us, I expected to see an old-time sailing ship come running around North Cape. That part of the coastline remains the same as it must have always looked from the sea.

We were leaving the relative security of Northland's east coast, for the unknowns of the Tasman Sea. As *Swirly World* sailed hard on the wind on the port tack, slowly working out past North Cape, I stared at the empty horizon to the north, and hoped there weren't any more cyclones brewing. Once around the top there was no real shelter till Golden Bay, or the Marlborough Sounds at the top of the South Island; New Plymouth was a potential leeshore only to be sought in the best weather. I had decided to sail out west from Cape Reinga until we hit longitude 172, and then go south down the line. Sounded great in theory. Now I had to do it. Mile by slow mile. That far out would keep us a good 100 miles from the west coast, in case some mean southwesterly wanted to push us onto one of those unsympathetic surf beaches.

That evening we beat magnetic north, away from the two capes. Everyone always seemed to make a big deal about the tide race and associated overfalls off Cape Reinga, so I sailed *Swirly World* well away from land to avoid the worst of it. As the sun set, silhouetting the Three Kings in the distance, we went about and started beating out towards Sydney.

During the night the tides helped and hindered us, and by the next morning we were about 5 miles north of Cape Reinga, and in sight of Cape Maria Van Diemen. The northwesterly was slowly increasing, and I had to do my first sail change since leaving Auckland; later being forced to learn how to reef again. At 8.30 that night, with the Three Kings lying north of us and the North Island nowhere to be seen, I set our course south. Relieved to be going in the right direction, apprehensive about what the wind might have planned for me.

The barometer was dropping, so we had to make the most of the northerly sector wind before it backed west or southwest. The basic stuff a sailor gets passionate about. For the next two days we ran with a 25 to 30-knot northwesterly on our starboard quarter. More basic stuff sailors get . . .

Our best 24-hour run was 127 miles by the log, which beat the previous best of 96 miles on the way to Sunday Island. The true run would have been about 110 miles given the adverse current, but without sunsights I was unable to confirm it.

With a fair wind to Wellington, the gate was at last shut behind us, and the attraction of retreating was gone. Surprisingly, no seasickness, even though the seas were quite lumpy, probably because I'd been able to adjust gradually to a little motion up the east coast. It was good to be back in that tiny fragile world again; progress and isolation dissolving previous doubts about continuing and enduring. I lay strapped in the bunk, the lee cloth holding me secure as we rushed blindly down the liquid hills. Back again in the sea hut. Fully loaded with vulnerable moments. Pop your head into the Perspex viewing dome above the bunk and watch the plywood cocoon gracefully riding the waves. You're inside . . . From the bunk you can check the windflow on the sails without having to get out of the sleeping bag.

Often asleep, face down, I'd have a vivid sensation of gliding in the air, over a great river gully beside a railway bridge. Flying. *Swirly*

World dropped down into a trough and rose onto a crest and it was as if I was floating through pockets of turbulence.

On the evening of Monday 19 January I began a serious search. We were filling up with water. Slowly. Nothing a sponge and bucket couldn't fix, but still technically taking in water. After a thorough sponging of the bilges, a few hours later I found lots more salt water slopping around inside. You start worrying about seams opening up, split sheets of ply . . . I threw everything onto the forward bunks and tediously inspected all the underwater fittings, but nothing seemed to be leaking. Luckily, a sudden lurch revealed a loose inspection port in the cockpit letting in copious amounts of unwelcome salt water. A most welcome find.

Progress was slowed by calms with a big confused swell. Life became emotionally taxing. Attending to the demands of fickle zephyrs, and the associated noise and rolling about on the restless sea's surface is most definitely one of the most negative aspects in long-distance sailing.

The swell subsided as a moderate easterly picked up, which was quite unexpected, but did at least make the east coast of Australia our lee shore; some 1100 miles away. The easterly decided to torment me by going around the compass all night with gale-force rain squalls and a formidable lightning display in the vicinity of Kawhia, which slowly moved away further southeast, much to someone's relief.

For most of the night, so often that it became impolite, I'd lock the self-steering onto the desired course, get the sails right for what felt like a steady breeze blowing out of the blackness, then retire below, take off my cold, clammy wet-weather smock and try to sleep. I would then be raised in a rush to tangle my way into my safety harness, climb out into the icy driving rain, release the sheets to bring *Swirly World* upright again, claw down the sails to stop them flogging to pieces, then relieve the wind vane of its desire to sail us to Sydney, Noumea or Manukau Harbour, depending on the new wind direction.

About 4 a.m. I gave up and let *Swirly World* drift around with the helm lashed hard over, and the No.2 jib sheeted in. I lay below and lost consciousness for a little while . . .

Another day of calms with a falling barometer brought on a strong desire for accurate position fixing. With a sunsight and an RDF bearing on the Waitara beacon near New Plymouth, I found we were 20 miles closer to the coast than anticipated. I put this down to the current that sets up the North Island and seems to follow the curve of the coast. We were 80 miles northwest of New Plymouth. The weather forecast that morning was for 35-knot northwesterlies, followed by 25-knot westerlies, which meant all downhill sailing, so that night we headed on course for Cape Farewell to clear Cape Egmont by at least 60 miles the following day.

I still hadn't graduated to a single sideband radio that would bring a more up-to-the-moment weather forecast. In the 24 hours between the daily 5 a.m. Relda Familton AM National programme broadcasts, my depression racing over the Tasman was deepening into a 'very deep low' of 975. I thought she was talking about my frame of mind. It was expected to cross the South Island near Westport, 200 miles south of *Swirly World*. Oh dear, we were in for it.

As the northwesterly increased, our sail area decreased, so that by dawn on 22 January we were running under just the No.2 working jib, doing 5 to 6 knots with the tiny storm jib hanked on rather overcautiously, ready to go. By 7.30 a.m. I figured the wind to be at least 35 knots but was reluctant to admit to any more as the Met team weren't expecting anything nasty.

That morning the wind got up more, blowing a velocity of raw air that hinted of far greater consequences, especially when you're tired. The wind vane had been doing its best to keep the wind and waves on the quarter but was frequently overpowered. Twice *Swirly World* was pushed over, the viewing dome half-underwater. Knock downs. It was surprisingly subdued inside, but poke your head out to have a look and it was a fully alive, cold, wet world carrying on in a thoroughly uncomfortable way. All the crests were rushing down the waves, while the clouds raced overhead; seemingly not much higher than the masthead.

Now and then an extra big wave would lift *Swirly World*'s quarter and slew her a little sideways along the top of the water ledge. Once pointing higher, she would fight to pull downwind again, but the correction needed was more than the wind vane could muster, so at 11 a.m. I reluctantly put on all my gear, climbed out into the cockpit and locked the door to my hideaway world inside. I clipped the safety harness to the deck-line and started hand steering down the big jumbled seas. The barometer had fallen to 988 millibars, and shortly after my taking control, a 60-knot rain squall came through that destroyed my faith in the Met office. The sea went white-out, and I expected the old storm jib to blow out. After a series of malevolent squalls, the wind suddenly backed to the west and the sky cleared, the wind remaining steady at 45 knots.

I nervously chewed my way through half a box of barley sugars while steering towards the empty southeastern horizon. It was great progress, but we had sailed into an area where the sea bed shelved from deep ocean to 200 metres. Crossing into shallower water was inevitable, but doing it then was bad timing. With the sea bed shelving and the backing of the wind, the seas became steeply breaking, with large westerly waves mixing with breaking northwesterly waves. Around 2 p.m. a breaking surf-beach sea reared up out of nowhere to menace *Swirly World*. It was quick but it seemed to take ages to topple down on top of us. There wasn't time or steerage to turn us away from it, so I convincingly grabbed the handrail, braced my body into the cockpit, and took air into my lungs. I looked on with mixed emotions as it came down.

The wave filled the cockpit and pressed me against the side. I felt *Swirly World* stop dead in the water, and a few seconds later was sitting up to my chest in warmish water (compared to the chilling wind), attentively surveying the deck. The worst of it had landed on the port side, bending one weather-clothed stanchion right down to touch the Perspex dodger, thankfully still intact. Nothing else was damaged. The water quickly drained out of the cockpit and *Swirly World* surfaced again, quite undaunted by it all. I had a desperate look inside, half expecting to find a foot of water swilling around, but the floorboards were still visible. Was this the beginning of something far more unpleasant? I steered us on and around wave after wave of shrieking westerly wind-driven water. During occasional lapses of concentration I savoured the taste of barley sugar sweets soaked in salt water. I started getting used to them.

Chapter 5

The wind, the moon and light rain

Teenage miles of heavy-weather dinghy sailing came into their own as *Swirly World* surfed down the steeply confused seas, touching 9 knots at times. Apart from contemplating the threat of imminent extinction, it was the most exhilarating sailing one could hope for. You're sailing for your life now, no cups or trophies, handicap winners . . . sailing to stay alive.

The pressure of physically maintaining the right course while combating the waves was fatiguing. Then suddenly here we are caught between two wave trains and *Swirly World* broaching sideways . . . That dead feel in the water again and for one ugly instant it seemed we were going to be rolled over by the next wave. If the wrong wave had followed, we would have gone over. I instinctively leaned up against the stanchions, ready to move onto the keel had it been necessary, but the following wave forgave. Teenage training hadn't allowed for the safety harness clipped onto the deck restricting my mobility.

As the day progressed, the seas became more even and the wind vane did its best again while I hid inside. That evening I heard on the radio that New Plymouth Airport had been closed and also some surf beaches along the coast. At Thames on the Coromandel a seawall had been washed away. It was encouraging to get confirmation of the severity of the gale; so much so that I clambered up into the dusk to pull on a bigger headsail for the night. That first sail increase after a gale seemed to symbolise the celebration of defiant survival. A feeling worth believing in.

By night I adjusted *Swirly World* to steer us further south again, not wanting to be caught too close to the Patea coast if the wind backed southwest. All night we reached with 30 knots on the beam and a great interest in the possibility of being run down.

At 5 a.m. I tuned into the Met man in Wellington. I often taped his forecasts for the various areas to put together a rough wind chart of what was going on. His sombre tones always instilled the greatest seriousness in me. It was as if he was personally involved in our survival, and imparting such valuable information forged a psychological alliance. It seemed like that every morning as I lay there fatigued and on edge, by myself in a void of pre-dawn darkness, rushing down the waves, water noises everywhere.

Over the last week or so he had insensitively forecast gales, severe gales and more gales for Cook Strait. Now we were closing in on the area, and it felt as if we were being sucked into a vortex compared to which the previous day's gale was only a warm-up. He made me feel even more uncomfortable . . .

Shortly after the forecast I sighted the lights of two large fishing boats slowly heading northwest, and for a short confused time, before realising they were moving, I thought one of them might have been the oil rig off Patea. I had been getting an RDF bearing from Patea during the night which was very clear, yet according to my booklet, we should have been out of its range. Being unable to pick up the Stephen's Island signal seemed strange because it was supposed to be twice as strong as the Patea one, and we were within its range. Considerately, just after dawn, I heard the faint Morse sounds of Stephen's Island directly ahead of the bow. Sanctuary was beckoning. All morning we ran under the No.1 jib, with only 25 knots of westerly wind behind us. A Japanese fishing boat came up astern, then turned away towards Nelson, rolling terribly on the steep seas. I didn't envy them.

Swirly World has a viewing port made of inch-thick, bulletproof Perspex in her bottom. I'd kept it covered up, finding the deep blue sea a bit disconcerting, but the colour had now changed to turquoise, meaning we were into the 100-fathom area. We were about 40 miles away from Stephen's Island, then at 11.45 a.m. I sighted the high hills of D'Urville Island emerging from a low cloud bank. I suppressed my expression of pleasure in case some sadistic ex-sailing entity was flitting about waiting to test my endurance, but marvelled again at the wonders of navigation that can bring one accurately across nowhere noticeable.

Unfortunately, I didn't suppress my attitude well enough. If the wind had stayed as it was we would have had a good ride down through Cook Strait to the Wellington Heads, but we had been tailed all morning by an evil-looking squall, which finally decided to move in for the kill. The wind picked up to 35 knots before the rain hit, and I assumed that would be the most it would blow. I still had the No.1 jib up, which was pulling us along at 6 knots, when dramatically the rain squall was upon us and blasting through at 50 knots. The whole rig strained as the sea went white-out. Not having the safety harness on, I didn't want to go forward to drop the sail in case I got a bad score. With an unsympathetic exploding sound, a seam of the sail blew apart and the cloth flogged out ahead of the bow in long, tattered streamers. The rig shook violently, and I had to go forward and drop it anyway. After that, the wind increased all afternoon until, contented at 45 knots, we were again running under the storm jib, in big, breaking seas. Hand steering was still easier than the previous day, but twice breaking chunks came rushing down the face of waves and over the stern to fill the cockpit and dodger, and shunt *Swirly World* along in a mass of broken water. The wet force was frightening. How bad could bad be? Will it get any worse? Not sure if I want to be here right now.

Stephen's Island gradually grew more defined, but as we closed in, the seas became worse, most probably from an adverse current. Often I'd hear a deep explosive sound, only to look round and see the leftover foaming remains of a deceased breaker. I witnessed a huge curling crest explode 100 metres away — thankful we weren't under it. It was Russian roulette, racing along, not knowing when or where the next mast-breaker or hull-tripper was going to pounce. Vulnerable was a very appropriate word.

After another tense, barley sugar-chewing time, we reached the lee of Stephen's Island where huge willie-waws of lifting spray raced unpredictably all over the place. It was only then that I realised how rough it was out there. I looked back at the mass of shining white-crested turmoil beyond the island and felt relief in having managed, as planned, to run down to sanctuary in the Marlborough Sounds. If we had gone down the east coast we would have been blown out to the Chatham Islands.

It was just starting to get dark and there was no time to relax as *Swirly World* had yet to face a night-negotiation of Pelorus Sound. I went to start the engine, but found that the exhaust valve had seized up, as it was prone to do if not used at least every four or five days. The only way to unstick it was to take the head off, so I set *Swirly World* self-steering down towards the sound under the storm jib, as I maniacally performed heart surgery. Every so often a willie-waw would strike, sending *Swirly World* onto her side and the nuts and bolts all over the place.

I got it going, only to find the water pump wasn't working because the main fuse had blown from the odd gallon of water sneaking in from the flooded cockpit incidents. Having no fuse, we were destined to go in the proper way, the wind in our sails . . .

I had cut my finger on the engine casing, creating a trail of blood everywhere I went, so while I reefed and set the main and No.2 jib, I also, in my disassociated fatigue, finger painted a pretty crimson pattern over the previously unblemished fabric.

The moon was trapped behind a cloud bank over Cook Strait, and Pelorus Sound was absolutely black. There was no distinction between shoreline and sea, so I kept *Swirly World* as close to mid-channel as I could, while we tediously worked up the mouth of the sound, either racing along over-canvassed in fierce gusts, or drifting back on the tide, in the lulls. I was trying to find Waihinau Bay, which was tucked under the hills just inside the entrance, and although there were a few shore lights about, none of them gave any indication of the right bay. I wanted to get up past the bay before turning in to anchor, as there was an unlit reef off its northern end. The only navigation aid was the outline of ridges silhouetted against the sky, and by tracing the highest peaks on the chart and comparing them to our position, I found we had overshot the bay. As we worked back, gusts came from all directions without warning, and we were constantly tacking onto various wind shifts with the alacrity of a racing sailor. There was the odd distant flash of lightning, but the momentary illuminations never lasted long enough to help much. On the flat sea *Swirly World* turned gusts into acceleration, then we encountered a consistent breeze blowing down the sound, and reaching across, pushed out a bow wave of phosphorescence, leaving another glowing green behind us. *Swirly World* was perfectly balanced as she sailed along, and in my forced state of application I perceived the wind at last as my ally, and was pleased I had been denied the ease of motoring in. Finally, at 2 a.m. on the eighth day out from Matai Bay, we ghosted in close to a lonesome shore light. I dropped the anchor over the side, pulled the sails down, and greeted the silent darkness of the surrounding bay.

As if they had been invited to attend my isolated celebration, the moon crawled up out of its cloud bank, and light rain began to fall.

After a real sleep, I was woken up by an H28, *Basil Brush*, which came alongside in early daylight to kindly demonstrate the wonders of SSB radio, and send a telegram through to Wellington for me. The rest of the day I cleaned up and dried out the squalor of the previous few days, and tried to reacquaint myself with the concept of appetite. I had continued to eat very little on the way down. Nothing really appealed, and I knew I hadn't got far to go. I fried up some greasy eggs and chips and stodged out in a big way. Eating. There's a lot to be said for it.

The weather cleared up, but the gale-force winds continued to rush through the strait. I finally relaxed. Safe in a bay with an anchor attached to some shingle below. No motion or water noises. Still security.

In the evening a fisherman gave me a new 15-amp fuse which brought the engine back to life. Five a.m. the following morning brought a forecast of 15-knot northwesterlies, with a southerly change expected that afternoon. At 8 a.m. we were off Cape Jackson, and set for an easy run through Cook Strait. I could see Cape Terawhiti out across the strait, and the clear run downhill looked inviting, but I had become overly cautious now we were so close to home. I didn't want to run into the strait to encounter a southerly, and the associated seas I had witnessed before from the safety of the Wellington shore. Instead a run into Queen Charlotte Sound and up through Tory Channel to anchor at the entrance, and wait out the southerly front until a favourable wind returned would do. I hand steered down the sound, past craft no bigger than *Swirly World*, while on my lap I viewed the chart bought when I was thirteen and first developing a fascination for the edge of the land.

Off Dieffenbach Point, at the beginning of Tory Channel, the wind fell light and a new 40-ft racing yacht from Picton circled us. 'Where you from?' They could tell by the windowboards *Swirly World* was the business.

'Auckland.'

'In that?'

'I hear there's a southerly on the way?'

The foredeck boys looked unmagnetically about, started pointing to the northern horizon. 'I can see a few clouds building up down there . . .'

The tide was just starting to flood, which meant 6 hours of opposition in Tory Channel. With the light breeze pushing us along, I poled out the genoa on the opposite side from the main, and we worked up the channel, a few feet away from the shore.

After 6 attentive hours of creeping along the cliffs to avoid the current, we arrived at the entrance to Cook Strait. The wind was still blowing 15 to 20 knots from the northwest and the Met team had changed their minds about the southerly front, postponed until tomorrow. So, after a 9-hour scenic detour, we popped out on the start of the ebbing tide, to sail the last 35 miles home.

There was a cloud bank down south, and I watched it diligently to make sure it wasn't trying to creep up on us. With the wind and the tide our allies, *Swirly World* sailed over the flat sea, heeled over, the fresh breeze rushing us along at 6 knots. The tides run rapidly in the strait and I didn't want us to see *Swirly World* becalmed and pushed down towards Cape Palliser. Concentrating on driving *Swirly World* as fast as possible towards Cape Terawhiti was the order. The wind was filling the sails to surge us forward, and though the radio was on down below, I registered only the time signals sounding each hour. It seemed as if only a few minutes passed between each one. Trance sailing . . .

The wind slowly veered to the north and dropped away at dusk to leave us wallowing off Devil's Gate. We'd already been pushed south by the tide, as the Cook Strait ferries were passing well to the north of us. Start the engine? A light northeasterly filled in and we started beating towards Baring Head. We were being swept southeast, and I gambled on the wind holding on as we headed further east, before tacking back in towards the coast. Soon the familiar lights of Owhiro Bay and Island Bay came into view, then at last we were far enough east to put one big tack in towards the lights of Kilbirnie. Gradually the coast came closer until we were almost sailing directly into Lyall Bay. It was my shoreline. I'd done twenty years there, bicycling round those bays, staring at the empty, often turbulent southern horizon. I recalled numerous occasions parked at night, looking out at the navigation lights of some sailing boat making its way towards the hostile Wellington Heads. I remembered following their progress up the harbour to surreptitiously share in the final stages of another Cook Strait crossing. Whoever it was never mattered, just knowing that it was being done.

Swirly World's navigation lights dipped about on the swell, as we skirted along the rocks with the light offshore breeze.

At midnight, we sailed in past Moaning Mini and Barrett Reef, and the scent of damp bush drifted out across the water to greet us. Inhalation, exhalation.

Swirly World slowly worked up past Scorching Bay and rounded Point Halswell to drift down Evans Bay with the dying northeasterly. Good old Evans Bay. I'd done a lot of capsizing on that water. Sandwiched between suburbs, you learn to sail the windy Wellington way. Sounding a feeble warble on the foghorn was an appropriate gesture. I started the engine to take us over the last half mile of windless water. No wind in Wellington. We were lucky. After 21 hours of hand steering we found a mooring, and I retired below for a little more sleep. There was nothing to get up for in a few hours' time, thankfully.

The next morning Cobham Drive was noisy and alive with Workerland cars speeding by. I closed the hatch and dropped the folding coracle onto the water. A couple of photos of *Swirly World* elegantly at rest and fully disengaged from duty, then the paddle to the wharf, across the water where many a centreboard had been lowered on leaving, raised on returning. I folded up my faithful transport, then breathed in the bay and deserted yacht club. It was the view common to many an idle sailor's stare through the seasons. I'd seen it all before but the bright green boat was new to the view. *Swirly World in Perpetuity* had finally arrived.

Chapter 6

Where steeples spike the sky

Within 24 hours of the rain's arrival, the river swelled a serious shade of muddy-brown, sweeping debris down from inundated under-growth. All night, logs and nail-ridden planking came by on the current, scraping sinister salutations beneath us. It kept raining, and the little vein of the land turned into the varicose kind, increasing in height and speed until it was undoubtedly a swollen, nasty piece of debris-carrying fluid.

Being unfamiliar with potential flood levels, the mooring stakes had been hammered into a section of clay bank 6 ft above the wa-ter. With six inches left, we pulled up stakes and let the boat turn out into the swift-flowing water. Boats had sometimes been lifted ignominiously into the surrounding paddock. With full throttle and a fearfully vibrating engine, we slowly pushed upstream to a shel-tered bend and currentless corner beside the West Molesey Sea Scout headquarters. Safe from that rushing wicked liquid. The gentle sanc-tuary of a corner of weir-free dead end, tucked away from rainfall currents pushing fast for the sea.

We'd landed on the other side of planet earth and gained access to the freshwater fast track thanks to a decaying 28-ft, mahogany motorboat built in 1958, called *Moonfleet Smuggler*. After a battered life of hard holiday knocks from apprentice drivers, she ended up forlorn and for sale, until the English summer of 1987. It would be easy to lose a few years riding the curves of the Thames non-tidal riverside. The 50 miles from Wallingford to Teddington were waiting.

Moonfleet Smuggler was luxurious by mud-flat standards. Two cabins, standing headroom, a four-burner stove and oven, hot water, shower, TV and a 2.2 litre BMC diesel engine to charge the batteries and move about at the turn of a key. A mobile home parked in the backyards of many rich and famous people. Better to keep moving, not invoke any unfavourable impressions. Not visually violate their expensive views. The need to run the engine most days to charge the batteries, combined with the expense of a permanent live-board mooring resulted in a life always on the move. Every 24 hours, for 36 months, we moved between riverbank moorings. It wasn't far and there were no waves to worry about.

Delivering songs to northern ears transmuted into a lengthy re-evaluation of what was worth delivering. While brewing potions of self-expression, subsistence existence oscillated between moonless raids on pumpkin fields, fondling riverbank plum trees and airless rides on crowded rush-hour trains — to and from the money-paying workhouses.

Harrods, a grand spectacle of choice, service and expensive prices, wanted extra slaves for the Christmas rush. There were lots of backstage rooms and backstage jobs. Tristram Jones, a renowned solo ocean sailor and social adventurer, had lived in the hot, noisy boiler room of Harrods in the late sixties, eating discarded food and planning an epic South American sailing adventure. He had returned there in 1975 to write half of his book *The Incredible Voyage* in the same boiler room. Our fortune needed topping up, so I took the opportunity to become a 'Harrodian Charioteer' in the tunnels of Knightsbridge, whilst searching discreetly for a trace of Tristan Jones. It's not too demanding dragging round a rola-truc, loading up with cartons of Christmas crackers that cost £80 per box of ten. Carting pallets of exclusive toilet paper for exclusive bottoms, exclusive pet food, delicious handmade chocolates . . .

Life in the labyrinth of underground passageways was often busy and often boring. A lot of time was spent waiting on ancient tradesmen's lifts in slow-moving, talkative queues.

Were the working class workmates deprived? For an outsider with an Antipodean accent, Great Britain appeared to be built on a shifting foundation of social segregation. Speaking reveals one's legacy of learning or non-learning and the company you have kept in culturally defining and socially confining ways. Not so for everyone but 'so and so' for many.

My parents had escaped West Bromwich in the West Midlands in 1949. They were still rationing butter in England then. A long voyage via Panama and Pitcairn, eventually direct into Wellington and handstands on Owhiro Bay beach. I'd revised their immigrant lives in the old dark-green photo album in the front room, off and on, through my years of being a boy. Shots of the land a long way off, from seaward. Pitcairn Island traders in their open boats, a long way down, from the rail of the ship. Romantic and adventurous if you came from the West Midlands Black Country.

In pre-dawn darkness, *Moonfleet Smuggler* would be left in favour of crunching the frosted towing path that led to a train full of strangers, with blank looks of sleepy resignation. Each morning I listened to 'Caroline's Fingers' (Cocteau Twins) privately loud, then out of the underground to greet the flags and cold dawn over Knightsbridge. Expensive shopping. Each evening another crowded journey back — underground, overground, thigh to thigh and totally detached. Uncomfortably close to unknown others, our mutual motivation money.

Thirty minutes of food-chewing time each day allowed me a regular inspection of the Serpentine Lake in Hyde Park, to watch the wind on the water and imagine *Swirly World* responding to the gusts.

Sometimes a posse of glistening carriages pulled by immaculate horses would race through the lunch-timers, but the park didn't really come alive until November, with fresh southwesterlies setting in to disperse acres of fallen leaves in a frenzied, rushing tumble.

Heavily subsidised Harrodian staff meals meant many elderly adults carried about the surplus weight of their overindulgence. They'd given in to that primary legal physical addiction — food. The boring routines of workplace existence day after month after year, had led them to fixating on the pleasures of eating. They were experts — virtually a full roast dinner for morning tea, lunch and afternoon tea. You could see where they put it. Their bodies had come to expect it.

Others were prone to illegal addictions. Hashish backstage at

Harrods. Groupings of furtive young males had rooftop pauses and clandestine meetings, emerging with glazed eyes and improved demeanours. They were stoned and in control of motorised vehicles steering pallets of Harrodian toilet paper around the subterranean passageways. Functioning in a state of artificially assisted gleefulness seemed to suit them.

I found Tristan's boiler room and experienced the unpleasantness of spending time in there. The heat and noise were memorable. Tristan had done a lot of safe, dry hours in there. He'd plotted out a sailor's sense of purpose and gone for it. I met someone who professed to having worked with Jones, but not surprisingly, there was no trace of him. I searched for the steel plate he had reputedly scrawled the calculations for his voyage on. Nothing obvious to be found.

Chapter 7

King Roadie . . .

King Roadie . . .

I got a job in the British music industry. The same industry that all
sorts of famous pop stars are a part of. I got a job as a roadie. It was
a promising start. I could work up from there. A new-age serf. Moving musicians' things around, setting them up, putting them away
again. I'd had a lot of practice in the past, working for myself in
New Zealand. I was a natural at moving things. I could think of
better things to do with my time. There was the possibility of brief
encounters of the rock star kind, Paul Weller, Whitney, Puff Daddy,
all in different lifts . . .

Pete Townsend of The Who wanted a keyboard taken to his house
on Richmond Hill. White van man, drive as fast as you can. Pete
shocked me with his oldness. 'Come on, close the door.' I'd heard
he'd turned bisexual. I wasn't sure about closing the door. He wanted to keep the public out. He had a great view on Rock Star Hill
with his neighbour, Mick of the Jagger kind. A minor little hill in
generally lump-less London, looking down on a wooded slope to
the last of the tidal Thames beyond. No day jobs required, wealth
on their own show-off songwriting terms. It makes me sick!

'Where do you want it?' I couldn't get the keyboard stand to
stand still without wobbling about. It was completely buggered.
I'd brought the wrong stand, the bad one, the one that should have
gone in the bin. Somehow I had the one that never went out . . .
'I'm sorry Pete, I'll have to fetch another one.' I never got back

inside again. Someone took the good stand off me at the front door.

Jose Carreras was backstage with me at Mohammed al Fayed's daughter's 21st in Knightsbridge. He was booked to perform along with a band of Turkish rock stars. I moved their things, made them go, hung around in case something stopped going.

Mohammed the father was polite but became more insistent. 'We don't want it too loud . . .' It was a familiar theme. Jose started complaining about the air conditioning. His throat was apparently very temperature-sensitive, he kept telling anyone standing near him. He even told me. I could relate, I was a singer too. He became even more unhappy. 'They're smoking!' It wasn't my place to make him feel better so I watched. How could that much noise come out of a little un-miked man? It was like a circus freak show. You had to clap at the sheer volume of the man at times.

He did an expensive fifteen to twenty minutes with encores and long periods of monotonous clapping. Lots more expensive clapping, then he was gone. Jose had left the building. Unfortunately I had to stay. The Turkish band had a few sets to get through. It seemed a long time until the last beautiful drunk stragglers finally got the picture from the stern, 'English as a second language' hotel staff that the show was over. The band stopped and I took off the company dinner suit, Cinderella roadie, put it all away again.

Coiling leads like halyards on other people's stages. As long as you pay me. Richard Thompson started to. He was a singer/song-writer/guitarist, who unlike myself had an enduring global audience. He was doing a UK town hall tour. The roadies had to travel and sleep in a bus. Tourbusland. Tinted windows somewhere between venues. Free food and grog, your own berth, braced to the roll and braking of the bus as you speed through sleeping English suburbs en route to another backstage parking spot, berthed in a new port. No motion to speak of. Parked behind a town hall, asleep in a still anchorage.

Later in the morning daylight, wincing at smart elderly security men, flashing the sacred laminated tour pass that gets you in no matter how disreputable your appearance. Down the bland heated civic centre corridors on a mission to find the toilets, wash your face . . . Where's catering?

It's not far to walk to get to the stage. Set up the band gear, same as last night and tomorrow. Show time 5 hours and counting . . . Basingstoke, Bristol, Nottingham, Liverpool, Leeds . . .

It was just another tour for Richard. Evidently some past emotional warfare had rendered him premier league status of 'emotionally most travelled'. It came out in his songwriting, and he wore his sorrow well — a folk-priest elder statesman, with electric credentials.

And then there's the guitar hero. His guitar solo. Sounds that make a human feel special things . . . He had his moments every night. 'Hard On Me.' Please don't break a string. Every night sourcing an unusual melody vault, otherworldly scaling . . . never the same, eyes rolled off somewhere in his head, sweaty frets, spontaneous soloing . . . in public.

It was the kind of soloing my born-again friends from the late seventies would have found disturbing. 'It's like he's in a trance . . . when he does that he's letting other spirits in. He looks possessed.' I'd never been convinced about possession theories. The Christians seemed to have a monopoly on sorting the problem out. More supernaturally relevant than the rest of us, the born-again sixteen-year-olds seemed to relish leading the discussions around to the dire consequences of evil, self-confident in their answers.

Richard had a summer folk festival to do in Belgium, Flanders Fields, Dranouter. Lou Reed was playing after Richard but his crew arrived before us. The Americans had already established a bridge-head up to the backstage loading ramp and were monopolising it. Their massive Transam truck had run aground 50 metres off the beach, up to its axles in mud. They were far away enough to need a local forklift truck to ferry loads of flight cases to the ramp. Their truck was too big and too full and so was their chief roadie with a headband, who started yelling at the local Belgians. 'You're outta here buddy!' The unfortunate man had been having problems understanding the American signals. The locals didn't look impressed.

I was there with the British team. There were three of us. We were outnumbered from the start. The backstage loading bay was all snarled up with 'Lou Reed' this case, 'Lou Reed' that case. Simon, the monitor engineer, suggested the hospitality bar. He was more experienced than me, so I had to agree. We'd been given two long rolls of free tickets and became determined to see what we would get in return for them. It looked as if it would be a lot but turned out disappointing.

Weak. Hard done by. Some Australasians might have called it 'gnats' piss', it doesn't really do much to you. You're gonna need more than that. We used as much as we reasonably could in the circumstances, and headed back, pausing to empty bladders, then back at the black boxes, lifting lids, making sure the stuff goes . . .

Richard delivered, preaching to the unconverted. Festivals are always like that. How often do you get to play to people who haven't specifically paid to come to see you? I got to go on stage carrying guitars, and later had the pleasure of trying to solve a footswitch problem while the crowd watched. The show went on, and Richard finished on time. I was ready for my turn . . .

Now it was Lou's turn. His seven-man crew rolled out the carpet for him. Replaced the front of house desk, and took an hour to do it. They were running late. Once everything was absolutely impeccably right they fetched Lou and he sauntered down the backstage tent corridor in the anticipated leather-waistcoat look. An elderly Action Man doll. Overly skilled session musicians underplaying in classic Lou Reed style. The Belgians were politely attentive, but something was missing. He did a little mime thing and occasionally moved his shoulders, but most of the time settled for being the day's most inanimate man. No one expected anything more. Lou's all right in small doses but his hour or so bordered on an endurance test. We thought so with our feet up in the bar watching the backstage video version.

Hours after it had turned dark we got driven to our local accommodation, the Hostellerie Kemmelberg. It appeared to be on a hill. I could make out that much. We were a bit worn out by then. Something to do with the copious amounts of weak grog.

All the young dead men from those past conflicts would have envied the overnight simplicity of our mission. It was only music after all. I could almost hear them laughing.

The hill the hotel was built on (after World War Two, not to mention the first one) would be a rare lump on any military map and destined to much attention. The land had obviously seen a lot of death and destructiveness. All that brutality and displacement in a 'civilised' way. The history of our species built on taking or being taken. Organised layers of men slugging it out, killing as many of the others as they can. Moment by precious human moment being paid to be as professionally unpleasant as possible. Fighting men. All those years of childhood nurturing snuffed out in a brief frenzy of state funded and organised fatal competition. A dangerous species. Some might say flawed.

My passage through Holland and West, then East, Germany, disguised as a white van man, went unchallenged at the borders. No one on guard any more against an enemy. I pushed on into Leipzig unopposed, a few hours before dawn. I was there for a gig, unfortunately someone else's. A new band supporting Tina Turner in a disused USSR fighter plane-manufacturing hanger. In the now wooded park next door, Napoleon's fighting men had met the Prussian forces and spent three days hurting each other with deliberate intent. We were as close to the 65,000 dead and wounded as you could get. I walked with them amongst the trees.

Outside in the very cold air between the venue and the trees was a lonely, tall gold tower topped with a large red star, emblem of another former caretaker's time. The complex was virtually deserted. An empire's industry vanished. Lots of foreign investment downtown. Building site cranes everywhere; new premises, with no one able to afford to be in them except government agencies, just like before.

At least the American economic occupation was bringing them real-life Western media imports like Tina. Well, almost real life. After two years on the road doing the same well-rehearsed version of her hitsville life, it almost wasn't real life any more. More like a choreographed theatre production.

The American roadies were counting down the days to home time. They were somewhere on earth, it didn't really matter to them. There was little integration with local cultures. Their self-contained, mobile, international celebrity rock show rolls into a city, set up and lit like an alien spaceship, beguiling the locals with otherworldly entertainment spectaculars. Same show different country, backstage catering carries on regardless, supply lines established, a team of calculator faces adding up the international income, door sales, merchandising.

In the park the trees were occupied with more mundane matters. A bitter wind kept them moving, swishing about for no material gain.

The seasons drifted by in the Thames Valley. Life passed, interrupted only by occasional floodings and inconvenient westerly gales. It seemed we were forever destined to move past the familiar garishly lit Bell Inn at Hampton, the night cloud silhouette rows of ornate chimneys over Hampton Court Palace, and the eternally paddling fleets of flying water scavengers.

Backstage I was working on my guitar playing. I was on a left-handed mission to learn to play better. The cheap acoustic had little time to itself. Songs were sourced in the relative isolation of the rural towing-path world. Nice place to do it. Unselfconscious singing to coots, Canadian geese, swans, even ducks.

Back in town we played the occasional live gig and beavered away at our first version recordings of new songs, called demos. The paths to recognition were clogged with aspiring bands journeying from all over. Coachloads of ardent, out of it, hometown followers crowding into small 'new band night' venues to stir the attention of record company scouts. The Dublin Castle, Monarch, Underworld, all the places aspiring musicians were using to attract attention to their style of bothering. It's like a talent quest each night in Camden.

Best thing about that part of London is the plaque on the wall of number eight Royal College Street. Rimbaud, the French poet, had lived there with Verlaine in the summer of 1873. He'd worked his words into the poems that constituted his sense of purpose at the time. Doing word work oblivious to the cut and thrust of commerce.

Seeing Rimbaud's ex-lodgings made threading Camden's tedious one-way system worth it. He would have been appalled by today's traffic speeding noisily past his dirty street windows. Same place, louder lifestyle.

As the months became years, our saga of unsatisfying demos led to a greater understanding of the cliché 'musical and personal differences'. Our differences were absolute. Sick of each other, languishing with our mutually unrequited ambitions. Mockers no more.

Camped at the gates of the marketplace Londinium we discovered what we didn't like. Personal learning curves. Each starting somewhere different. Lots of waiting for trains. Riding on, then waiting again for trains. Confined defining moments.

Chapter 8

My view of the universe
My view of the universe

We exhausted our attraction to the non-tidal Thames. It took three and a half years. After getting the clutch operated on at Maidboat's in Thames Ditton, where *Moonfleet Smuggler* had been designed and built thirty-two years before, we set off for a last minor journey — down on the tide to clean and paint her bottom on the grid near Kew Bridge. Underestimating the time it would take to run the few miles down from Teddington, we arrived thirty minutes too late to have enough water left to get onto the support beams of the grid opposite Oliver's Island. *Moonfleet* was forced to spend the night against a 30-ft wall at the entrance to the Grand Union Canal in Old Brentford.

As the tide surged relentlessly back, we cast off and were soon high and dry on the crossbeams, *Moonfleet's* hull clean and painted, in time for the next convenient inrush of salt water. Floundering around in the mud while working underneath the hull was character building, knowing that all the houseboats upstream in Brentford were legally discharging their digestive leftovers into the river. Too bad. That's the way the law stands at the moment.

Just after midnight the cupboard doors creaked open as the silent tide lifted *Moonfleet*. She gently rose free of the old paint-splattered crossbeams and floated off upriver. It was a still, timeless evening, ideal for riding up through the dark isolated stretches beside Kew Gardens. There were no buildings or bridges to gauge our place in the river's history, only the dark silhouettes of flanking trees. Thirty minutes later the salt water swept us round the bend to witness the grand contrast of the floodlit riverbank steps and buildings of Richmond. On a previous visit we'd been reduced to baking scones at an intimidating angle of heel as the departing tide left *Moonfleet* tilting down a mudbank. (I had again underestimated the swift departure of the sea.)

Moonfleet was slipped and surveyed as part of the trauma of selling her. As the surveyor armed with his trusty prodding and probing tools tapped away beneath the hull, I did my best to live a normal life in the aft cabin. His incessant tapping was punctuated by lengthy pauses and the sombre tones of talk between the cautious buyer and himself. For two strangers to have such an intimate knowledge of the state of *Moonfleet* felt vaguely violating. Eventually I could endure no more, and retired to the sanctuary of the heated Richmond public library and their shelves of atlases.

Hastings, on the southeast coast of England, provided a week of recording demos beside the seaside. Once home to a wind-driven fishing fleet, now there is a motorised line-up, launched and retrieved each day from the open shingle beach east of the town. Up from the shore, tucked under the cliffs, a replica of a sail-driven fishing boat stands beside a tiny chapel/museum. The stout, squat lines and heavy, practical fixtures were more aesthetically appealing than most racing yachts. A secure, sea-kindly chunkiness.

After days in a damp basement surrounded by musical things, I took to the ridge above the fishing village and found a sheltered spot to consume hot potato and chunks of thickly battered fish. Hastings is one of the lucky places to have a fish and chip shop that cooks the food while you wait, instead of the widespread vulgar British practice of keeping pre-cooked edibles under a heat lamp to stay warm but unpalatable.

A cold wind kept the waterfront promenade empty and set strings of gaudy party lights swaying their redundant summer colours out over the model boat lagoon. East of town, flag halyards slapped monotonous rhythms against fishing-boat masts, and invisible seagulls shrieked above the submerged sewage outlet.

From the top of the cliffs I could hear the swells dropping onto the gravel shoreline. Directly above, a clear autumn sky made it easy to define the flight paths of planes coming in from the Continent, some 50 miles away. The presence of the stars was intensified away from the glow of electric London. Several shooting stars burned their final brightness that evening, and as I watched the celestial show, a thin lid of high cloud crept over the southern horizon to slowly smother my view of the universe.

Twelve miles out, one of the busiest shipping lanes in the world kept the horizon lit with a constant stream of floating traffic — no sleep for solo sailors out there. The darkness beyond Beachy Head led to wherever you wanted to go, no tickets or bookings required. Ancestors had journeyed by wind alone to all parts available. So many similar memories cast obsolete by the passage of time.

Chapter 9

Back to the sandbank

Grey clouds moving through outrageously clear light-blue twilight sky. Mt Roskill, with its cluster of phoenix palms and neon crucifix, looking sacrificially exotic. The distant evergreen growth of the Waitakeres standing in dark relief against the warm tones of another throwaway Southern Hemisphere sunset. It looked like another planet. The narrow sandbank of Auckland dividing the Tasman Sea and the South Pacific Ocean. The Southern Hemisphere of planet earth. Ponsonby Road.

Six years had passed since I met Michael Brien and his audience of kittens on the rotting veranda of Avondale Road. Michael died in 1988. A letter arrived almost three years later, the day before we left London. The founder of the Church of Physical Immortality had gone out. He wouldn't have liked the irony.

I made it back to the row of tall defiant trees towering above the neighbouring sections. Where the front lawn, veranda, house and garage should have been, there was nothing but long seeding shoots of waist-deep grass. The old echoing kauri floorboards, the meditation chamber beneath the floor, rooms crammed full of the residue of activity through the years, 'UFO Jamboree' painted 15 ft high down the side of the house . . . all gone. Maybe the spacemen had reciprocated his interest and lifted him and the old place up and away for sanity experiments. He would have preferred it that way.

I hung around foraging for discarded memories, then braved the next-door neighbour's dog to find out what had happened. 'Oh yeah.

Michael had a stroke, massive stroke, died a week later.' In September 1988 he had a stroke and died in hospital. A few months after, half the house burnt down — the rest was demolished later. Today a group of tidy townhouses stand on the site of Michael Brien's Church of Physical Immortality. He never really got it off the ground, people didn't seem to believe him.

An overnight train to Wellington, dozing away the darkness sitting in my upright seat, uncomfortable but dry, listening to anonymous coughs, snores and the clatter of steel on steel as we jolted into the Roaring Forties. Now and then slowing, stammering to a halt, disembarking passengers disturbing us with the slamming of doors. Daylight let me inspect the back yards of rural New Zealand, moving through the small towns of Levin, Otaki and onwards past Kapiti Island. Wellington was still where it used to be, and a short detour round Oriental Bay and Point Jerningham took me to Evans Bay, where, looking neglected with faded paintwork and a patchy cockpit cover, *Swirly World in Perpetuity* waited.

In 1987 the Evans Bay Club Captain, the late Peter Brommer, had found a spot for *Swirly World* to sit for what I thought would be eighteen months. After two years had passed, my friend Mike Britton and cohorts moved *Swirly World* to a new corner beside the Flying Fifteens. Another two years passed before I returned at the beginning of 1991. By that stage *Swirly World* had almost become a permanent fixture beside the clubhouse and I expected to find her converted into a children's adventure playground with slides and gangways coming out her sides. I was keen to turn her back into an active sailing entity. So many boats deteriorate into disrepair while their owners focus their attentions elsewhere.

In four years the only threat to *Swirly World*'s existence had come from my own negligence in parsimoniously choosing borer-infested timber to make the cradle. The previous year a broken, borer-ridden support post had to be replaced. Under faded paintwork *Swirly World* looked in good shape. All Dynel-covered joints remained fast and no movement could be found between the keel and the hull.

With anticipation akin to an early tomb robber, I scaled the shaky cradle and removed the cover. A pool of stagnant water had accumulated on the port side of the cockpit where the slight lean of the hull had defied the call of the drains. Surprisingly the padlock still had moving parts, and, hatchboards removed, I was back inside, savouring that sea hut full of forgotten memories and the damp scent of neglect. I half-expected to find Mike Brien waiting for me.

The yacht club hard area stayed deserted during the first few weeks of January. With most people away on holiday, their racing calendar was postponed until later in the month. For a few days a Sea Scout regatta was savaged by southerly gales and northwesterly willie-waws. Scores of waterlogged adolescents made their way past *Swirly World* en route to dry clothes. Many found time to halt at the sight of her short, stout green hull and engage in discussion about her size and shape. Comments were projected in loud, self-confident, almost authoritative tones whenever I happened to be out of sight, inside or under the hull. 'Look at this one, someone's chopped half of it off.' Most believed she could have done with another few feet stuck onto the back, as the angled cutaway stern seemed peculiar.

Wellington had done its best to impress on me its unsuitability for small sailing craft, by continuously whipping Evans Bay into an intimidating froth as gale-force northwesterlies monotonously preceded the arrival of equally unsavoury southerly fronts. The only days that came close to reasonable were always at the tail end of a southerly blow, when the clear cold air slowed up to leave Cook Strait heaving itself lethargically onto the southern coast. Twenty-four hours was all it took before another faint northwesterly would find its feet and work itself into another afternoon of frenzied gusts.

As one more southerly gale rattled rain onto corrugated-iron roofs I managed to track down the spray-painter, and by the time the sky turned blue and the wind slackened, he was ready to make *Swirly World* glisten with all her former glory. A 10-knot southerly persisted and was enough to make me fear for the paintwork of nearby parked cars, the overspray floating as a fine green mischievous mist.

Late January saw no sign of easing winds so I arranged for the long arm of a Titan's crane to have a go at quelling the tempest, early one morning. The driver was determined to impress with his machine. He positioned the truck where its crane arm would have to be extended over a row of Flying Fifteens in order to lift *Swirly World* back and above.

A spot was cleared for easy access to the north, but the driver insisted on providing his audience with value for money ($140 an hour), by soaring *Swirly World* high over the other boats. The only consolation was the attractive angle to view the hull. The driver retracted his extended arm with *Swirly World* hanging at the end of it, then suspended her a metre off the tarmac. With the boat dangling in front of the cab he drove down to the Elephant House (Wellington Sea Rescue headquarters) and extended the arm out over the still water. By 10 a.m. on 13 January the wind had yet to reach unpleasant proportions and *Swirly World* touched down without difficulty. I removed the fabric straps from under the hull and pulled her over to the wharf. With the aft quarter tied down to a pole, I encouraged the engine to see if it would function like a real one. It sounded good so I let go the line and steered us round to an empty marina berth.

Swirly World looked so much smaller in the water, and after *Moonfleet Smuggler's* deck area, she seemed absolutely tiny. Without mast or gear, she heeled drastically with the slightest movement. I'd installed a new Wasp log, and as we puttered over the calm water it registered 3 knots. Slowly the mileage meter moved on from its pristine four zeros. It worked, and that mattered.

We picked another pre-wind early morning to step the mast. I took *Swirly World* in against the breastwork where my press-ganged brothers Rob and Mike held the mast upright while I tried to arrange turnbuckles and shackles in the correct manner. We got it to stand alone, although still in need of adjustment. By eleven that morning the wind had picked up enough to send an uncomfortable high tide jostling in amongst the boats. I moved *Swirly World* back to the marina berth and stayed on board doing other odd jobs. After an hour I was lethargic and lacking motivation. Seasickness was upon me while still tied up to the marina. Karyn arrived and extracted me, leaving *Swirly World* to readjust to the improved stability offered by the hefty mast. I wasn't sure I really wanted to do this anymore.

A few days later Australian sailor Phil Goden led the way in stay tensioning, marvelling at Michael Brien's vision of a durable rig. As we tightened up the starboard sidestay a loud crack initiated a search for potential disaster. A shackle pin had given way. A closer examination identified a deep, well-tarnished and ancient hairline crack that had secretly survived many stressful miles.

That evening the annual Wellington to Nelson yacht race was to start in Evans Bay. The wind was blowing with its usual intensity, a strong gusty northwesterly promising an uninviting black night beating into short steep headseas for the 40-odd miles from Karori Rock to Stephen's Island. Undaunted the crews all turned up and sails appeared on booms and foredecks. All at once the water was churning with large racing machines tearing their overcanvassed way about the bay. They beat up past Greta Point and Shelly Bay to round Point Halswell close in, waving and hollering final goodnights to an armada of binocular-toting friends and relatives. It was a windy evening by Auckland standards, but the yachts went unperturbed, quickly hoisting spinnakers to rocket them out of the heads and into the wet dark hours to windward.

I kept ferrying bundles into *Swirly World*, and as the weathercloths, self-steering and various deck fittings took up their stations, she began to look like an active sailing entity once more.

I often found my way to the southern edge of Wellington where the northwesterlies grimly funnelled down the gullies and out into the empty ocean. Out past the fishing boats in Island Bay, I watched the horizon fade to darkness, leaving only Tapuaenuku on the South Island outlined to the west in orange and pink receding light. The fairy glow of a Cook Strait ferry moved rapidly out from Baring Head, passing across the night to drop from sight behind the familiar arches of Devil's Gate.

Sailing out to embrace the solitude of an empty horizon felt less appealing than before. Contemplated in overpopulated Europe, no problem. Sitting there beside the reality was another thing. The weather during my summer stay in Wellington was stern stuff. The thought of one-day sailing into that isolation so far removed from the human chaos of rush-hour commuters had served as a pressure release valve on discontented occasions. Being finally there on the edge of all that salt water, I was struck by the gravity of the dark, wind-buffeted scene before me. I peered out and wondered how it would feel to be back in *Swirly World* with a small headsail up and the self-steering moving us down the waves.

I feared the easy ways of motorboating on the relatively tame and secure Thames had redefined my concept of 'pleasure' forever. Perhaps the rigours of keeping a small yacht moving in the desired direction by wind power alone would be beyond my matured definition. February and March seemed the most benign months windwise, and I hoped the continuous fronts rushing across the Tasman would have relented a little by then.

Before leaving Wellington I took *Swirly World* out for a couple of short rides. On both days, southerly blows made way for clear skies and light airs. Off Cobham Drive I rediscovered the simple sail-tending systems, and quickly had *Swirly World* flapping the stale odour of neglect from her sails, and heading off downwind past Shoal Pile. Racing had recommenced and yachts slid about working the windshifts over the flat water. We sailed around to Scorching Bay and experienced the responsiveness to the wind that had originally endeared me to *Swirly World*. She was finally restored to a sailing state, almost four years to the day since leaving the water.

Chapter 10

West out of Wellington
West out of Wellington

The wind creaked the house about and I knew that outside a north-westerly was doing its best to intimidate me. It was succeeding. The sooner I could get out there, the less time for negative conjecture. I'd decided to try for Auckland the long way, round the South Island and Stewart Island, which was ambitious by most standards, so I refrained from expressing my intentions to people. The usual story. Shout about it once you've done it.

In 1973 Gerry Clark had gone south alone down the west coast of New Zealand to the Auckland and Campbell Islands in his 21-ft Ballerina-design twin-keeled yacht. I viewed *Swirly World* as buoyant and as seaworthy as that Tucker design. Was I? Gerry was the precedent, setting (or discarding) the limits of what you could do.

The early hours of Friday 15 March 1991 brought rain squalls ricocheting off the roofs and roads of Wellington as the inevitable southerly front replaced the northwesterly. I woke up with numbers on my mind, 2182 hz, 4125 hz, 2045 hz, 2638 hz . . . A 9.30 a.m. appointment at the Lower Hutt radio frequencies building had the wind and rain driving me down the leeward shore of the Hutt motorway. Beside the road, rows of small, disorganised white-capped waves slapped themselves onto the jumbled retaining blocks. Another southerly gale.

My memory performed its recall on demand and within twenty minutes I was out to greet the puddles and gale clutching my bits of paper, the proud owner of a new call sign.

I did the responsible thing and got an SSB that would allow me the convenience of long distance two-way communication. The antiquated double sideband unit was virtually redundant as a transmitter and had never been properly adjusted to send a signal any distance.

I found a cheap 35-watt AWA 110 SSB in Newtown, and rendezvoused with a technician in the pouring rain at Evans Bay. Inside *Swirly World* he wired up the relevant pieces and made adjustments for maximum aerial loading. One channel refused to register any transmission signal, so it quickly disappeared into the rain for a workshop inspection. It was late on Friday afternoon, and being keen on departing as soon as the wind moderated, the job was dealt to with some urgency. It was mistakenly deduced that the channel was faulty, so the frequency was moved to another.

On reinstalling it, test transmissions had everything sounding and looking right, this time with immediate aerial loading signals, and the problem was considered solved.

In the last hours of summer daylight saving I loaded a hefty collection of stores, divided into plastic-bagged subsets, into *Swirly World*. The wind had eased back to 25 knots and the rainbearing cloud had begun to break up. *Swirly World*'s bow was prone to nose-diving whenever any bundle of weight made its way forward. There was a lot of gear jumbled over the front berths, most of which needed to be repositioned further aft. I was moving in and it would take some time to adjust to living in such a confined, cluttered space again. I cleaned the 1987 kerosene soot from the deckhead and attempted to stow provisions in order of accessibility.

Over the past few days I'd made the acquaintance of the marina watchman. He took an interest in *Swirly World* and was genuinely uncomfortable about her size and ability to cope with wind and waves. Auckland via the east coast of the North Island? That I intended to head west out of Wellington and then try for Stewart Island, a few hundred miles south, was too shocking a proposition to mention.

On Saturday morning a moderate southerly blew fresh oxygen through the lungs of Wellington. I attached the windowboards, tied the folding dinghy to the foredeck, then pulled out the last vital ingredient — sails. Without those and the wind we wouldn't be going very far.

I was on schedule for clearing the Heads at midday, to arrive at Karori rip in time to catch the tide up through Cook Strait. I stepped back onto the mooring for a final change of perspective on my future home. She had never appeared so out of place and vulnerable as she did there, in the company of the many larger craft.

I pulled the mooring line in and stepped back on deck. Weighed down, she felt solid and stable. I dropped all but the starboard stern line, then manually pivoted *Swirly World* around in the berth to face the light southerly breeze. Phil and Steve Raea provided appropriate grins and words of fine encouragement as I started the engine and throttled us out of the tangle of mooring lines. Off Cobham Drive the flap of rising sails replaced the mechanical vibrations, and we bore away for Shoal Pile. How many times had I aimed for Shoal Pile? To a twelve-year-old mind, Shoal Pile (with no shoal to be seen) was an awfully long way. The hard of Evans Bay was barely visible from there. A sense of achievement in getting there and back. Now try going from the slipway to . . . Auckland.

The 12-knot southerly brought long breaks between the clouds and it looked as if we were in for an ensuing period of post-gale tranquillity. As *Swirly World* ran down the bay I stood supported by the Perspex dodger, steering by the pressure of my foot on the short stainless-steel tiller. We slid by the house-topped ridges of Hataitai and Maupuia. A keeler race was about to start at Point Jerningham and the yachts were luffing about waiting for the gun. I steered in close to Point Halswell and exchanged farewells with family. The yacht race started and from the wind shadow of Kau Bay I watched the stretch of white sails slowly fan out across Evans Bay.

The breeze and the wake of a Cook Strait ferry reached us simultaneously, setting *Swirly World* off towards Eastbourne over the short swells. The rapid lifting and dropping delivered the unpleasant aroma of petrol back to the companionway. My attempts to deal with the old gap between the petrol breather pipe and the inaccessible tank outlet had failed again. The morning blossomed into a glorious late summer afternoon and the memories of Scorching Bay and Worser Bay Yacht Club slid past as *Swirly World* steered herself back and forth towards the Heads. Her sole unfortunate occupant was inside, transferring fuel from the main tank to cans. I'd done this stretch of water over and over, got a very good fix on its northwesterly nuances and southerly onslaughts. Raced my glorious OK dinghy against Ricky Dodson, Leith Armit — the most efficient wind users imaginable.

But none of us sailed at night. Everyone back in the bar by then, or at home tucked up . . . never a thought for staying out there, once it became dark and not very nice . . .

The level of fuel crept low enough to stop further spills in larger swells, and I resumed hand steering in the clearer air near Barrett Reef. I couldn't see any other competitors.

I thought back to the contrasting scene there in April 1968, when the 286-ft inter-island ferry *Wahine* had been driven onto the reef by cyclonic winds and seas, to capture my five-year-old imagination as it lay half-submerged, thrashed to death off Steeple Rock light. How disturbing the wind could be, and there I was committing myself to such potentially malevolent uncertainty. Apprehensive was the word, especially after a four-year interlude. The whole enterprise was going to take a little adjusting to, or so I hoped, feeling a little unadjusted. Maybe I had severely readjusted my concept of pleasure after living in England, safely tucked up a freshwater river away from the sea.

After the southerly, the swell through Cook Strait was still quite lumpy and on rounding Moaning Mini, *Swirly World* reached along at 5 to 6 knots, heeled over, along the slopes of the little liquid hills, full main and the No.1 jib.

We sailed well inshore of the ferry route, and off Island Bay the wind eased, calling for a change from jib to genoa. *Swirly World* was then framed on the same patch of blue sea behind Taputeranga Island that had been gazed at so often by my greatly interested eyes, from our garden up the valley. *Swirly World* was now part of the view that had led me to Evans Bay to learn to sail, sixteen years earlier.

Off Owhiro Bay I remembered my father's story of finding pieces of yacht on the surf-pounded beach in January, 1951. A wicked southerly had come through and devoured the *Husky* and her four crew, while they were running for the Wellington Heads. It could be a wickedly serious piece of sea. My climate of maudlin reflection would not do.

The practicalities of steering through the gentle jobble of the Karori rip in a failing breeze saved me from my own imagination. Once clear of Karori Rock the breeze freshened and *Swirly World* slewed her way northwest down the slight seas. There were no boats or humans to be seen, only the high dry land of Mount Misery and Terawhiti Hill beside a benevolently blue Cook Strait. I retired to the starboard quarterberth and lay braced against the side, listening to the new sounds of an old environment. Centimetres away, I heard water rushing past the thin plywood hull, while the log spun with the rapid clicking that denotes 5 knots of boat speed and the mast-head light wire slapped its audible nuisance sound inside the hollow alloy mast. It all smelt familiar. The swinging gimballed stove, swaying bags of hanging fruit, the lockers packed with nourishment necessities. A self-contained, user-friendly corner, once you've adjusted . . .

On deck, sitting on the plywood seat on the pulpit, *Swirly World* rolled along with no hands on the helm. The sun was setting behind the Marlborough Sounds and the western sky shone orange about the dark defined ridges. Tucked away behind Mana Island, the lights of Plimmerton twinkled a distant farewell. Under the boom, to port, the stern utilitarian sweep of the Brother's light reminded me of the diligence darkness would require.

I fished out the pressure lantern and got it hissing our presence, hung from the Perspex dodger, for all who needed to know. By its bright light I returned to the quarterberth, hooked up the lee cloth and filled in the log. Cook Strait was providing a dignified welcome back to life for *Swirly World in Perpetuity*.

We slid gently northwest, alive again with the fluent sound of forward motion. Life became continually interrupted by the shrill clatter of a new egg-timer alarm clock. At varying intervals, depending on the acuteness of caution, it would wake me to survey the watery environs for anything untoward. In relatively confined Cook Strait the chances of being run down by a ship were greater than away from land, so I checked out for the enemy regularly. Four swept by that night, their respective 'glows of life' rapidly approaching then receding into the darkness.

In the late hours I called up Wellington Radio to announce our departure from Cook Strait. I had been putting off calling since leaving Wellington Harbour, as providing trip details such as intended destination and ETA seemed like tempting fate, and audibly exhibitionist. I called them up, but they couldn't hear me. There was no loading signal on the aerial meter and the transmissions were starting to deplete the small 12-volt battery. I stared back upwind at the distant lights of Plimmerton. It would be hard on the nose all the way there, and I'd be in Sunday morning, which meant waiting until Monday to get the radio looked at. By then the usual westerlies may have returned, and I'd have lost the lift we were getting out into the bight between Cape Egmont and Cape Farewell. Every mile gained west was precious. I had a rare wind for Cook Strait.

I tried once more, and for reasons unknown, the radio decided to perform. Wellington Radio acknowledged our existence on 4125 hz and enquired as to my ETA for Stewart Island. I pointed out that a small sailing boat unaccustomed to motor sailing and relying on the random movement of air made it difficult to set an ETA at that stage.

In the early hours of Sunday morning *Swirly World* sailed out past Stephen's Island into Tasman Bay. The night's moderate southeasterly had eased, leaving a slight swell to heave us west. It was going to be a safe day for sightseeing in Tasman Bay. A severe contrast to our turbulent arrival at Stephen's Island in 1987. The prospect of encountering those steep breaking waves toppling their broken crests into *Swirly World*'s cockpit again was something I chose not to embrace at that point. We'd have to cross those waves when we came to them.

The patchy southeasterly got us across the bay, then the wind left us to roll about, sails strapped down on a tame piece of sea, a few miles northeast of Bush End Point, the tip of Farewell Spit. The view was warm and settled, nothing threatening to be seen. The afternoon rolled into evening and a seal came up to check us out. It circled and surveyed *Swirly World* with large appealing brown eyes, observing us with an inquisitive, intelligent stare. It took a large breath, inhaling with a human-like sound, then dived directly down dissolving into the distant depths of its blue playground.

I'd been swotting up on how to nail sunsights and calculator operations again, and the day's collection of sextant-clutching episodes reassured me I was indeed looking at Bush End Point. We had stayed more or less stationary and been treated to a protracted view of the lighthouse nestled in macrocarpas, floating alone like an oasis on the horizon. It was a sight Adrian Hayter must have clocked a few times on his voyages about that region. Hayter had been here and done this. He was a source of great inspiration in my chosen field.

He had sailed solo from England via the Mediterranean and the Red Sea in 1950, to arrive six years later at Westport and eventually Nelson, New Zealand. In 1961–62 he sailed the folkboat *Valkyr* alone from England via the Panama and Pacific, again to Nelson. His experiences are available in the books *Sheila In The Wind* and *Business In Great Waters*. Hayter, like Gerry Clark, David Lewis and Johnny Wray, all using the wind on the sea in a very competent way.

In 1986 I heard he was living a reclusive existence in a caravan in the Wairoa Gorge, near Nelson. Keen to make his acquaintance, I sent him a paperbag full of poems. A year passed and having come to terms with my rejection, I received a letter. He was now in his seventies and had spent the past year coping with having part of his body diagnosed as cancerous.

Shortly before, I had been in a second-hand bookshop next to the Hampton train station and found a pristine 1960 book-club version of *Sheila In The Wind*, complete with pamphlet introducing the new author. On bringing the existence of a book-club version to his attention, he wrote that he'd never been notified of it, nor received any royalties. He felt there had been a long-standing cover-up by his original publishers and seemed intent on pursuing compensation. My burst of fandom it seemed, might have served another purpose, other than my own.

He sent me some copies of his latest book, *The Missing Piece* (1983) to distribute to whoever was interested. It seemed a waste that it hadn't been professionally published and promoted. It contained philosophical discourses and a brief account of a 100-day sailing sojourn from Nelson up the west coast of the North Island to the Kermadecs, then on to a coincidental mid-ocean meeting with a sinking yacht. He rescued its sole exhausted occupant and sailed him 500 miles to the sanctuary of the Bay of Islands.

It was what Hayter was trying to find in a spiritual dimension that imbued him with the most relevance as a solo sailor. Sailing between societies, astutely observing the religious and social complications, trying to get some kind of epiphany from his accumulated experiences. Thinking up a better way of modelling a society so that everyone gets a lot more out of it. Hayter died in June 1990 at *Tejada* in the Wairoa Gorge, at the age of seventy-five.

For 48 hours the tail end of a tropical cyclone had been sitting north of Norfolk Island and drifting slowly south. Cape Reinga had 35-knot easterlies and most of the North Island was experiencing easterly quarter breezes to a varying degree. The low pressure didn't appear to be hurrying down to our latitude, so things looked good.

Under the cover of darkness, a light easterly had set in to sail us parallel to Farewell Spit, out west, away from the shallow water bight between the South Island and Cape Egmont. With the mainsail one side, the poled out genoa the other, and the self-steering guiding us before the wind, *Swirly World* sailed away from New Zealand at 5 to 6 knots.

Asleep on the move, I drifted between noisy wave-slapping surroundings and silent surreal dreams, on the edge of blank chasms of exhausted mental disengagement. Whenever a new noise supplemented the volume of passing water, I'd be drawn back to investigate. That night a group of unusual sonic sounds pulled me back from the silence. Sea creatures were chatting in our vicinity. The dolphins had arrived.

Off and on they joined us, moving out before the freshening easterly, making eye contact, whenever possible, with well-timed swimbys and body rolls. With the wind blowing us away from Wellington, we headed for the imaginary line 100 miles west of Westport, before turning south.

Sailing a heavily laden small boat had made one aspect clear. It was slow. Travelling at a little more than walking pace took a lot of getting used to; as did the cold hard reality that without constantly monitoring and attending to the actual sailing of the boat, one wasn't likely to get very far. The obliging easterly was unusual there, and a lack of anything threatening set my mindmites pondering how bad it could be . . . The breeze finally deposited us, wallowing about on the shiny, sloppy sea, 100 miles true west of Cape Farewell at Lat 40 20' south, Long 170 15' east.

Through the thick Perspex viewing port in the hull, I examined the cold steely-blue colour of the water below. Quite a serious shade of blue. Apart from clouds, the empty horizon held no prospect of company.

My appreciation of the view was tainted by the distraction the radio was becoming. I'd assured Wellington Radio I'd make contact every 48 hours but the SSB was preferring to deem when this should be so. I'd have to spend five to ten minutes testing and depleting valuable battery amp hours before it would cooperate. As an emergency transmitter it was virtually redundant. The forecast was for moderate northerlies in the Foulwind area, but they were reluctant to arrive.

Becalmed in the evening I watched the sun slip out through a line of grandly lit horizon cloud. Inside the radio vibrated with the sound of foul-mouthed fishermen exchanging home life on 4143 hz.

'Never seen it so good on the coast.'

'Went to Carl's birthday, Janis got so pissed . . .'

The sky was settled, no rushing clouds, the barometer high and steady; it looked as if our pause at that latitude was to be longer than anticipated. The fishermen liked it, a flat workbench for them. No wind, no miles for us.

For 48 hours the SSB refused to transmit. I feared that faced with my enduring silence for what could have amounted to some time, I might have agitated Wellington Radio's concern to unnecessarily expensive extremes. Their enthusiasm for position reports had impressed me. I didn't consider going in closer to the west coast to make contact lest the wind should seek to savage *Swirly World* on that frequently leeward shore. The alternative to backtracking through the shallow bight to Nelson was equally unappealing. One hundred and fifty miles northeast, New Plymouth jutted out on the Taranaki coast. I had sailed there in the Paper Tiger Catamaran nationals and remembered the salient land features and port access as user-friendly. But for the moment there was no going anywhere, as the wind had lost interest, and my fuel supply wasn't going to move us far. I had to lie it out. I wasn't sure which way to go. It was more an emotional crossroads than anything else.

Swirly World was a self-contained bedroom riding the swells, all facilities within arm's reach. I tried working the odd fleeting zephyrs but the sails were perpetually robbed of their power, collapsing to the random slight cross swells. If the northerly they predicted filled in, *Swirly World* would probably be able to run down to Milford Sound or Jackson Bay before any ensuing fronts arrived to delay us. That was fairly optimistic. I hadn't got a life raft and I'd lost radio contact. That was fairly pessimistic. I was undecided so decided to let the wind decree the course. Wherever the next consistent breeze blew, we would go. Downwind or across the wind, either would do.

A light southerly eventually put me out of my misery and set *Swirly World* pointing for New Plymouth. The self-steering, full main and genoa moved us quickly over the flat surface. Finally being able to go somewhere was a relief after drifting like a becalmed Tasman trespasser for two days and nights. The wind gradually backed through to the southeast and we broad reached north. I took to the quarterberth and passed out as per usual, whenever the sails were full and drawing us forward with balanced ease, self-steering slewing us more or less on a compass course, closing in with the land.

In the dark early hours Wellington Radio forecast that a deepening low was expected to rush across the Tasman from Bass Strait to coincide with our intended arrival at New Plymouth. Running in for the breakwaters with an onshore gale was one scenario, so I headed *Swirly World* north to stay out well beyond the shelving 200-fathom line until I could get a more accurate report of what was coming, and when. I didn't want to get washed up on the shores of Cape Egmont. If it was going to rough up, the fewer obstacles the better. I'd bounce it out in deep water without the company of rocks or oil rigs.

My appetite for weather forecasts became insatiable. They all prophesised strong northeasterlies direct from New Plymouth, and as we had a willing 15-knot southeasterly, I set about sailing *Swirly World* as fast as possible towards the Taranaki Coast. Every mile made good by tight reaching could save us tortured hours to windward once the wind shifted. *Swirly World* moved well balanced, heeled over and sliding through the sloppy seas, the self-steering adjusting our course relative to the wind's nuances; the hull was riding responsive and buoyant, lifting her lower chines to windward. The motion of harmony. The original flotation chamber. It was what I was there for.

Twenty-four hours on a starboard reach led us to dawn 60 miles northwest of Cape Egmont. I woke to the sound of a windless sea setting sails flapping unviably. The sun was elevating through the east, and the outline of the upper slopes of Mt Egmont stood above a wash of low misty cloud. The northeasterly came up off the unseen windward coast and my nostrils registered unmistakable rustic aromas. The smell of the land.

On port tack I hand steered the day away, sailing over a long southwesterly cross swell that seemed to lift us windward with each passing rise. The light faded to dark and I harboured great expectations of seeing the welcoming glow of New Plymouth ahead. The Waitara aero beacon had been bleeping out its bearing dead ahead but the loom of lights had yet to come over the curve of the earth. The Motunui methanol plants shone out further north up the coast but at first I thought they were squid boats just over the horizon. Our walking-pace progress made their approach imperceptible. New Plymouth had to be there, and later was, glowing its collective brightness into the clouds above. Music was appropriate for such a dark, starless occasion, so I put on the Walkman, only to discover its motor ran erratically, slowing the songs then speeding up unpredictably. I had to make do with the usual symphony of sea slapping sounds, until closer in, the local FM stations emerged. Low disjointed lights appeared from over the horizon and I again mistook them for fishing boats. Further in they became clusters of buildings and obvious parts of the town.

The wind backed north and freshened, sending *Swirly World* reaching for the Sugar Loaf Isles, while I retired below to indulge in great slabs of satiation. Appetite was well adjusted to the degree that I conjured up feasts of fried kumara and potatoes. I'd pressure-cook a pile in the day on the single burner, then leave them for a highly appreciated fry-up in the dark early morning hours.

Grey daylight brought an audience of neon-lit office windows, watching *Swirly World* from a distance, tearing in for what I thought was the breakwater. I had hand steered since the previous morning, with no more than 2 hours of uninterrupted sleep in eight days.

My sense of distance had become peculiar. I was convinced the long man-made rectangular shape about 2 miles away was the southern arm of the breakwater. It was stationary at the right angle. I got out the boathook for jumping a mooring. Dark clouds were moving low over the coast and they quickly took the form of veils of heavy rain, blocking out parts of the shore. Fearing an overcanvassed, out-of-control stagger in the harbour entrance, I made my way about *Swirly World*'s small deck, reducing sail. With wet-weather gear on and safety harness hitched, I was resolved to do battle. We sat comfortably dead on the sea, undercanvassed, as I waited for the first sheets of cold, refreshing rain and wind to move over us.

In the middle of the deluge, the breeze shifted but stayed light, making it difficult to lay the port. The big rectangular breakwater in the meantime metamorphosed into a large ship, a lot further away than initially envisaged. I pulled up more sail and held our course, hard on the wind for the harbour. The ship appeared to be motoring northward but as we closed in, I saw it was anchored and a current was pushing us southwest down the coast.

The sky settled into an overcast shade of grey and as we slowly sailed closer, the green tones of grass-covered land became visible. Small runabouts raced out towards solitary fishing buoys, and I felt the physical reassurance that comes with the proximity of land.

I'd come to know the approach to New Plymouth from the north or south, along the usual roads leading from the show the night before in Hawera or Hamilton, driving a rental van full of hangovers around all the bends leading to Taranaki. Coming in by sea was a novelty.

At 10 a.m. on Sunday, *Swirly World* reached sedately in between the breakwaters, nine days and 560 miles by the log from Evans Bay. I spied a small finger marina that had sprouted since my last visit, and steered *Swirly World* in to sample its parking opportunities.

Alan MacGregor had woken up dehydrated early that morning. It had been another big night at the New Plymouth Yacht Club. En route back from the freshwater tap he gazed out of his front windows at the expansive Tasman Sea before him. Offshore he saw a tiny sail and through his telescope he could make out *Swirly World*'s small green hull. When I later stepped onto the marina he greeted me on behalf of the New Plymouth Yacht Club and with parking details dealt to, I departed to experience his family's house and hospitality on the nearby cliff top. The MacGregors were used to having sailors stay. Alan, a sailor himself, helped organise the Solo Trans Tasman race every four years. They had a guestroom and I found myself in it.

Decontaminated by a hot shower, I inspected myself in a mirror. A lack of sleep partially compensated for by repetitive catnaps had induced an exhilarating edge to my existence, and it showed. The psycho-killer look. The clouds lifted by lunchtime, and a very nice lunch it was too, thanks, Linda.

The front never lived up to its publicity, the wind stayed polite and the low surprisingly dawdled and dissolved mid-Tasman. That afternoon I nailed two of my immediate priorities in life — chocolate and Ballarat apples. It was late enough in the season for the cooking apples of my desire to be ready for raw, sharp tasting. Sugar and vitamin C.

On Monday morning I couriered the SSB to Wellington, then roamed the port and Moturoa for five days, letting the tones of contented crickets and the scent of slaughtered grass assail my senses. Land. Freshly appreciated land. The week showed little sign of consistent sailing breezes, the Tasman was going through a quiet recuperative phase after its summer of furious fronts. I sat out on the breakwater and thought about my sailing options. I had lost the inclination to go south into autumn. The calms and our detour to Taranaki had set us back later in the season than intended.

I would also have preferred to head south in the company of a life raft, or at least something that was immediately launchable from the deck. Before leaving Wellington my small two-man US Air Force life raft had been checked by a company in Newtown. They found the CO_2 automatic inflation cylinder was empty. They couldn't fill it and the replacement part to make it work would cost US$1000 — not having a spare US$1000 on me at the time, I was resigned to manually inflating it should the need arise. An efficient permanently attached hand pump could do the job in five minutes. Off Cape Farewell I had partially inflated it, constricting it into a bundle on the forward berth, small enough to exit the companionway in a rush. It was a dubious arrangement but I had developed a matured sense of self-preservation, and it seemed safer than relying on the internal buoyancy bags alone.

I settled on the soft option of a trip around the top of the North Island and back down again to Auckland. I would have my solitude in less serious latitudes. The SSB had been tested several times in Wellington and the problem deemed untraceable, so it looked like the fault lay in my aerial wiring. Before couriering it back to me, they gave it a final look and fortunately discovered the problem, an offending dry joint. For my inconvenience they installed the crystal for Auckland Radio free of charge. My reticence to run south was real. I was valuing the concept of preparation and the prospect of continued existence a little more.

On Thursday the wind blew moderate, direct from where we wanted to go, but they forecast a change to the southwest that evening. I spent some time gratefully eating with the MacGregors, and poring over the course charts of some of the solo trans-Tasman New Plymouth to Mooloolaba yacht races. A big trip across all that sea, between the land. The Solo Tasman Race had always appealed. Twelve hundred miles non-stop northwest. Maybe one day I would do it. Not in *Swirly World*, she's too small. I doubt I could carry enough food and water without being too sluggish. It's a long way when you're going slowly.

The wind stayed northwest, direct from Mooloolaba, making it even further for a sailor. I retired to *Swirly World*, sleeping at the ready, tuned in for the change that would allow us to sail free for Cape Reinga, 250 miles over the horizon. I felt a 'serious feeling', but tried to get to sleep. The change came before dawn, light rain on deck bringing a southwest shift. Awake and engage. No lying in this morning. Pre-dawn dark. A difficult start.

By 6.30 a.m. we were sailing through a jumbled mixture of small waves near the Sugar Loaf Isles. I was steering 310 magnetic, the shortest route to the deep water beyond the 200-metre line, aiming well west of the top of the North Island.

We passed Good Friday reaching under full main and the No.1 jib. There was nothing on the horizon in any direction but New Zealand wasn't far away, 60 miles at most. I spent most of my moments in the lee berth feeling queasy, unsure if it was caused by the sea's motion or my dwindling supply of Ballarat apples. Throughout the hours of day and night rain squalls drifted across our path, drawing me from the warmth of the bag to readjust sails or wind vane to cope with fluctuations.

One hundred and eleven miles in 24 hours took us away from the Taranaki Coast and into deep, dark, steely-blue water again. The wind took most of the Easter holiday off, leaving me to work the odd puff, imperceptibly north, on top of an obliging current.

The sea softened into lumps that once resembled waves, then all that was left was a smooth, unruffled skin. Flat. Slow became stopped. An orange and yellow filter of sunset filled the western sky and reflected onto the calm, mercury-like sea. The whole show turned orangey-yellow. The horizon was indistinguishable, and it looked as if we were floating suspended in the colourful fluid atmosphere of another world. What year? Where are we? Doesn't really matter. Certainly looks quite interesting at the moment . . .

On the last night of March a northeasterly arrived to tight reach us on starboard, parallel to the Kaipara coast, 70-odd miles over the eastern horizon. For three days and nights I lay strapped up to windward against the lee cloth, living life lying down as *Swirly World* ploughed along under the double-reefed main and No.1 jib. I just lay there most of the time. Suspended animation indoors. I read stories of social angst on coral islands, ate slabs of root vegetable fried in olive oil, and forever set the egg-timer alarm to divide my life into an endless succession of short catnaps and horizontal thinking.

My allies at Auckland Radio expected the wind to back to the westerly quarter, so I kept *Swirly World* steering parallel to the land until, on the third night of April, we went about onto port tack and aimed in the direction of Ninety Mile Beach.

Heavy rain clouds moved up all morning to windward, so I dressed in waterproofs and reduced sail. Bad weather on nearing land was not what I wanted. The rain came torrentially and the wind went north, eventually pushing the waterlogged clouds away to leeward and the Northland coast. Fifteen miles ahead, poking up through leftover mist, were some rugged-looking hilltops. It came as a surprise to encounter what could only be the Three Kings, 35 miles northwest of Cape Reinga. Loose navigating.

I'd been optimistically relying on cross-bearings from the Kaitaia aero beacon and the Cape Reinga beacon on my RDF. While Kaitaia faithfully bleeped its signal, Reinga refused to make itself heard. In the overcast conditions I hadn't bothered with taking any sunsights, and combined with an underestimation of the current up the coast, we had moved further north than I had expected. A GPS would have made things different, but it wasn't a fiscal option then.

The sky cleared further to reveal Great Island and we set off, broad reaching towards the cloud bank hiding the top of the North Island. Cape Reinga appeared 2 hours later, then became a flashing light for the night as we ran before the wind and into the early hours of my mother Irene's birthday. Even at a short distance off-shore the RDF still failed to pick up the Reinga signal.

Turning southeast off North Cape, the wind turned southeasterly and blew at 30 knots. The early daylight hours had us heeled over hard, punching into and falling over short, steep waves. Strapped up in the lee cloth to windward, I wearily registered the overpowering gusts staggering *Swirly World* to a sideways slide until the self-steering recovered its composure to correct the luffing and keep us moving. Slow, slower, slowest. Very dull, and no fun at all. Slamming into short seas, dragging it out, beating to windward. Hard on the wind, hard work.

A large ship intersected our course en route for somewhere east. I periodically braced myself against the side and peered out of the small Perspex viewing dome at the vision of North Cape gradually receding, as we slogged into Great Exhibition Bay. Our short test of endurance was rewarded by the wind veering west at lunchtime to allow a reach down the coast under clearing, fresh, blue sky. In the distance the Karikari Peninsula, where I'd buried my message in a plastic bag, stuck out from an otherwise empty, shimmering horizon. From grey distant headland to headland we sailed at 5 to 6 knots, reaching before the moderate westerly. By dark the pressure lantern hissed at passing ships, while I steered from light to light in a faltering breeze.

Warm morning sunshine showed up the contours of the sparsely populated Whangaruru and Mimiwhangata coast beside us. The aroma of damp vegetation and wood smoke once again drifted out over the water.

Coming down off the Whangarei Heads, the gentle morning breeze freshened enough to make me reduce sail again. An audience of dolphins clustered around the bow and eyeballed my every move. They were larger than most I'd met and swam powerfully, often in long torpedo-like rushes at *Swirly World*. They always politely avoided bumping us.

Sleep was moving up on my list of immediate priorities. I hadn't had much and I was enjoying the twilight zone my fatigue-enhanced life was bringing me, but energy reserves were low. The breeze fell too light for the self-steering to cope, so I settled in for a final night of hand steering. Staying awake some more, for a change. Cape Rodney ushered us into a calm spot from where I had the extended opportunity to view the late night lights of Leigh.

The northwesterly came back at 1 a.m. so I poled out the genoa, restrained the main and set *Swirly World* self-steering, flat off for Flat Rock light. The noise of the bow wave and log cable whirring called me hypnotically to sleep. I pumped the lantern to keep the bright white glowing to its maximum for all to see and hopefully avoid me, then hit the quarterberth, setting the egg-timer alarm to allow me thirty precious minutes of silent restoration. Disengagement. My battery on fast charge.

I passed out and into a dream, where I was gathered with friends, all dressed up in the uncomfortable social costume that denotes an official engagement, in this case a funeral. It was Mike Brien's, the First World President of The United Planet, from Avondale. I'd found out about his real-life death back in London, a few months before. A letter passed on at a party, friend of a friend. 'Are you moving to London? I've got a letter for Andrew Fagan.'

'Doubt if I'm going to see him.' That was strange enough, but someone put something in my drink and it all seemed even stranger. We saw this kind of shimmering light solidifying into something else by the very unclean gas stove. Geoff the bass player made a run for it. I stayed to see if it would be him . . .

Now here he was again, this time in a dream. Bright sunlight was coming in through the windows of a room where we waited, and all seemed ill at ease. We were informed the proceedings had been delayed — then I remembered I was supposed to be somewhere else — looking out for Flat Rock light. I seeped quickly back into *Swirly World* and checked the time. I'd been dead to the world for an hour and a half, sleeping through the alarm. Numerous rocky outcrops had been waiting for the wind to shift slightly and sail us into peril, no hand on the helm.

I sprung above and surveyed the darkness expecting to find Flat Rock light flashing in the spreaders. *Swirly World* was still moving along before the 12-knot breeze and looking back beyond the phosphorescent trailing wake, more than a mile away, was the flashing light. We had missed it even though we had more or less been aiming for it when I fell asleep. Luck? Or was Michael Brien still hanging around, too keen on staying, enjoying the sailing . . .

The wind had freshened as forecast from the northwest and sailed us on course, to pass Flat Rock close by . . . How close by? Ahead, Tiri light swept its white shaft through the darkness, and past it, the glow of sleeping Auckland defined the outlines of Rangitoto and the Whangaparaoa Peninsula. No adjustments needed, *Swirly World* sailed on course for the end of Tiritiri Matangi Island, as she had done so many times before, returning from journeying about the Northland coast with Michael Brien's hand on the helm. To punctuate my suspicions the pressure lantern faltered, then went out, the darkness dramatically consuming us.

Forty-eight hours after clearing North Cape and eight days from New Plymouth, we ran flat off, with only the genoa poled out, through the Rakino Channel. It was getting light and heavy rain squalls moved across from the East Coast Bays. Motutapu, Rakino, and Waiheke wore fresh shades of rain-regenerated green, against the now familiar greys of sea and cloud.

RIGHT: Andrew, aged twelve, with his first P Class, *Tin Ribs*, at the Evans Bay Yacht Club, Wellington, in 1974.

BELOW: . . . And he grew into sailor man Andrew, who liked to live at sea.

Andrew the Mocker, in dress up mode for a 1985 *Rip It Up* cover.

A very different cover shot, taken on Andrew's return from Sunday Island, in June 1986.

ABOVE: Got there! *Swirly World* at anchor, Sunday Island, 1986.

BELOW: The welcoming party from the Sunday Island Meteorological Station, who had been keeping an eye out for *Swirly World*'s arrival.

OPPOSITE: Andrew and *Swirly World* off Westhaven in Auckland, in a fresh southwesterly.

Aboard *Moonfleet Smuggler*, at Sunbury On Thames, 1990.
Another hemisphere, another watery home.

A. Fagan, Kiwi entrant in the Messiah World Championships,
Garden of Gethsemane, Jerusalem, 1992.

LEFT: *Swirly World* craning towards the sea again after four long years – Evans Bay Yacht Club, Wellington, 1991.

RIGHT: *Swirly World* rafted against eventual race winner *Chinchilla*, New Plymouth 1994, as the contestants prepare for the Solo Tasman Race.

BELOW: Andrew and *Swirly World* preparing to leave Moreton Bay Boat Club marina in Brisbane, about to become the smallest boat to double the Tasman solo.

Andrew on *Swirly World* before setting off from New Plymouth on a compass course for
Mooloolaba, Queensland, Australia, only 1200 miles away . . .

The rain caught up to us off Park Point and we gybed in a cold downpour to drift along in the lee of the shore into a calm and silent Huruhi Bay. The water clouds moved out over Maraetai, leaving patches of mist in the gullies and loud streams pouring down vigorously from the bush onto the gravel shoreline. Distant dogs and birds made themselves known, but no humans could be heard.

Within fifteen minutes of the frontal rain passing through, a fresh southwesterly came across from Howick to expel the stillness. A swift change of wind direction. Having hooked onto a mooring, I filled in the log, 1258 miles on the new milometer. I packed up the kitbag and unfolded the dinghy on the foredeck. The new wind had set a slight jobble into the bay, and getting myself and baggage into the flimsy, undulating dinghy was the most difficult part of the trip.

On the anniversary of *Wahine* Day, 10 April, the wind commemorated the fifty-two drowned in Wellington Harbour in 1968 by blowing itself into another severe southerly up the South Island and through Cook Strait, blasting cold and wet as far north as the Hauraki Gulf.

That morning the first rays of sun had been banished behind low-flying clouds. Anticipating the worst, I got into a wetsuit, ready to paddle the folding dinghy out to *Swirly World*. Already the southerly was blowing little breaking waves into the bay. I couldn't have rowed against it without our low freeboard being swamped. I launched the dinghy well upwind of *Swirly World* and paddled out with the little waves liberally slopping their tops onto my legs. When I reached the boat I'd accumulated a healthy-sized paddling pool around me.

They were forecasting 40-knot rain squalls and Tamaki Strait was already uncomfortable with a short wind and tide-induced chop. I hoisted the relevant sails and soon had *Swirly World* plunging to windward, the appropriate balance of reduced cloth keeping us going at 3 to 4 knots. Solid sailing. Heeling over, locking in, maximum boat speed, balance, drive, pointing up the steep little waves, then driving down their backs . . . slam on through to the other side. My 1200-mile reacquaintance with *Swirly World* had confirmed to me my suspicion that sailing is physically addictive.

We beat under the sheltered cliffs of Musick Point, mere metres from Auckland Radio headquarters. I had conversed with them from 500 miles away on my improved radio in the past few days. Now they are no more. Centralised and economically more efficient, broadcasts come from Taupo in the central North Island.

As the rush-hour traffic tailgated along Tamaki Drive, we reached inshore off the Bastion reefs, the wind blowing fiercely over the flat water, heeling *Swirly World* to dip the boom in the sea as we raced along. Nasty squalls almost lifting spray to leeward, no sea to speak of, but a lot of noise as I eased the mainsail to flog itself through the worst of it.

In the lee of the downtown wharves and the towering steel bows of ships, I removed the sails and motored towards Princess Wharf. *The Rainbow Warrior II* was leaving harbour and took advantage of the strong breeze to fly its sails. It was blowing, and it looked undercanvassed, but made a fine futuristic sight moving out past Devonport at 10 knots . . . sailing ships once more.

I later inquired at the Hydrographic Office in Takapuna as to the state of the Reinga Beacon and found it listed out of order in the navigational warnings on 15 April. Having discovered it was out on 3 April, I was remiss in not reporting it earlier. At least I'd noticed it. For its absence to have gone unreported for so long stands as testimony to the more unfortunate consequences of automation.

Chapter 11

Sailing with a seawolf

'Why do you want to live on Waiheke?'

'It's quite nice compared to other places I've seen.' The opposite of overpopulated England, it can only be approached by sea or air, and you drink the drips that fill the individual water tanks. With a boat, you can't ignore Waiheke. There's sheltered holding all around the narrow isthmus of Oneroa and Blackpool.

The volcanic land affords privacy in gullies and valleys on a scale American tourists call quaint. At night the glow of Auckland City lights is sufficiently distant to allow the universe to beam brightly with overbearing intensity. The real dark. No electric glow, horizon halo . . . as dark as it really is when we stand or float, on a moonless night, in the enormous gap between earth and the rest of it. More constantly reminded of the universe as we know, or think we know it.

It was cheaper to sail to Auckland than catch the ferry. But the quick cat only took 35 minutes. The best *Swirly World* could do was 3 hours from Blackpool (Huhuri Bay) running or reaching. It was 5 to 6 hours on the wind against a westerly. The cupboards were getting bare in our bach on Waiheke but the price of imported food on the island was offensive, so I tight reached to Foodtown across Tamaki Strait one overcast midwinter's day. I anchored one high-tide night at Mellons Bay near Howick and walked the ridge to the less expensive mega-aisled competition.

Staggering back through the suburban streets with kitbags full of cans, weighed down, I gave up the idea of making it a regular venture by foot. I overestimated my packhorse ability, and silently castigated my masochistic self-denial in passing the beckoning taxi stand at the shops. A few locals mistook me for a scruffy bag-person intent on setting up a cardboard home in their garden. Or a highly successful thief. Upfront, self-confident hostile looks at me staggering past their front windows, weighed down with a bulging bag of booty.

The wind abandoned play, and left us to putter our bright green way back through myriad tones of grey. Twilight brought haloed streetlights along main ridge roads, and a low mist about Mt Wellington and One Tree Hill. As it got darker, the grey lid of cloud grew pink and orange with reflected city light, then we rounded the point and Blackpool revealed itself, sparsely lit with streetlights, relatively empty and deserted.

In the black night east, the faint flicker of Kawakawa Bay took me back to the milkman's shed where I'd found *The Prince of Innocence*. That 30-mile trip in 1982 to Cox's Bay had taken two days in light airs and became a bit unpleasant to my inexperienced 'coasting' self. Auckland more or less to windward all the way had seemed a marathon. Sailing years had since passed and the jigsaw puzzle pieces felt a little more connected. The darkness beyond Devonport wasn't so daunting after all. You just had to keep looking a bit further, then you'd see it.

Eighteen nights in a row singing songs took me to a summer-coated South Island. I stole away one Sunday morning from the Turf Hotel in Stoke, to visit *Tejada* where Adrian Hayter had spent his final years, a few miles distant in the Wairoa Gorge.

It rained hard going along the unsealed windy gorge road. It was a mild cold front and I barefooted through brown puddles to open and close the farm gates that led to the riverside plateau. Waist-high brown grass hid a forest of native saplings and looked grateful for the liberal sprinkling it was getting. There was no sign of Hayter's caravan, which had been his home from 1986–1990.

Of three attractive alternate dwellings, only the mudwalled place looked to be occupied. I talked to a woman and Great Dane, who were renting the abode, but they'd only been there a few months.

She agreed with me that we needed the rain.

Driving back, I stopped on the bridge high above the gorge to close the last gate. The sky was still dripping and the water felt special. Mist hung round the ridge line, and far below, the night's rain ran clear and fast towards the sea; same as it always had. I didn't need to actually see Hayter, it was as if he was there anyway.

Seven gigs later it was Dunedin. The Commodore of the Otago Yacht Club, Austen Banks, having read a sailing article of mine, took time to make himself known, and toured me around the edge of the land and assorted boatish places. He was being hospitable in a 'sailing secret society' way. He had appeared out of nowhere after the afternoon sound check at Sammy's nightclub. It was similar to being frogmarched away by the headmaster for showing off in a public place. He had boats to show me, mainly his. He was an enthusiast, either that, or he was a born-again Christian picking his moment to have a go at me . . .

On visiting the small marina in Deborah Bay where his 38-ft Farr yacht was living, I noticed a familiar looking folkboat. Austen was directing my attention elsewhere but the folkboat distracted me.

Except for an extended coach-roof, it was the same as the one Hayter had sailed from England via the Panama Canal to Nelson in 1962. It was *Valkyr*, there in Deborah Bay, after all those miles and years. The same small foredeck where he'd toiled so many times with unruly sails, by day and dark, in solitary confinement while he sailed the world. Here it was. Hayter had led me here. I reached across and held the bow, the hull gently moving in the water.

Another weather front was coming over the southern Tasman Sea towards Fiordland, and the humid northwesterlies preceding it had been freshening their way down from Lord Howe Island, hundreds of miles away. The entertainment was done, and I escaped to a night of no humans, on the end of the wharf at Lake Wanaka. The warm wind stirred Antipodean willows alive and tumbled lake water onto the tideless sand. The sky was clear and dark, stars conspicuous. An excellent view of the universe. I thought of the people I knew who had stopped, and breathed the moments with the potency the inherent brevity of existence demands.

The next morning the rain came loud before daylight, washing down the deserted streets. Indoors we sat, at a tower-block break-fast table with friends and a handful of elderly tourists kick-starting their hearts at 6.30 a.m. with bowls of black coffee. The harsh neon lights above made the sleep-creased faces and freshly smeared foundation unpleasantly conspicuous. And that was just me. The head waitress picked immediately that the party I was with were coming to the end of an evening's amusements. She adopted a headmistressy manner towards the social mutineers contaminating the premises. We were aesthetically inappropriate. Someone wanted to order a bottle of wine, it was the wrong thing to say . . .

Out through the windows, the grey early light seeped through layers of low-moving cloud. Lake Wakatipu came into sight, looking authentically severe in whitecaps and rain. It was worth staying up for. We were only there for the view.

The sun was slipping out for the night as I rowed my resurrected plywood dinghy out to *Swirly World*. Huruhi Bay is exposed to the south and southeast but the usual westerlies and southwesterlies can be avoided near the marae.

A friend, Frank, had lost his 30-ft Piver trimaran on a trip from Waiheke to Motuketekete. Hard-pressed in a southwesterly squall, one float swamped and the trimaran slowly rolled to submerge on its side. The wreck went unretrieved (not without a struggle) and had last been seen drifting north past Little Barrier Island. Frank wasn't happy but he heard that it might have come up, months later, on Great Barrier Island, at the north end near Catherine Bay.

Hearsay was enough and not having a lot in my appointment book for the next few years, I volunteered to go and check it out. That evening, in receding tones of twilight, *Swirly World* was quick to bear away around Park Point and reach northeast out past the white flashing light of The Noises and into the clouded pitch darkness of the gulf. A darkness that, with accumulated experience, no longer appeared quite so bad. A light westerly over the outgoing tide kept us moving under the wind vane, while I cowardly sat on the companionway steps, hatchboards in, head sticking out into cold air. More inside than out. Another damp winter night on the make. It made a change to be awake at night compared to the usual day rhythms of writing songs in the kitchen and wandering gullies plucking neglected fruit from holiday-home trees. Waiheke was good for that. Unpatrolled trees. Feijoa trees shaking uncontrollably from below for no apparent reason other than me.

The breeze was light to moderate so the dinghy stayed trailing behind, no likelihood of irregularities as I lay relaxed inside, away from the wind and winter air outdoors.

Near Cape Colville, at the end of the Coromandel Peninsula, the fetch had increased sufficiently to raise a slight sea that interfered with the dinghy. It would occasionally surf up behind and clip the stainless heel on the self-steering rudder. The pull of the dinghy's painter was getting heavier but I lacked interest. The sea motion had the better of me. By dim lantern light, lying on the quarter-berth, I feebly willed a body to go outside and feign involvement. It made it out, and there lay the answer, a dinghy half full of liquid and well on the way to sinking. One of the earlier encounters had punctured a hole in its thin plywood shell. I pulled it in and bailed a little bit before managing, in a last energetic flicker, to drag it up and onto the foredeck. It was too much for me so I had a good throw-up to emphasise the point. All sorts of unpleasant pieces just gathered there, not quite over the side, as I would have preferred. A pause, faint sense of recovery, then slithering back inside onto the bunk again. Thoroughly unenthused.

This time out on the Hauraki Gulf I was transporting a silent, unhappy, captive passenger. I was sailing with an animal that couldn't (or wouldn't?) speak English. A pet dog saved from death row at the Onehunga SPCA. The form said 'colour sable' and it sounded easy, so thanks to us, Sable, every moment's a bonus. She had resigned herself to a long wait lying on the sail bags up front. No scent of land, no hint of liberation. Sensing my disturbed being she pushed in on the action, wedging between body and hull. They never warned us about this at the SPCA.

As *Swirly World* sledged into another anonymous dawn at sea, I lay incapacitated by standard seasickness, but at least kept warm by the body of the hyena-face stretched out beside me; dog hair all about.

Half-hearted navigational efforts throughout the night had me anxious to locate various rocks before daylight. Seasickness makes me a very apathetic navigator. If *Swirly World* went down that night the court of enquiry would have slaughtered me. It didn't happen, and with the sun came the divine view of distant things. The horizon behind was empty. Auckland and Waiheke had disappeared. Little Barrier Island was a large island to port (left), and the outlying Port Fitzroy islands of Great Barrier were close at hand off the starboard (right) bow.

By 10 a.m. a glob of underwater epoxy had sealed the dinghy leak and my passenger impressed with her eagerness to board the shore-bound shuttle well before being invited. Catherine Bay looked quiet. A cluster of houses but no humans about. On earth again, the seawolf relished each nostril-stimulating encounter with whatever, while I trod unsteadily over low-tide rocks, depleted from vomiting episodes. Not enough fuel left inside to really enjoy things — a body out of tune with the motion of even the mildest swells.

When the unsealed road looked set to enter 'densely wooded' parts (according to my ancient chart from the 1920s I'd found tucked away in *Swirly World*), the seawolf managed to trigger the madly barking interest of a pack of well tied up local canines. I was relieved they were well-tied-up. Their dreadlocked master emerged to settle them down and I met Roy, who revived us with hot tea and dog biscuits. Each to their own.

Roy hadn't sailed before, but he made it clear he wouldn't mind trying, so that afternoon Sable socialised with heavyweight pig dogs while *Swirly World* slid out past Bird Rock and down to Miner's Head. Roy hadn't heard about a wreck but a low-tide look around the rocks might spot something.

One kilometre east of Miner's Head, at eight minutes past midnight in thick fog on a wild night in October 1894, the 87-metre *Wairarapa* slammed onto the rocks and 130 people died. Waves swept passengers, crew, and sixteen horses from the deck. Thrashing horses kicked people to death as the water washed amongst the rocks with heavy wreckage and bodies. Many ended up in Catherine Bay. All those horrifying moments, emotionally seared on the atmosphere of the coast. That's how it was. The final moments of many, right there. We had it easy, plenty of visibility, no significant swell.

There was no sign of the trimaran. The choppy sea dissolved Roy's application after an hour, and one decent flattening from a misgauged gust had him doubting my competence in getting us back. The wind was picking up.

That evening *Swirly World* was anchored in 3 metres, close under the slight lee of a northern point in the bay. The wind had veered back to the west and blew onto the exposed shore. The sky looked tame enough. We went ashore.

Time travelled, and I found myself leaving Roy and partner later that night. Exactly how much later, it was hard to tell. I was a bit under the weather. Roy's hospitality had seen to that. I eventually deduced the wind coming out of the darkness had freshened considerably. Leaves on bending trees were letting me know all about it. The tide was fully in and the first obstacle between a path along the cliff to the dinghy and me, was the dark wet sea flowing swiftly up the mouth of the stream. After much persuasion, a timid sea-wolf reluctantly joined me for a hand-paddled ride in a borrowed dinghy across to the other side. We were going to have to get wet. The wind-driven high tide was breaking waves all along the shore and up the little clay cliffs around the headland. Our path at the foot of the clay was covered. In I went, torchbeam unable to penetrate the murky salt water splashing about bare thighs. Things didn't look good for the four-legged one. The sensory overload of rushing, frothing, cold salt water surging in out of the darkness at neck height was too much. She refused to participate.

Naked and wet, and grimly keen on seeing if *Swirly World* was still where I'd put her; I physically encouraged the beast to join in. Lifted from her cowering rock ledge perch, it still required persistence on my part to complete her passage up, over and occasionally through the water. Eventually we made it up to the sheltered undergrowth. It had to be done. Canine character building.

The rest was dry and along a dark uneven path, identifying treacherous roots by torchlight, the seawolf nosing ahead, nostrils alive with undergrowth aromas. The trees thrashed their intermeshed canopy of wind-inspired chaos above. The sound of the air rushing through the woodwork and surf on the nearby rocks animated the night — and all because of our invisible antagonist, the wind. *The wind, the wind, the invisible wonderful wind . . . you can feel the wind, but you're never going to see it.*

And all because of the wind, I hastily shunted the green dinghy into the shallows and somehow convinced Sable that returning to the sensory-depriving floating green kennel where she occasionally got to sleep with humans was an appealing thing to do. *Swirly World* had use of the only slight lee in the bay. Here there was some shelter from the steeply breaking swells surfing in to inevitable destruction on the exposed beach. It wasn't so much shelter, more a deflection of impact.

The wind was gusting hard off the point and threatening to lift spray. A good wave set was driving into the rest of the cove and *Swirly World* lay rolling and lifting on the waves rounding the point to windward. It was a dubious deflection.

The passenger knew the exit drill for disembarking from dinghy to cockpit could be difficult. By darkness, in 35 knots on a short, uncooperative sea, it could be hazardous. Clutch the stanchion, standing up, one arm under the hyena's chest cage, lift and pivot. Can't afford to miss or allow animal to splay limbs, thereby stalling procedure. The swing and pivot point when the creature is elevated becomes crucial. With the passenger under my arm, the dinghy began backing away, and as our combined weight went aft, the gunwale (edge) sunk down and water rushed hideously over and in. The ejected passenger landed half a body on board, the rest undignified, and kicking for something solid. Without the extra ballast the dinghy recovered.

All night we lifted, lowered, rolled and veered to the long anchor chain stretched out to the oversized Danforth anchor dug down deep into the thick sea-bed mud. Held secure, if uncomfortable, as the seas rushed malevolently into the rest of the bay. It was easy to imagine the wind and waves as the work of an emotionally disturbed entity from the wreck of the *Wairarapa*. Totally dedicated to disturbing my reality, tucked away in the far corner of *their* Catherine Bay. The hours went by and I lay half-awake, listening for the sound of something going wrong. It didn't.

At first light the wind still gusted hard, and the waves rolled impressively in. Severely geared down, two reefs in the main, No.2

jib. With dinghy strapped onto the foredeck, the well-dug in anchor was retrieved from the mud below and *Swirly World* reached off on starboard into the bay. It was a lee shore of unpleasant proportions, a short, steep sea pushing in towards the rocks with slopes and troughs of water just the right size to halt our drive to windward. I didn't like the look of this at all. I shouldn't have stayed the night, should have got out before dusk, even if it meant staggering out another night somewhere vaguely near Little Barrier. Now it was too late and this was not the place to be.

In the time it had taken to pull up sail and anchor and clear the lee of the point, the fierce northwesterly had eased and backed to the westerly quarter, making it a dead beat to windward out of the bay. *Swirly World* moved lethargically through the waves but with the eased windspeed we were undercanvassed. A feeling of under-achievement beset us. We couldn't gather enough boat speed to round up and go about. After bearing away and losing ground to gybe onto the other tack it appeared we could only hold our own against the waves. Between gybes, we reached across to the rocks on either side, shaking out reefs as we went. The headsail was still a bit small for a masthead rig, but more mainsail got *Swirly World*'s momentum up and we gradually pushed to windward through many a wet, crumpling crest. The seawolf didn't realise life inside a ken-nel could be so uncomfortable. It took us an hour to clear the bay. Once past Separation Point, in deeper water, the waves were fur-ther apart and the motion and progress less wretched.

On a tight reach against a fresh clearing westerly, *Swirly World* cleared the southern headland and aimed to the left of Little Barrier, slamming along at 4 knots, on course for the empty horizon and the unseen coast of Waiheke Island. It always looks so far when you can't see it.

Another sailing day in the *Swirly World* time machine. Trance sail-ing. Absorbed in the view of heeling hull, telltale windflow wool-lies on the headsail, and the hypnotically compelling feel of the sails drawing us over the sea — feeling it through the tiller.

Fifteen hours later it was night once more, the wind relenting to a dysfunctional strength, and *Swirly World* was left drifting next to Haystack Rock beside Rakino Island. Out of it for free on fatigue.

The passenger had lost interest hours ago, but registered no complaints until we came into the aroma zone of land. With the familiar light clusters of Bucklands Beach and Beachlands set in black and beckoning down the Motuihe Passage, I managed to get the wind vane activated in a more permanent northwesterly airflow. A clear, cold, star-filled night, 2 hours till daylight.

Relieved of the helm, a fatigued body lobbied the brain for relaxation. The view couldn't hold my attention, so I opted for a 20-minute wind of the egg timer and stretched out inside. Up on the forward sail bags the passenger stared impassively at me with forlorn disenchantment.

I'd spent most of the night steering, focused on the slowly approaching dark line of Waiheke. It took a long time. Periodically the sky over the land flashed unexpectedly, like sheet lightning in a cloudless sky. I'd seen it before over Waiheke and once in Little Oneroa, the night instantaneously illuminated as if a huge flash bulb had gone off. Peculiar electrical discharges. The sporadic flash of otherworldly entities entering our frequency spectrum. Something like that, or so I've been told. I hope so.

I awoke forty undisciplined minutes later to the fact that I'd not returned to consciousness when the alarm had rung. Oh no, not again near land . . .

The wind was still present as the water was gurgling past outside, but which piece of water was that? Let's have a look, quickly. Up on deck the dark skyline of a surrounding amphitheatre of land was disturbingly close at hand. *Swirly World* had sailed round a rocky point and was heading for the beach in Home Bay on Motutapu Island. Not a good look. Wind vane disengaged, then bearing away to gybe on to a course for Park Point at the entrance to Tamaki Strait. No obstacles in our immediate way. Consider yourself fortunate. Remember, 'You're not there until you get there, and near the end, beware.'

Back in Putiki Bay on Waiheke a short compact keeler arrived to catch my eye the way unusual little boats do. It was *ROC* (*Roger's Offshore Cruiser*). A 19-ft ferroconcrete Donovan design, full-keeled yacht that had sailed in the 1974 Solo Tasman Race from New Plymouth to Mooloolaba, north of Brisbane. It had taken thirty-five days with Roger hand steering after his wind vane was damaged early on.

Marcus, a young enthusiast, now owned *ROC*, having found her ashore and disused at Ahiwa Harbour near Whakatane. After a first attempt to cross the Ahiwa Bar resulted in being completely rolled and dismasted, he finally made his engineless way to Waiheke. The full-standing headroom inside was a novelty in such a short boat and the concrete certainly slowed things up. But having done the Tasman, the boat could do no wrong in our eyes. Marcus was a fellow enthusiast. He knew about the Solo Tasman Race. It was a cult thing. A specialist sailing experience.

In the mid-seventies, sailing Starlings in Evans Bay, I'd cut out the articles on the earlier races and thumbed through them on many a dull, gale-beset Wellington school holiday. Australia. There by boat and wind, alone. Imagine being out there now in this north-westerly. If *ROC* could do it, could *Swirly World*? Equally important-ly, could I?

The seawolf and I had been motoring for an hour against the flooding tide up past Matiatia through the Motuihe channel. We were going nowhere for no good reason. Finally clear of Motutapu, the engine gave a no-fuel hiccup and died, leaving *Swirly World* wallowing on a glassy smooth surface behind Rangitoto. This time I hadn't thought about fuel, the forecast had read wind so we should eventually arrive in Auckland. It didn't look good. The clouds weren't going anywhere and the outgoing tide looked set to suspend us in the gulf indefinitely. The hours of afternoon daylight crawled by with no progress to mention, in any direction.

No physical course worth steering . . . for me or the boat? Be-calmed, my application became internal as I reflected on my lot. The years were drifting by and the cycle of recording and perform-ing was becoming stretched out. Slowed down. A lot further in be-tween segments of the cycle. Still no CD recorded. Treading water, glum in paradise. In between audiences. Who needs an audience anyway? I had to concede I did.

The songs had to be exorcised from my mind, and until they were satisfactorily recorded and irrevocably released, they wouldn't go away. It was always like that. The duty to song. Not to be found in a bottom drawer of forgotten demos. It was an odyssey of collaboration. Musicians, engineers, producers, record company sales people, record shop retailers, radio station programmers, DJs, commentators; all partially responsible and undeniably relevant to one's 'marketplace context'. All contributing or not contributing to the 'marketplace validity' of your self-expression. But you have to have an audience to fund your endeavours. It's the difference between a hobby and a career.

I needed a mission. Some self-determination without strategic alliances. Run away with the wind and waves. Any voyage would do. A primeval odyssey. Dark moonless nights far away from my own earthly ambitions.

The sun went out through the low North Shore coastline, and the cloak of a dark long night descended. Cold and becalmed. A band of electrically lit lounges and streetlights stretched south and north from the city. All those private, expensive, extensive sea views curtained off. A nation united in its centralised, televised infotainment and amusement channels.

A light westerly filled in and we finally started moving again, tacking towards the land. Having gone without, the wind is always most welcome. To get up Auckland Harbour I needed fuel to make the opposing tide inconsequential. While most of the lights were going off like the end of a *Flintstones* cartoon, I anchored off Mairangi Bay and walked the ridge to a late-night petrol station. There were humans asleep all around me, but I didn't let it deter me. *Houses are but badly built boats so firmly aground that you cannot think of moving them.* Arthur Ransome, 1922.

Wairau Creek in Milford is one of the redeeming features of the Auckland's North Shore. Its down-market tidal marina is accessed through a narrow entrance that almost entirely dries up at low tide. Before the Harbour Bridge was built, much of the Shore had sported holiday baches, just like Waiheke.

After months of rushing for the last ferry from town to Waiheke most evenings, one of the few remaining baches in Milford became campaign control centre and home. The wooded corner property had been sold and the townhouses were coming. It was only a matter of time, but for that time we would be the last tenants. Firmly aground. *Swirly World* found a mud berth in the creek where the radar reflector could once again be seen from the window. With the creek bed drying out, a unique weir barrier retains a certain sea level in the marina area. When the tide returns it eventually floods the basin, lowering the barrier to allow deep keels in and out.

Being able to step aboard *Swirly World* in eternally calm conditions was good for the manual aspects of getting things done. All those jobs I'd put off. Quiet hours of preparation before an audience of private North Shore suburban windows. Preparing for the distant possibility of sailing to Australia.

I was back in Auckland with a band again. *Swirly World* remained tucked away from the elements while we laboured the days and nights into months, finding sounds to colour in the tonal landscapes of those precious three-minute emotional capsules so often dismissively called 'pop' songs.

After three months the collection was complete and the record company wanted a video. Absolutely. The song was called 'Jerusalem', so if we were truly going to do justice to the lyrics we shouldn't hesitate to embark at once for the Holy Land.

Chapter 12

Would anyone be looking?

Would anyone be looking?

After many hours hurtling above land and sea, Israeli security police greeted us at 2 a.m. Tel Aviv time. They were looking for drug carriers and singled me out for special attention. I believed him but he didn't believe me until, obliged to disrobe, he could tell by the cut of my genitals that I might be on his side. I was encouraged to sign a declaration written in Hebrew testifying to something. He understood my reluctance. Welcome to the Holy Land.

A lot of people think it's all going to go down in Jerusalem. The big one. Second coming, messianic deliverance on behalf of us all. A lot of the locals appear from the outside to be doing their best to manifest some kind of showdown. Humans who feel they might have a historical role to play can be very dangerous things. Humans fed on historically divisive ideologies are very dangerous things.

New testimonies of lifestyles and attitudes described in the Dead Sea scrolls and Gnostic gospels, only discovered in the last fifty years, point to another possibility for human spiritual expectations. That Christ died of old age, had four children and a wife who left him, is heresy to a lot on planet earth. What they found in the caves says it might be so. No one's got a monopoly on the truth, even though they advertise it so. A 'Son of God' only in so much as we all could be, at one level.

The Gnostic gospels contained techniques for attaining self-knowledge they called *knowledge of divine power within*. They conceived of gnosis as a subjective, immediate experience, concerning themselves, above all, with the internal significance of events. *Whoever achieves gnosis becomes no longer a Christian but a Christ.* Those who expected to become Christ themselves were not likely to recognise the institutional structures of the church as the ultimate authority. Hence their virtual deletion from history by the Roman Catholic Church. They had their own agenda, and still have. The Cathars were onto it and paid for it with their lives. Orthodox religion as a social control mechanism — centuries of hypnotising the humans with fear of consequences. Get your God here. Sacred this and untouchable that. All a bit sad really, unless of course they're right?

They thought we were there to shoot a music video. That was what we told them. Anyone who asked. 'See the guitar? Song's called . . .' I couldn't tell them the truth, it would jeopardise the whole enterprise. I was part of a covert invasion force. You don't need guns to successfully overrun resistance. Guitars are far more diplomatic. I was in actual fact in the finals of the Messiah World Championships. The competition was run along the lines of a pentathlon. My next event involved making an unmolested appearance on the Mount of Olives, down in the Garden of Gethsemene, then more audaciously at the blocked-up Golden Gate itself, no less. Gold suit mandatory. Would anyone be looking?

Israel, the tourist bus commentator, remembers his 1948 War of Independence, which created the state of Israel. He had a sense of purpose in having participated in claiming, then consistently maintaining, exclusive sovereignty. He'd been at it again in 1967, carrying his weapon into the Judean desert and down to Qumran on the edge of the Dead Sea. Israel was adamant about territorial sovereignty. He didn't like the other team and wasn't in favour of giving them bits back. He was brought up as a persecuted chosen person and some emotional animosities are hard to erase. If you didn't share Israel's attitudes, he didn't seem very interested.

'Did the Essenes who wrote the Dead Sea Scrolls reject the Jerusalem of their day?' He didn't seem to hear me. 'I heard that they rejected the theological competition, and built a new Jerusalem, a scaled-down replica and were dismissively tagged as Seekers of Smooth Things.' Israel wasn't impressed. I was glad he didn't have a weapon. He didn't want to know. Apart from pointing at the crumbly white cliffs and announcing the location of the discovered scrolls, Qumran and the Essenes were irrelevant.

The other heresy of the scrolls is the idea that the crucifixion of Christ the terrorist, the 'man of lies' and the 'Wicked Priest', took place at Qumran (then also known as Jerusalem). Under the care of Essene herbal specialists Christ recovered and went into hiding, making various exclusive 'appearances' throughout his mobile life. At least he didn't get overexposed.

The pre-dawn call to Islamic morning prayers had followed our rental car, echoing around the hard, silent slopes of East Jerusalem. The Dome of the Rock temple has a good, if slightly distorted, loudspeaker system. Still, pre-dawn darkness echoed its monopoly around the Mount of Olives. Setting up the camera and Messiah contestant mere metres from the sentry box and barbed wire on top of the Golden (Essene) Gate went unchallenged. Our torchlight trips carrying guitar et al amongst ancient graves appeared to have taken them by surprise. By prophetic decree, the Messiah can be expected to arrive at the blocked up Golden Gate in East Jerusalem, overlooking the Kidron valley.

He is expected to enter (once the blocks have been removed) and take up residence on what is now the Islamic Dome of the Rock site. That was the tricky part. Who wrote that bit of the script? That the Prince of Peace would have a little hostility on his hands as his followers competed for worship space seems to have been overlooked, or the definition of a compassionate Messiah has become confused. Perhaps everyone should have a go.

Camera and sound on standby, all that remained was the sun's impending rise from behind the Mount of Olives. The Palestinian poultry were loud in their anticipation of daylight. The cars had yet to commence their noisy procession sidling up the Mount of Olives. It was showbiz time. I was doing the playback for myself to mime to on a ghetto blaster gaffered up to a 12-volt battery and mini DAT player. It was behind a gravestone beside me and looked suspiciously like a home-made bomb.

Down the path from us I noticed something else hiding behind another large gravestone. It looked like a human. With the guitar slung from my shoulder instead of a machine gun, hopefully my intentions were obvious. I plucked a peaceful chord or two, just in case our secret audience was open to emotional persuasion.

A well-presented Palestinian eventually stepped forward and politely introduced himself as Mohammed, the night watchman. Pressed casual slacks, shirt collar, slip ons. In unaccomplished English he pointed out the sacredness of the spot from a Palestinian perspective, then squatted down and lit a smoke, listening attentively to my song on the ghetto blaster. His initial concern receded. 'Like Michael Jackson?'

'Yeah, sort of . . .' Torchbeams amongst the headstones were his business and permits expected. With no paperwork we were winging it and relied on the collusion of Mohammed to film without interference.

Dawn joined us and the sun finally rose from behind the Mount of Olives, casting its soft yellow light over the graffitied ancient Golden Gate. The moments passed and finally with enough light for filming, I sang my 'Jerusalem' to Jerusalem. In the valley the traffic built up quickly, sonically desecrating the early morning atmosphere of the Garden of Gethsemane. So did I.

We marched on Qumran late in the morning but met with little resistance at the gate. The excavated ruins of the Essene community were fenced off, you have to pay to experience their plateau. It's not hard to believe Christ could have experienced his crucifixion agony there, surrounded by steep rocky slopes silently witnessing . . .

It was very badly hot. All close and oxygen depriving. A lot of people had done their living there, all zealed up on their own alienating opinions. A community alone in the wilderness, dedicated against orthodoxy. Setting up their version of how to do your life. Slugging it out with ideas, belief system battles. No cars, a long way to walk, all worked out in pedestrian time.

Our cameras and tripods were all they expected from tourists. There was no wind that morning up the north end of the Dead Sea, 38°C. I'd brought a big flag to fly whilst silently addressing all who had been there before to pay attention to what I had in mind. The usual messianic stuff.

The flag initially refused to fly, a major hitch — no wind. Then an obliging light air filled in from off the Dead Sea to stream it out fully, white and purple cloth flowing fluid against the heat-parched red and yellow rock. Qumran had fallen with no casualties, it was obvious to the true believers that we held a spiritual mandate. Israel wouldn't agree. Surprisingly the armed gatekeepers offered no comment when we eventually withdrew our unofficial occupation. They hadn't been looking.

Retreating, drenched in sweat, gulping cold bottled water and heading for the air-conditioned sanctuary of the car, we had underestimated the heat. Qumran wouldn't have been worth defending anyway. No reliable water supply. Some might say the same for the whole region.

Any further desert missions had to conclude early or the low altitude oppressiveness would get the better of us. Swooning, they used to call it. Our Qumran campaign also revealed that the pole carrying my rather large flag would not stay upright in the ground without some mallet and stake attention. The props department (consisting of myself) would have to sort it out.

At 3 a.m. we were back, 17 hours later, driving down deserted desert night roads through the West Bank occupied territories, overtaking lone Israeli jeeps as they crawled along, mounted machine guns trained on the dark, unseen Judaen desert. On isolated ridges, overly lit barbed-wired fortified Jewish settlements stuck out like Asian squid boats suspended on giant, dark, Southern Ocean swells.

We closed on the checkpoint soldiers at their most vulnerable hour, just before dawn, on the edge of the Dead Sea. A cursory wave of the hand from a disinterested nineteen-year-old, doing part of his obligatory two-year military service, watching the flickering night lights of Arab lives across the water in Jordan. Small fires were boiling their tea kettles black and steaming; heavy metal Western democracy rock music blasting out from the elevated lookout seat. Just like the usual heroic American 'Nam' war movies. They'd probably seen them all, relating to threatening proceedings in a universally primate male way. Basic competition ethic.

We drove our air-conditioned base camp into the unearthly Dead Sea salt hills at the foot of Massada and had the flag-bearing pole anchored and upright as the threatening red and orange wash of dawn over the Moabite escarpment turned into overly intrusive sunlight. With the solar radiation substance came wind, 15 knots off the water and enough to raise the fine chemicals from the sandy surface, dizzying our senses. Involuntarily breathing toxic salts in unpleasant amounts.

The flag flew fiercely, flexing its upright pole in a most satisfactory manner. An army helicopter appeared from the hills and came low, tracking overhead. I had erected other smaller white flags and they all flew defiant and unidentified. We thought about a rocket launcher but that would never do. The 'camera pointed at guitarist scenario' defused their suspicions of an impending invasion. They veered off up the coast towards En Gedi. We decided to let them go.

Having established our foothold in the sandhills, we decided against forming a bridgehead and landing reinforcements on the edge of the Dead Sea. The army had thoughtfully signposted their landmined zone between the road and saline liquid.

In these overpopulated years all land might as well be called Holy. It's becoming that precious. Holy water is anything that drips out of the sky fresh and reasonably free of pollutants. In the 'space lifeboat' we now perceive the earth to be, all the basic natural ingredients rate as sacred and special: no group more chosen than the other. One species, different stages of emotional development. Exclusivity over living space always makes for a dismal contest: a bloodthirsty sense of purpose emotionally contaminating those left grieving, while training more recruits in the grudge-match mentality: us and them.

The Essenes were right to clear out of old Jerusalem. Too much volatile theological competition. Better leave them to it and try again somewhere less contaminated by divisive opinion. Colonise the sea. Might as well. Most of the land comes with too much emotional baggage these days. Better grab the best latitudes and go for it. Miles and miles of steel islands . . .

At the air terminal exit there was an unmanned booth with free booklets on aspects of Judaism. On the cover of one magazine, written in French, was a 'prophetic' drawing of the Temple Mount with a Jewish synagogue replacing the existing Dome of the Rock structures. They appeared to have been removed. Somehow it looks as if it will end in crying. The sign above the booth read 'Judaism with a Smile'.

We woke up to the sound of chain saws in the garden. The time had come to defoliate our private corner of Milford. One of the last pre-Harbour Bridge North Shore baches was on its way out. By that evening the old overgrown timbers had fallen. Meg the poet's tired plum tree never to plum again, one wooded corner no more. No longer a private backyard, instead indecent exposure. The foundations of the first townhouse, metres away, promised noisy activity for some time to come.

That night I steered *Swirly World* over the Wairau Creek weir barrier, pushing the last of the incoming tide. It was late and most humans were sleeping again. Lone cars raced up the coast hill road as *Swirly World* slipped out close under the overhanging pohutukawa, down the narrow creek and out beside the channel markers. It was flat calm but a slight leftover northeasterly swell heaved small phosphorescent breakers onto shallow rock ledges. Two hours by monotonous motor took the seawolf and me to Woody Bay on Rakino Island and two more hours brought morning sunshine streaming its unwelcome way through the viewing dome. I knew any sign of consciousness on my part would stir pet interest to an irritating extreme. Psychological mutiny. There's a lot of it about. After her compulsory shit and stroll the beast looked ready for long hours confined aboard *Swirly World*. She didn't have any choice.

With dinghy on deck it was out of the bay into the sun, still rising over the Coromandel Ranges. Destination Tryphena, Great Barrier Island, 45 miles away. The wind blew moderate out of the east-northeast, putting *Swirly World* hard on the wind, close-hauled for a slow beat to windward. All day we heeled on starboard tack, either lying in the lee cloth suspended to windward on the quarterberth, or hand steering with dog hair in the cockpit. The seawolf couldn't smell the land, and as it was minimal by mouth, she didn't really need it for any biologically compelling reasons. Nineteen hours later she had become predictably interested in disembarking as we puttered over the still surface to anchor off the deserted late night Tryphena wharf. The light winds had made it seem a long way.

Great Barrier Island is far enough from Auckland to make the land you're leaving disappear over the curve of the earth the further away you get. As you move out near Cape Colville and Channel Island, the land greys to a low horizon line, then it's gone. It feels further away than it really is. With nothing behind you, was it ever really there? Near Great Barrier, the east coast of the Coromandel Ranges stretches down to Whitianga and the low grey lumps of the Mercury Islands.

It was sunbathing weather in the outer Hauraki Gulf: late summer, empty bays, crickets and cicadas. The breeze had stayed moderate onshore but cloud had come in gradually over the ranges to the west, a thickening high veil. The air was humid and hinting of an impending something. A noisy broken surf pushed in onto Medlands Beach, on the ocean side of the Barrier. The vitamin D sunlight bake and frequencies of crashing wave sounds combined with atomised surf clouds of negative ions . . . disengage at the beach.

That evening the bus rattled back down the shingled hillside road to Tryphena. The bay was flat and securely sheltered. The sky was clouded up and closing down with an otherworldly hue escorting the sun into the evening sea. The kind of sky that turns a sailor serious. The wind was gusting harder offshore in the lee of the hills and locals were tying down the blades of their wind generators . . . something was coming.

I caught the weather map in my friend Julie's living room on a 12-volt television. A tropical depression south of Norfolk Island and tracking down towards North Cape. Cyclone Polly. Northland was battening down. By the look of it so was the Barrier.

It got dark and the wind picked up, gusting down the gullies and rushing about in the tall secondary manuka growth. It was a northeasterly, freshening all the time and blowing fair for Auckland. All downhill (in a positive way) for a sailing boat. The depression was still a way north of New Zealand but tomorrow would be too late. The lights were green for a dash by dark, running flat off back to the city. The seawolf knew Thunderbirds were go and lay resigned on the sail bags, shedding hair everywhere. The anchor came up and I tied down the dinghy as *Swirly World* shy reached slowly across the bay, hove-to with the jib backwinded, heeling hard at times to the unseen attacking gusts. With the quick flashing Tryphena light behind us and Channel Island light ahead, *Swirly World* slid again with one reef in the main through absolute darkness. No stars tonight. The odd solitary curtainless Barrier window receded, flickered, then finally disappeared over the horizon. Always that slow farewell to relative security when sailing a small boat.

All night the phosphorescence of following waves glowed its supernatural show, and grew grander, leaving the lee of the Barrier and extending our fetch. *Swirly World* sat on 6 knots, being hand steered down the little waves. It was full throttle with the constant wind-pressured sails pushing and sledging the hull through the water. No need for an engine, the wind providing ample energy. Sailing.

The radio batteries were low and only Pete Sinclair's love songs on the AM band beamed in. All a bit melancholy, but each hour the mood was punctured by the urgent realism of the repeated 'battening down scenarios' going on to the right of me over the horizon on the relative safety of land. There was a cyclone warning out, Northland was closing down.

By the early hours we'd covered most of it, and had the choice of various exits to sheltered waters, should the velocity of the following air increase. There were the eastern approaches to Waiheke, giving the long lee of Waiheke and Tamaki Strait, Motuihe Channel past Rakino to tuck in behind Motutapu and Rangitoto or the direct route straight to North Head.

A couple of hours before dawn the wind increased substantially and as the tide was leaving the gulf, a short, steeper sea built up. Believing in my abilities to hand steer light to light till daylight I had dispensed with formal navigational duties. As we neared the electric glow of Auckland, the low hump of Rangitoto showed up dark and defined against the city halo. We were closer in to the Noises Islands than I anticipated, the clear red glow of their beacon alerting me to the easterly drift I had allowed through the night. Pull up, pull up . . . Coming up onto a tighter reach, we roared along at maximum boat speed over the ideal steep little surfing waves and troughs. Off Rangitoto the hint of first light made the Coromandel Ranges behind almost discernible. The single-reefed main remained more than adequate to rush us satisfactorily and without any stress towards North Head. I didn't yearn for sleep, the need to stay awake and survive was more compelling. The moments felt like ones worth remembering. Phosphorescence and surfing waves, a sense of urgency in a private race against well-forecast impending doom.

At the beginning of her 6 a.m. breakfast stint the generic radio DJ, Kerry Someone, was quick to pay tribute to the wind's ability to savage her sleep last night. In the lee of Bayswater, fierce gusts threatened to lift the surface of the sea. The mainsail plastered against the stays was too much sail, but we'd run our minor gauntlet and an overcanvassed stagger in flat water didn't rate on the danger spectrum. While the wind threatened to lift spray from the surface of the bay, I picked a disused mooring, flung the anchor out as a second chance, and rowed the seawolf ashore, 10 hours after leaving Tryphena. It would have been impossible to anchor off Wairau Creek or enter with the onshore wind.

Back in Little Shoal Bay the tide was out for the seven thousandth time since I wrote my 'I Am Nothing' trilogy poem while writer-in-residence there, aboard *Mylene B*. John on his Ron Given catamaran was up early and invited me to a restorative hot breakfast aboard. The hyena seemed quite happy following her nose about the mud flats while I feasted on hospitality.

It blew hard that day, but Polly veered southeast away from the coast and out to eventual dissolution alone in the southern ocean, living out her emotional problems where no one else could see.

Once again I ended up keeping *Swirly World* in Little Shoal Bay, as the townhouses finally consumed our piece of pre-Harbour Bridge North Shore. Back to the other side of the bridge. A basement flat, more like a cave, in St Mary's Bay.

Now and then I released *Swirly World* from her mooring and sailed about the inner harbour, keeping my hand in, working the wind again. Checking out the edge of the land, far more compelling than the rest of it. Off Herne Bay, near Watchman's Island, I found a 22-ft boat that reeked of character. *White Heron* was an old Laurent Giles Barchetta design, a centre-cockpitted cutter with a small spoked wheel and self-steering vane. She had crossed the Tasman four times in 1974 and '78, having sailed in the Solo Tasman Race twice with her original creator, Joe Davison, from New Plymouth. It was less a yacht, more a working boat, with a bare minimum of yachting chandlery, quite unusual by most standards but incredibly robust. *White Heron* had floated for four years on death row, worn by westerly wind against tide conditions, her pushpit and self-steering badly rusted and a long luxurious growth of underwater cling-ons. I returned to my ancient teenage folder of solo sailing articles that evening and there she was. 1974. New with a big black number three painted on the side. An active seventies sailing entity. Poor old *White Heron*. She'd been out there once, doing the miles, out of sight of land; she weathered cyclone Hal in 1978. The Solo Tasman Race. If *White Heron* could get to Australia, so could *Swirly World*.

In January 1994 I saw an ad for the Solo Tasman Race, run every four years by the New Plymouth Yacht Club. A test of resolve financially, physically, emotionally. I wrote away and got a copy of the rules. A minimum length had been introduced, 7.62 metres. *Swirly World* was 5.4 metres long. Back in New Plymouth I'd made the acquaintance of Alan MacGregor, the race treasurer, so I rang him and sounded out the possibility of an exception to the rule. 'You want to do it in your boat?' Talking on the phone we both made it sound possible, 1200 miles from New Plymouth to Mooloolaba, just north of Brisbane. There, and not to be underestimated, back to Auckland. I had two months to go before the start on Easter Monday. I had a lot to do.

The first effort involved prices, paperwork and phone calls. I would have to borrow money and beg . . . find a sponsor. The first hurdle was a Category One Certificate — a thoroughly comprehensive Warrant Of Fitness inspection. To race offshore you have to have one. I'd by-passed it before, it was one of the reasons I'd gone to Sunday Island, no officials to tell me off for not having Cat One clearance. Life rafts, emergency beacons, flares etc are expensive items, hopefully never actually activated. But nevertheless they are still mandatory.

Sponsorship proposals were drawn up and likely candidates approached. It didn't look good. The old 'size equals safety' chestnut loomed large for the uninformed businessmen. I was prepared to cloak *Swirly World* in alcoholic colours in order to sail the Tasman, but no offers arose. Sailing in the lee of the Auckland Whitbread stopover, it appeared likely sponsors were all boated out and the miniature odyssey I had in mind didn't quite rate.

While phoning for finance behind boardroom doors, I went about doing whatever immediate preparations I could afford. *Swirly World*'s mast was plucked off one still afternoon at Birkenhead Wharf and sized up for new stays to replace the original 20-year-old ones. I motored *Swirly World* across to Westhaven and at high tide we drew her from the water on a modified Soling road trailer.

My eccentric sailing friend David Ingram had several Olympic-class Solings he had collected over the years and left lying around his backyard. Winter months were spent restoring them to a pre-sentable state. I sporadically appeared to hold the odd spanner and offer encouragement between late-night recording sessions.

The Rangitoto Sailing Centre at the Hobson Wharf Maritime Museum had recently come into being, and getting paid to take people out sailing seemed a fairly satisfactory proposition. First I would have to do a weekend course to qualify as an Academy Club Instructor, sanctioned by the New Zealand Yachting Federation to teach sailing. A practical test racing Lasers around a small course and tight manoeuvres around the rescue inflatable reminded me of the thrills I'd forgotten centreboarders were capable of. Could I do it like I used to? I hadn't used a hiking strap for ten years. Staking out, balancing the wind's influence, it had always looked the coolest thing a human was capable of. All the 1970s *DB Yachting Annual* pictures. Ricky Dodson at fifteen, in an OK Dinghy, Andy Knowles in a 470 on the trapeze wire. A 'Lyttelton tussle-haired dockside worker, Peter Lester' transformed into World OK Dinghy champi-on, bare arms and an open waistcoat life vest . . . the wet sea warri-or carried up Takapuna beach in his boat . . .

Pattern response memories. All those seasons pulling up savage-ly flapping sails — wetsuits wet from the morning's race. A strong northwesterly whipping Port Nicholson Harbour into a frenzy of hard work to windward. Wellington. The ideal survival sailing train-ing ground. All those first wet waves of the day exploding on the bow and sending the shock of cold salt water drench back over the stacked-out helmsperson. Wet stuff down necks and up sleeves. All those sea hours spent putting in the moments of application that lead to knowledge, practised feel and refined sensitivity to working the wind.

I passed my certificate and started taking different personality types up and down Auckland Harbour, acquainting them with the pleasure and compulsion of sailing.

David Ingram generously let me widen one of the Soling trailers and its double-axled dimensions matched well with *Swirly World*'s shape. If a sponsor clambered onboard then *Swirly World* would be towed south to New Plymouth. It might take weeks to sail up around North Cape and down to Taranaki and the countdown was ticking away.

A certificate had to be manifested prior to arriving in New Plymouth so I arranged for the Auckland inspectors to do their preliminary physical checkout of *Swirly World* as soon as possible. If *Swirly World*'s hull wasn't up to their standards, the mission would be thwarted before it began.

Rob Carpenter and Co. were thorough in their physical evaluation. 'Have you been offshore in her? She's small, Andrew. Bloody small.' It was a taste of talk to come. They had eyes for detail, poking and thumping about the outside and inside, pausing to examine all corners with knowledgeable intent. Toe rails would have to be added to the foredeck and a two-way main hatch latch-lock fitted. They'd be back two weeks later to tick off the list of work done and items purchased. Moments were tumbling by and still no offer of finance.

De Amalfi Survival Ltd in Beaumont Street is the nautical survivalist's dream shop. From the survival suit-clad dummy protruding through a mural of breaking seas, to the shelves of electronic 'know where you are' and 'come and get me' devices, De Amalfi reeked of relevance. I'd priced all *Swirly World* needed but couldn't afford to buy it — close on $15,000 worth of safety items. As if synchronised by unseen actors, David Manzi of De Amalfi identified with *Swirly World* and our Tasman challenge. He was enthused enough to equip her with flares, emergency beacon, life raft, Mustang Survival Suit, GPS and emergency food bars for the duration of the race and return voyage. An 18-ft yacht doubling the Tasman. 'If anyone was going to need it Andrew, it'll be you . . .'

'Good on you David, I appreciate your confidence.'

The campaign was building. The 'Fund Fagan Society' was formed to deal with finance borrowing and long-term loan problems. The 'Bank of Mother Irene' had a special pre-race interest-free offer, available only to offspring. Three weeks and counting. A deadline looming. The race to get to the start line had started. Many manual labouring moments followed, sanding, epoxy, sanding epoxy, painting, sanding, painting, spending money that wasn't my own.

Late February/March the band had a series of shows around the Auckland colleges. A hit-and-run schedule had us setting up in assorted playing fields, prefab-fringed quads, and frequently under the windows of suspicious teachers. Come bell-time, hoards of enquiring adolescents would gush forth from previously silent and deserted corridors to receive our brand of guitary sonic assault.

We drove our ambulance into the 'emergency access only' alleys between school buildings and set our sonic trap for soon to be lunch-timing locals. Some teachers were convinced opportunists had arrived uninvited and gate-crashed their educational domains. 'Are you sure you're supposed to be here? There must be some mistake. Who gave you permission?'

Two days before *Swirly World*'s big drive to New Plymouth, I found myself in an all-night vigil finding stowage space for the gear the inspectors expected *Swirly World* to have. A university club gig reached a sweaty halt at one in the morning, then numerous heavy black boxes had to be individually carted down two flights of fire escape stairs. The return of King Roadie . . . Loading the gear out, then loading it back in to the practice room off Symonds St. Harder still returning to *Swirly World*, the bright electric light bulb, inside at 3 a.m. finding corners for items still showing their price labels. The sun came up and a few hours later at 8.30 a.m. the inspectors returned. They were on my side. They wanted to make sure my project was together enough for me to have a reasonable chance of getting to Australia.

Armed with a checklist, all the buckets and buoyancy aids were accounted for, apart from a storm trysail considered necessary in the event of a broken boom. A 9 oz rescue orange cloth, 2.6 square metres. Tiny and expensive.

To avoid bouncing the keel on the road trip south, Peter Funnell worked a steelwork wonder and created extra supports for the hull. He could always be relied upon like that, the problem-solving backbone of an engineering project.

At the last hour the riggers returned *Swirly World*'s mast, complete with new standing rigging. The old stuff had been all right but you never can tell when 20-year-old stainless is going to deceive you. With seven days to the start gun we set off, towing *Swirly World* in a rental-van voyage to New Plymouth. First we drove round the block from our temporary campaign headquarters at M & G Engineering in Daldy Street to the De Amalfi showroom. We got David Manzi to move his van and parked *Swirly World* strategically in front of his Mustang sea mural shopfront. It was *Swirly World*'s first photo session, proudly wearing the large white name and No.12 race entry numerals on the hull. The show looked good, all bright, gawdy green and white.

A reflective, post-summer evening guided *Swirly World* south over the land. In the still darkness seaward of Te Kuiti a full moon made it up out of the mountains to silhouette rugged Taranaki ridges against a cool, clear, brightly glowing universe. The river led to the coast and there it eventually was, waiting in the pale moonlight — the Tasman Sea. It was waiting for me.

Swirly World had turned in a fast passage by most standards, 366 km in 7 hours. It was almost midnight when we arrived at the beginning of the Port Moturoa breakwater in New Plymouth. I ventured down to view the opposition already gathered for the race. The moon had met a cloud and it was darker than before. The boats were there.

Five large seaworthy yachts lay waiting for *Swirly World* to join them. It made me feel uncomfortable. By comparison to the others, I appeared to have misjudged the scale of things. *Swirly World* was really going to be the odd boat out, the smallest ever to enter the race. Perhaps they'd let *Swirly World* hide away somewhere else until race day so we wouldn't have to look so ludicrous next to the others?

Out with the polish at first light, matching small patches of fresh bright green paint with the Wellington spray job. Keeping up appearances. By 8 a.m. the first of a gaggle of interested onlookers had gathered. For someone not unfamiliar with being the performing centre of attention, I felt strangely self-conscious with my silent attentive audience that morning. 'Are you going to Aussie in that?' They weren't there to hear me sing my songs. I had something far more serious to do. They knew it too.

People would arrive, circle, inspect, then wander off, keeping their opinions to themselves. The procession would only increase during the coming week. In the past I had always avoided parading my voyaging intentions prior to leaving. Preparations had been a private affair, free from the potentially psychologically contaminating opinions of sceptics. Not so now. 'Are you sure she's small enough?' Forget the audience and publicised ambitions about crossing the Tasman, just do it.

'Sure. Have you done it?'

'No.'

The engine wouldn't start. People were watching. They started waiting as well. Condensation was cleaned from the fuel tank and we had blast off. On with the wetsuit and *Swirly World* was guided back into the thoroughly cold sea. We motored out, minus mast, to the rusty steel barge at the end of the harbour breakwater and rafted up against the largest entry, Jim Lowe's 40-ft *Chinchilla*. It was an absurd comparison. *Swirly World* was almost the size of a lifeboat Jim could have been carrying on deck. With the other boats all over 30-ft long, I could understand the onlookers' fascination.

Jim Lowe immediately embraced *Swirly World* and me with a generous spirit of assistance and took an interest in my preparations. He was everything to aspire to in seamanship terms, thoroughly competent and experienced in all aspects of ocean travelling. A true sea man. He had faith in *Swirly World*. 'Great little boat.' The same couldn't be said for many of the spectators on the rusty catwalk overlooking our small fleet. Some were loquaciously convinced *Swirly World* should not have been attempting anything so demanding as the Solo Tasman Race.

They couldn't reconcile small with safe. The audacity to enter seemed to offend their senses. Who draws the arbitrary boundaries about when one should dare not to stop? They certainly thought they did. I disagreed, but didn't court the chance to defend myself.

Had they ever ventured beyond the security of their comfort zones? My intentions for *Swirly World* represented a perplexing challenge to their concept of reasonable human endeavour. 'He's not going in that, is he?'

'Is that it? He must be mad.' My sanity had often been the subject of speculation.

But in this field I had specialist knowledge, all those precedents they didn't know about. Shackleton south of Cape Horn through storm latitudes in his 22-footer, a deck sewn together from hides. Thomas Musgrave's epic voyage from the wild Auckland Islands south of New Zealand in a modified 15-ft ship's boat. Fred Rebel in his undecked 18-ft centreboarder across the Pacific through cyclonic seas. *Half Safe*, an 18-ft amphibious jeep around the world. *Ketiga* (21 ft), *ROC* (19 ft), and *White Heron* (22 ft), all there and back across the Tasman in the 1970s. It could be done.

Two of the other solo sailors were apparently against *Swirly World*'s involvement but chose to conceal their negativity in my company. Perhaps they felt *Swirly World*'s safe arrival in Mooloolaba might lessen the scale of their own achievement. At the time I wasn't in a position to dwell on it, there was too much to do and no one knew what the wind would bring.

Before the breeze picked up the next morning we stepped *Swirly World*'s mast, topped with a tri-colour navigation light and new stays. It was hoisted up on *Chinchilla*'s main halyard, then suspended in place while I screwed and sealed the electrical wires together under the foot of the mast. All went well until a tug-shoved ship moving into the harbour sent nasty swells across to violently roll the boats about. The mast leapt around and three humans weren't enough to stop the connections from wrenching apart. More fiddly wiring up, bindings against salt-water inroads. A second attempt eventually found success.

Jim had warned of the powerful southeasterly wind that had a habit of screaming down from Mount Egmont whenever the wind spirits felt like it. Prior to our arrival, a southeast gale had driven down so hard *Chinchilla* had waves breaking over her bow and spray flying her length. A cowl of cloud would gather threateningly on the slopes of the mountain before each onslaught. Time travelled during my moments asleep, and I awoke at 3 a.m. to *Swirly World* pitching and squeaking alarm sounds against *Chinchilla*'s substantial fenders. The wind blew from the southeast and sure enough, the telltale cowl of foreboding cloud clung to the distant, clear, moonlit mountain. Jim emerged at the same time and we agreed it would be a good idea to assign *Swirly World* to one of the moorings clear of the other boats and barge. For its first outing, the Mustang survival-suit jacket insulated well against the chilling wind. We pushed the bow away and full throttled out to the mooring. It was all a bit shockingly real. Jim seemed to think nothing of it, apparently always on 24-hour callout alert. The wind stayed fresh but thankfully subsided at dawn. It was becoming more obvious how serious this voyage would be.

Bleary eyes opened later that morning to calls from a collection of neatly presented gentlemen clutching clipboards and writing sticks on the barge to leeward. The first of the race committee official-dom had gathered to begin their own safety inspections. I rowed across to meet and greet and my wariness waned as I discovered the inspectors were genuinely trying to assist in my preparations, rather than condemn. Drill bits and beer would appear and attitudes of support quickly eroded any paranoid preconceived ideas. These people were here to help me get over there.

It was then that I had the pleasure of meeting Joe Davison, the original creator of the unique, small *White Heron*. Joe had sailed her twice before in the race and had gone on to build another larger craft and sail her in the following race. He had continued west after the race to sail around the world back to New Plymouth in eighteen months. At the time of the 1994 race Joe was building another overtly sturdy boat . . . He had the accumulated knowledge of a specialist, a true participant. What's more he saw *Swirly World* as the capable offshore cruiser she was. 'Oh yes, she's a little beauty.' That made me feel better.

The first informal 'meet the local race sponsors' function was held that evening at the yacht club. Once again Joe figured highly, sticking introductory labels on lapels and one on my only clean but rapidly soiling white skivvy. 'Introducing Andrew . . . Competitor'. It hadn't occurred to me that I was competing in something. In our case it was more a matter of getting there. Small is slow, and my race would be against the 20-day time limit. Competitor, sportsman, here with the free beer, tonight any label would do.

In the clubroom they wouldn't stop filling up my glass with that brown liquid. It just kept coming. Hospitality plus. Yachties like their beer. It's an established part of the pleasure ritual. The competitors weren't allowed to hold an empty glass for too long, it made our hosts uncomfortable. The way some of those old-timers looked at me and so readily poured the beer struck me as a little peculiar. It was almost as if we were taking part in some kind of sacrificial ritual. That was it. Those gnarly seadogs clustered about the bar were sacrificing us to appease the Wind Gods so they'd get a good four seasons of club racing. No wonder they looked as if they knew something I didn't. They'd seen us solo sailors before, descending on the Yacht Club for a couple of weeks, then gone for another four years.

As the headlights of another car came hurtling up to the judder bars on the road back to the boats, I concealed myself behind some rocks, maintaining the privacy of a few spare moments. The locals had got me quite out of it. They'd forced too much grog on me. Not so much onto me as into me.

Alone with the night, I perched on the north-facing breakwater boulders and listened to the gentle swell lethargically sucking up between the slabs of concrete below. The moon was shrinking and cloud covered most of the Tasman sky. It would be good to get out there again, far from the burden of others' expectations. A sense of purpose in simply surviving.

I'd been out there before, but I felt like I'd forgotten. Alone and invigorated, alone and frightened, alone and alive, with all the emotions in between. At least I'd have a chance to sober up. I slept well but woke early with a dry mouth and large thirst. Dehydration. Poisoned. That was it. They were saturating us so we'd be easier to sacrifice on Easter Monday.

With the amount of niggly jobs yet to do and small items to be bought, I had been neglecting my domestic arrangements. Every sea-readying crucial detail took longer than anticipated and eating and cleaning took a backseat to more pressing matters. It was back to basics, just getting it done. Invitation meals with my hosts, the MacGregor family, kept me functioning, along with a sack of surplus apples Jim Lowe slung into *Swirly World*'s cockpit. The life raft, flares, EPIRB and storm trysail had yet to arrive from Auckland. The specific 4483 frequency crystal needed to converse with the New Plymouth Yacht Club was also yet to arrive from Singapore. The start gun was looming, but had I paced the campaign right? I was bound to find out.

Chapter 13

Two hours and sponging . . .

The Race Committee thoughtfully arranged for the air force to come down and brief us all on their search and rescue procedures. It seemed the Orion flyers were keen on scrambling to find a distressed mariner, a wholesome sense of purpose compared to routine fisheries patrols. Flare procedure and flying patterns were touched upon, then the smart air force spokesperson was followed by Barnaby, the harbour tug driver and pilot. He was there to demonstrate the workings of a life raft and I was allocated the task of pulling the cord to inflate the raft inside the clubrooms. They always picked on me. Like I'd be the first to need it. It was longer than expected and I ended up pulling out armfuls of the stuff before it finally triggered the cylinders and expanded the tubes. The hands-on (bodies in) experience was strange, sitting inside the life raft inside the building as if we'd all been simultaneously shipwrecked out in the harbour. We were allowed to taste the survival food bars. Having gone without nourishment for many hours, I wasn't shy in sampling their dry, pasty nutritional content. Lunch of sorts.

The compass deviation card hadn't been updated since the Sunday Island trip, so I met with Barnaby (also a compass adjuster) the next day. I motored *Swirly World* alongside the imposing steel tug *Kupe* and collected his rather large self to putter about the still harbour lining up on various markers. He was huge, like a bear in the cockpit. His extra weight made the low-lying drains back-flood the cockpit in an annoyingly wet way. Barnaby pretended not to

148

notice. All was well in our alignments and gradually he adjusted to *Swirly World*'s tiny size. He didn't say a lot but he did say *Swirly World* would be the fun boat to do the voyage in. Hopefully.

Two days and counting, I loaded two shopping trolleys full of food on board and filled many new two-litre plastic bottles full of freshwater. The official Solo Tasman Race dinner was held on the Saturday night and the usually bare wooden floor of the clubroom was decked out with several long tables, all neatly arranged with tablecloths and cutlery. About 200 members and associated guests packed into the bar area prior to dining and consumed the mandatory jugs of beer. I heeded the call to be seated quite quickly, having continued to neglect my diet until then.

Fortunately, the head waitress must have noticed, our end was chosen to begin the queue at the servery. Jim Lowe was sitting opposite and was also not slow to respond. We hoed in. After our first plateful we rejoined the queue and indulged again. If I'm going to be sacrificed I might as well make the most of this bit. The threat of bachelor self-sufficiency brought out our appetite. Two desserts later, we were done.

After dinner each competitor was called forward and introduced. Jim Lowe rose admirably to the occasion and eloquently thanked the club for their hospitality and support. Adam Lambert, at 26, was the youngest sailor, an Australian professional yacht delivery and racing crewman who charmed with his address, endearing all to his Australian sense of humour. Theirs was the real race amongst the bigger yachts and the cut and thrust of inter-dominion rivalries would lie with them in the coming week. I on the other hand felt more in tune with the concept of embarking on a medieval odyssey rather than a race. I'd be happy proving to a sceptical audience that their pessimism had been unwarranted.

Reticent, and a little out of my depth in the company of the more experienced sailors, I shook Neil the Commodore's hand appreciatively and withdrew to the low-profile end of the room. Never mind, I'd blow my trumpet once I got to Australia . . . hopefully.

You've broken your own golden rule. Never announce your intentions until they've been achieved. Too late now, mate. Off you go. Good luck.

After the official part we were left to our loud voices competing socially with each other while a solo music performer dished out his renditions of well-known classic hits from his keyboard and drum machine set up in the corner. Usually that was me being a part of the noise in the corner. The level of background chat would have ignited me to aggravate my audience rather than condescend to entertain such a rude non-listening lot. But that wasn't the nature of what was required. Tonight was different. They were all there for another Yacht Club function. It was legitimate socialising for them. I was a guest of honour who had something quite serious to do, soon. The thought of it spoiled my evening entirely. Outside I knew the sea was waiting for me. Inside, people started dancing to the music, while most turned up the volume of their social intercourse. 'Sorry, what was that?'

Suddenly, from across the room, I saw him coming. 'Yeah that's right . . . I'm a singer.' Would I sing a song? There wasn't a guitar in the room and without one I was stuck. I didn't feel like showing off. That was someone else tonight. I declined. He was unhappy and returned to his table to deflate their expectations. Later on, as we all started negotiating our way out into the early hours of another Sunday morning, Joe Davison approached me and repackaged the request. I fell back seized with self-consciousness, unable to deliver. Returning once more to the dark harbour hideaway of *Swirly World* I knew I'd let them down. I had a lot of miles on my mind.

A cold squally southwesterly came through the next day, reminding us all that autumn was here. It didn't look good out there. Serious if not severe. Low cloud and rain, more wind than was polite.

Karyn arrived bearing the last of my Category One items. The new orange trysail, De Amalfi's 406 EPIRB, and the long-awaited life raft. Having given David Manzi such limited notice of my adventure, the Beaufort life raft ordered from England had sadly failed to arrive in time. David acquired a replacement raft but it ended up being a considerably heftier eight-man beast. It took two of us to lift it on to the deck. Even though weight was at a premium I was in no position to find a replacement, so I stoically lashed it firmly down over the main hatch recess. Stiff rain squalls savaged the harbour and the mountain was nowhere to be seen, hidden behind low, racing clouds. In that last wet evening twilight, fiddling with knots with a frown on my face I felt less than enthused at the prospect of setting out to sea the next day. I'd made my bed, now I had to lie in it.

Contrast is what the wind can bring, and the following morning brought a sky of sunshiny blue, where foreboding grey had reigned supreme. What's more the mountain was back, as if it had never left, only this time it stuck out, splendid in thick white snow, once again emphasising the change of seasons, another southern winter on its way.

Today was the day I had to go away. Three hours and counting . . . the six sacrificial victims gathered with loved ones in the cruising clubrooms to do the formalities customs officers like you to do before venturing overseas.

I returned to the boat after receiving clearance and discovered water over the floorboards. Undetectable leaks? A sinking at sea? Sabotage? It was water all right, but luckily fresh. Two hours and sponging . . . like a maniac. It appeared many of my new water bottles so precisely placed in difficult corners had not been quite as watertight as I expected. Better keep it quiet lest the rapidly gathering spectators on the breakwater got wind of it and suspected something was wrong.

With an hour to start time the motorboat arrived to tow us out into the harbour. All engine shafts had been sealed for obvious reasons — the wind being our sole motive power. Because *Swirly World*'s alternator is belt-driven off the shaft, requiring it to turn free to charge the batteries for the radio transmissions, it was allowed to remain unrestricted. With only six gallons of fuel on board, it was unlikely to drastically alter the outcome.

The forecast was ideal, the previous day's imposing southwesterly easing up as a slow-moving high drifted across the Tasman, bringing moderate southwesterlies with the promise of it backing gently to the south and southeast. Perfect conditions for reacquainting oneself with the ways and motion of a small boat sailing alone on the ocean — nothing threatening or immediately violent. I took advantage of the lee of *Chinchilla* and let *Swirly World*'s stern fall away to hoist the sails whilst still tied up and pointing head to wind.

I kissed my darling farewell and waved to our considerable audience gathered on the breakwater, taking pleasure in being the only boat manoeuvrable enough to sail from the barge moorings. The light southwesterly got us tacking and gybing about the harbour and I felt once more the familiarity of *Swirly World* under sail. I knew how to do this bit. Sailing. Perhaps my long-distance ambition was not totally unwarranted.

It does however remain a point of regret that my build-up campaign did not involve more practical application to the art of solo spinnaker setting. Faced with a flat run from the start line to a buoy about a mile down the coast off the township, it seemed only appropriate that we fly our multicoloured spinnaker to give the 2000 odd spectators along the breakwater and rocks a good look. Alan MacGregor with family and crew were out in their Ross trailer sailer, as were numerous others aboard racing craft considerably quicker than *Swirly World*.

I rushed about the foredeck packing the flimsy spinnaker fabric into a bucket wedged in the pulpit, arranged the sheets and pole, then hit my stopwatch to log the ten-minute gun. The race had been well publicised by the local paper and a lot of faces were perched all about the busy little harbour. The tug *Kupe* was crowded with people, one of whom was Karyn. It was doubling as the start boat. Everyone was looking.

Before the gun fired I pulled the halyard hard to drag the spinnaker skyward. Halfway hoisted, *Swirly World* began rounding up so I was forced to leave the halyard at the mast and dart back to the cockpit to bear us away on course. Of course, what were you thinking of? Without a halyard leading back to the cockpit and tiller you're doomed. I should never have entertained the idea in the first place.

While pulling the tiller to get us back on course, the partially raised spinnaker gained a life of its own and began flogging itself into a shocking, embarrassing tangle of tightly wrapped sailcloth and ropes. Disaster. My kite work, or lack of, revealed in all its amateur glory. A spinnaker halyard lead to the cockpit would have saved the day but I'd overlooked it in the past.

Avoiding eye contact with the nearby flotilla of craft, I returned to the helm and locked in the self-steering vane to broad reach us

downhill somewhere vaguely near the mark. They were still looking. Clearing the harbour breakwaters, the leftover southwest swell
nicely complicated my efforts, confining me to sit ignominiously
on the foredeck untangling the mess. By the time we rounded the
mark my fellow competitors were already far ahead, tight reaching
out to sea. *Kupe* was stationed off the buoy and Barnaby the pilot
gave three resounding blasts on the horn to farewell us out as we
gybed seaward. A shocking start, substantiating our underdog role.

Alan and co sailed in our lee for a while, snapping a few photos,
then waving farewell, went about and the last of our company sailed
back towards the land. Gone. This was it. The beginning. Some
might say a bad one.

Up ahead I watched the other five sails already hull down on the
horizon, slowly growing more distant. Following their lead we tight
reached out towards the empty horizon. *Swirly World* was sailing
well, 5 knots, full of food and water into the long-awaited Tasman
Sea. After an hour, one of the disappearing sails ahead looked a bit
bigger than before. There was no doubt about it, we seemed to be
catching. Gradually we drew closer, then the wicked truth became
evident. It was another unknown yacht sailing in from somewhere
else, bound by the look of it, for New Plymouth, back the other
way.

All afternoon I sat there meticulously hand steering while keeping an eye on our competitors disappearing west and leaving us in
their wake, our isolation a foregone conclusion. It was emotionally
more demanding than I had anticipated; their previous company in
harbour almost a cruel joke. It didn't pay to look back. Progress at 3
to 5 knots is slow. The mountain was still there behind us, I didn't
think it would go away.

At length the land did subside to a faint line, then was gone, leaving only the majestic white mountain and the Moturoa chimney
alone on a twilight horizon, as the sun went down ahead into the
first of many a slow, watery dive.

Further out from the Taranaki coastline but still in relatively shallow water, the seas were surprisingly large and sloppy, making it a
wet ride. Broken pieces of waves collapsed randomly on *Swirly World*,
flooding water over the decks and into the cockpit. At sea once

more, wetness everywhere. The transition was beginning. A sea-sickness pill that morning and acupuncture wristbands weren't enough to contain my delicate constitution.

All was well while focused on sailing outdoors but on descending downstairs at dusk to do my first radio broadcast, my wellbeing deteriorated. The rapid elevating and dropping over the sloppy swells did my unaccustomed stomach no good. Leaning out into the cockpit I deposited the last of anything undigested from my stomach all over the emergency waterbottles on the cockpit floor. At least I made it outside.

For those first few days the wind was as kind as it could be, slowly backing to the southeast and staying light to moderate. Away from the land with clear, uninterrupted horizon all around, we were at last left to our own devices. The hectic preparations of the past week had amounted to a last-minute campaign compared to the others. But we'd got there. The pressure of a deadline and natural apprehension about the undertaking had left me fatigued before the race had begun.

I now had the opportunity to adjust to solitary confinement again but this time it didn't feel as isolating as before, knowing that five others were doing the same as me on a similar piece of sea somewhere up ahead. Each morning and evening, a few minutes after seven o'clock, the radio would come alive with voices as New Plymouth Yacht Club logged our positions and probed our concentration and application levels. To be able to communicate regularly on 4483 (the crystal arrived in time) never ceased to impress me. My comparatively cheap 18-year-old crystal radio had been virtually condemned by the Auckland inspectors as obsolete, but with a little specialist aerial insulating advice from Jim Lowe, it did the job all the way across.

It became obvious some of the sailors were more astute than others at broadcasting the kind of lifestyle stories the newspapers liked; whales seen, potentially overbearing ships, large meals heartily consumed. I never anticipated that an incidental mention of trying to find some toilet paper would make it to Taranaki breakfast tables.

Less than interested in our surroundings, the 1200 miles on the chart looked a long way to someone travelling at little more than walking pace. I'd get us sailing efficiently, set the wind vane in action then retire to my sickbed, dozing or reading or listening to dull but reassuring New Zealand AM radio stations. Motion sickness, lack of nourishment and lack of sleep induces a bizarre twilight world of existence. It's like a physiological gate you have to go through before the concept of enjoying yourself re-emerges. Once a certain degree of exhaustion has been reached the brief catnap becomes physically regenerative and body energy levels begin to lift. But you have to go through it and it's not very nice.

The sea miles rolled by and the surface of that deep salty liquid sliding its soothing tones beneath us stayed relatively unruffled. The gimballed stove swung enthusiastically about trying to get my attention, but anything worth cooking couldn't stir my interest. Appetite itself subsided to an all-time low. Don't mention anything chewable.

The use of food by humans was well precedented so I forced myself to reach for one of the dark chocolate survival bars De Amalfi had provided. At least the preparation wasn't too difficult, remove wrapper and chew on an empty stomach. My insides could not have been more empty. All those miles of intestines had had a well-earned break from digestive duties. Piled up in their black plastic bags on the forward berths, large sacks of every conceivable foodstuff sat neglected and disillusioned. Now and then I opened one up only to smell a food-like odour and recoil in horror. Not yet.

The GPS De Amalfi had fitted in *Swirly World* gave our exact position at the push of a button and made my confidence in broadcasting our position twice a day out of keeping with my general lassitude. Previously those first few days getting away from the land would have gone by on a dead reckoning of our position until I had sufficiently recovered to find the motivation for sextant work. The induced lethargy of seasickness is not to be underestimated. I can't be bothered being here right now.

Sleeping or awake? Sometimes I couldn't tell. Personalities and faces encountered during the week in New Plymouth kept circulating through my subconscious. I'd never anticipated that so many helpful strangers would rally around *Swirly World*.

After some good 100-mile runs in 24-hour periods, the fickle wind dissolved to leave us riding peacefully up and down on slight disintegrating swells. The view from the bunk out the hatchway was blue sky and fine unthreatening anticyclonic clouds. The barometer high, the Tasman settled for the moment.

My fellow competitors were hundreds of miles ahead in a race of their own but the boat names were indelibly stamped on my mind from the twice-daily radio contacts. '*Chinchilla, Chinchilla*, this is *Gumblossom*, do you copy Jim? Over.'

'*Prospector*, this is *Electric Blue*, have you heard from *Miss Conduct*?' A parallel universe.

Becalmed, I managed to coax a little effort out of myself, realigning the weight of things inside to get the bow riding lighter. I sealed up the air vents on deck, a job that should have been done in harbour, and finally gave the Primus some activity, pressure cooking up a pile of root vegetables to fry later in olive oil. I pushed some into my body through the usual orifice but it could hardly be called eating. Appetite helps.

At eight o'clock that night a light northerly picked up, the forerunner of a shallow depression coming across from Australia. The breeze put *Swirly World* on a tight reach and for the following 20 hours we crashed away over building waves, steeply inclined, up and down, on and on, moment by moment. It gradually became more as I had been expecting. More uncomfortable.

At such an angle, with a relatively short, steep sea, every little job was difficult to do. I couldn't get much more speed by hand steering so I took once more to the quarterberth, strapped up in the lee cloth, almost hanging in midair as in a hammock, above the Primus and chart table beneath me. Every movable item tried to jump from its designated, wedged-in stowage, and many things were never where I'd left them.

The wind freshened and I kept changing down gears, reducing to two reefs in the mainsail and the No.2 jib for the night. As the low approached (centred north of us) the wind veered northeast and east-northeast, allowing us to ease sheets and broad reach west. With heavy rain the scene outside became breezier so I dropped the main to run under the jib alone. Five knots of boat speed was easily maintained without threat of overpowering if the wind increased.

From 10 p.m. till 2 a.m. the frontal system was upon us and hard rain squalls belted out of the darkness to windward, rushing *Swirly World* on towards Australia. The horseshoe life rings and 'man overboard' lights did their best to drag errantly in the sea so I banished them below. The Category One inspectors in Auckland had obstinately made me buy two of each and a long Danbuoy and dye marker kit to meet the regulations, even though if I fell overboard there'd be no one to throw them to me.

In the squalls the wind vane was getting overpowered and constant correction was required to recover from rounding up onto a reach, so I clambered into my Mustang survival suit and picked my moment to climb out into the windy cockpit, hopefully dodging the flying pieces of quartering waves. With safety harness clipped to the wire running the length of the deck I crawled forward on hands and knees to kneel on the bow, hanking the tiny storm jib to the spare forestay. With my weight so far forward and still sailing under the No.2 jib and self-steering, *Swirly World* slewed and veered about, tearing down the waves in a drunken manner. The glow of the spreader lights lit the wet deck but all around was concealed in absolute darkness. I could feel the incessant surge of speed as *Swirly World* slid along, but being unable to view the scene in context made it seem as if I was in a virtual-reality chamber.

Focusing on changing sails while moving in such a manner was demanding. Now and then *Swirly World* would plunge her bow into the back of a wave and send solid sea washing back over the foredeck and about my prostrate body. Water pushing at sleeve seals and trouser legs. More wetness than you really want to know about.

Reducing or increasing sail area to achieve the appropriate balances and harmony with the wind is the manual labour of which sailing is made. Sometimes it's hard to be bothered. Cosy in your sleeping bag, wind easing, boat speed dropping, more sail required. Just get up and do it — self-discipline of the primitively imperative kind. No one else to do it for you. Can't stay there forever, not enough consumables.

It's illegal in *Swirly World* to drip water on the quarterberth. I carefully extracted myself from the survival suit spacesuit whilst wedged on the companionway steps with the hatchboards and sliding main hatch firmly shut up, then returned to the warm, dry sleeping bag. In bed in the storm, on the verge of going to sleep, a long way from land.

Two hours later the rain had stopped and I could feel that *Swirly World* was underpowered. Back outside, this time naked to avoid the drama of the on again, off again routine. Down storm jib, up No.2 to maintain that 4 to 5 knots of slow but methodical progress. Sail changing — a 24-hour vigil, on call, keep the boat moving, make the most of the wind. That's what you're there for.

Chapter 14

Bleary and belligerent

Bleary and belligerent

The following morning it was as if the night's exertions had never been. The wind blew moderate from the east and throughout the day veered to the southeast, allowing full sail to be set. *Swirly World* was rolling along, her sole occupant inside catching up on the night's lost sleep.

Another flat, calm 48 hours later and it appeared I was coming around to understanding the concept of appetite once more. Let's do it. Let's eat. Lasagne built for four, consumed by one. As full as a shrunken stomach can get, followed by one of those tinned spongy puddings you're never normally keen on at home. Small and dry with sickly sweet stuff they call sauce parsimoniously slipping down the sides. Suddenly it was gone.

Repeat weather followed, freshening northerlies this time, peaking in the afternoon daylight with quickly growing confused seas pushing *Swirly World*'s quarter off course and calling me to hand steer through hard, driving rain, up and down and occasionally under short, steep gullies of salt water. In control, if undercanvassed, *Swirly World* seemed in her element — alive on a roller coaster of ever-changing sea shapes, sliding northwest, forever northwest.

With a dramatic change of opinion, the northeast wind suddenly left the scene, causing *Swirly World* to toss and tumble with nil stability on a churning confusion of pyramid-forming and collapsing seas. A truly agitated seascape with *Swirly World* an unsteady perch from which to view the turmoil. Within half an hour of thoroughly uncomfortable washing-machine treatment, faint gusts of air came from the south, followed by a magnificent clear sky. Sweeping in from the southwest came 40 knots of cold, ominous wind. The day's low, imposing, grey scudding cloud retreated north and the sea did its best to show me the real definition of uncomfortable. Unless you've been on it, you can't conceive it.

The leftover southwest-travelling waves met the wind head on, reaching new heights in steepness, their broken crests blown dramatically backwards. The waves, while not being excessively tall, were sheer and uncompromising. Upright in the trough, *Swirly World* would rapidly elevate up the back of a wave then get blown over hard on top, to fall heeled over sideways down its other face. And so on, and on, and on.

I stood on deck hanging on to the mast, admiring the grandeur of it all. It was special, all that stormy liquid thrashing about, the kind of steep awkward seas that could cripple a catamaran riding in the wrong position. But there were no catamarans or other craft about, only us, running the gauntlet a few hundred miles west of New Zealand.

With the wind side on and only the storm jib up we were losing ground to the north. *Swirly World* didn't have the drive to point up towards the wind and keep moving against the seas. It was time to see if the new storm trysail they'd insisted I purchase, would do as they promised and sail us to windward in those kind of conditions. Yes. I take back my economically motivated resentment. A trysail is worthwhile. *Swirly World* felt balanced and under control, just like full sail in far less breeze. If we were fighting to beat off a lee shore it could have been done. Directional control brings peace of mind. Content that we could go to windward, I let her fall away onto a beam reach to ride on northwest through the short, sheer gullies of southwest gale-driven sea water. *Swirly World* was taking a lot of liquid on top but as her insides were comparatively dry, I was happy to descend indoors and leave the wind vane to steer us more or less towards the promised 'Great Southern Land'. With the wind on our port side the quarterberth was downhill and very loungeable without the need for the lee cloth. Inefficient in ballast terms but . . .

Over 45 knots I find it very hard to judge wind speed without instruments. The dense, cold southwest wind had a severe aspect to it I had witnessed many times on the Wellington coast of Cook Strait. If it hung in we would be facing the kind of seas my imagination dreaded. Fortunately through the dark hours it began moderating, giving me a long, disturbed, attentive night, slowly increasing first one sail then another, until daylight found us moving slowly over an uninspiring, undisciplined sloppy sea. Another gale gone, never lasts forever.

During my trysail experience I discovered a treacherous water-spilling problem. Comfortably half-conscious, I had been rudely awakened by a large dollop of salt water pouring from the tightly closed hatch recess. Down it cascaded, oblivious to my protests, across the all-important SSB radio controls and onto the warm, dry sleeping bag (not to mention me). Sacrilege. No water shall breach the bedding. No exceptions. A law absolute. Absolutely broken. I was wet, in bed.

It appeared that the small windward drainage hole on the hatch recess had been letting liquid in and instead of escaping from the leeward hole, the violent motion had induced it to travel back over the closed hatch and into the cabin. Outrageously inconsiderate.

With a mixture of anger and irrational resentment, I donned my spacesuit and harness and exited the cabin intent on revenge. Someone was saying 'I've had a guts full of this.' Underwater epoxy poked into holes awash with cold Tasman Sea should have done the trick, but an infuriating repeat performance compelled me to return topside to remove the leeward plug, facilitating token drainage. Success, sort of.

As the wind eased the stainless steel self-steering parts jarred mercilessly (underpowered and overacting), so the saga of successive sail changes continued all night. Wind eases, big sea running, more sail, more momentum through the crests, up the steep sides, down the backs, back to bed. Feel the boat moving better, keep the boat moving better, make the most of the wind direction, it's on your side now . . .

Bleary and belligerent, I saw the dawn in while lying below listening to an unusual noise on deck. Something metal smacking against something it shouldn't. A new noise — danger, danger.

Upstairs once more, I found the starboard (leeward) inner side-stay hanging loose and unattached. During the night it had managed to unwind itself, the barrel detaching from the deck pin. Red alert. Not a good design and not a good look. Not the kind of example you want to set to the other stays.

While feverishly trying to rethread it, *Swirly World* went about on to the other tack, throwing all the weight of the thankfully light breeze on to my unfinished business. The mast visibly sagged to leeward, curving concave without the crucial halfway support of the inner stay. Emotionally I sagged inside. She completed a vague circle and gave me another chance to secure it, and I did. It was an uncomfortable feeling, hundreds of miles from land, holding something in your hand that should have been strategically secure. Vice grips and spanner restored my tenuous emotional balance. How suddenly and unexpectedly the whole trip might be rendered untenable. Steady on, get some sleep.

Having a radio on board with the frequencies most in our corner of the South Pacific were conversing on, made me realise how many sailors were out there, doing their miles, at any one moment. Kerikeri Radio, operating on 4445 Hz, was a private New Zealand station renowned for its great personalised weather forecasting service for yachts all over the Tasman and southwest Pacific. Each evening they conducted a roll call, locating the whereabouts and wellbeing of all on board. Weather details were collated, giving John and Maureen Cullen the most comprehensive, up-to-date information on wind system movements available. Underfunded, with no prospect of state assistance, they closed in January 1997.

Eavesdropping on the rest of the world one nondescript night, I heard the well-spoken tones of the legendary Gerry Clark, off the east coast of the North Island. Like Adrian Hayter, Tristan Jones and Johnny Wray, Clark was one of the legends.

In 1970 he sailed his 21-ft twin-keeled Tucker design, *Ketiga*, in the first Solo Tasman Race. The picture of his grinning wet self perched in his pulpit at Mooloolaba after the race had remained with me in my pile of inspirational torn-out pages. In 1974 he solo circumnavigated New Zealand in *Ketiga*, visiting the subantarctic Campbell and Auckland Islands and setting a precedent where others feared to go. In 1983 he set off on a three-year subantarctic circumnavigation of the world in the 29-ft *Totorore*. He lost masts, was rolled and intimidated, but made it. Gerry Clark was still out there doing those miles, reefing, unreefing, steering and bouncing about on the waves. Always going back for more.

In June 1999, wreckage from his vessel *Totorore* was found southeast of New Zealand, at the Antipodes Islands. Down in truly serious latitudes, he'd been dropping scientists off in exposed bays. He was later declared missing and presumed drowned.

Another 24-hour pause mid-Tasman gave me the extended opportunity to charge the batteries with a little motoring and finally restring my old guitar, which had been waiting patiently to make a noise. Only a couple of gallons of fuel were consumed on the trip, approximately 30 miles of advantage being calculated and the appropriate time penalty added to our final finishing time.

It took me an hour to restring the guitar, before I discovered its refusal to tune up in the conventional manner was due to the neck being twisted. It had spent many a month in curtainless spare rooms, the sun doing its silent, irreparable damage. Twisty-necked bad noise.

At dusk a light northwesterly came up and I had a choice of left or right, west or north. I opted to steer north, unaware that a northeasterly setting current would send us virtually backwards through the night. By that stage we were over the Lord Howe Rise and a substantial northeast set consistently retarded *Swirly World*'s progress. I started thinking superstitious thoughts. Michael Brien had often held court in front of his self-grafittied TV. Hogging the limelight and enjoying having an audience, he solemnly spoke once of towing a boat called *Sea Egg* out from Auckland up to Kawau in *Swirly World*. Englishman John Riding had sailed *Sea Egg* all the way from England. When Mike finally let him go, Riding was reluctant. 'He didn't want to go. He had a British girlfriend waiting in Brisbane, was leaving a new one in the North Island. Didn't even clean the boat's bottom. Said he had a gun on board, if he ran out of food or water he would do himself in.' Mike Brien saw it as a crisis of motivation. He was later convinced *Sea Egg* had got stuck over Lord Howe Rise, pushing a current they couldn't contend with. 'I astral travelled up a line from Cape Reinga to Norfolk Island, then down to Lord Howe. The hull wasn't long enough, not much waterline length. Couldn't beat the current. I picked up energy over Lord Howe Rise.' Riding never came back to tell us if Mike was right.

The current and who knows what else was against us. We were sailing fast over the sea, but over the ground below it was slow. Our first and remarkably last day of headwinds departed the following evening and a superb southeasterly freshened to 30 to 35-knot gusts, sending us broad reaching for the gap between Lord Howe Island and Elizabeth Reef. With the wind with us we'd get the better of any currents . . .

At that stage the other boats were closing in on Mooloolaba, some 500 miles ahead, and their close competitive racing was evident from the radio skeds (scheduled reports). *Swirly World* was going her fastest but I'd left our 'catch up and come from behind' burst a bit late. The southeasterly gave us our best run for the race — 113 miles in 24 hours. With the others so far ahead and *Swirly World* so far behind, a new urgency regarding boat speed crept into my consciousness. I wanted to go faster. Rising for the 7 a.m. radio sked, I'd do my weary best to sound on to it and together. I'd have a breakfast of muesli and water, make a packed lunch of peanut butter and honey-smeared rice cakes, then farewell *Swirly World*'s innards and move into the cockpit for 10 to 12 hypnotic hours of hand steering. Trance sailing, it just happens to you and you do it. Don't stop because there's no one else to take your place, stay here and steer, it won't last forever. What's twenty days in your life?

With a Walkman soundtrack playing the same selection of songs a little too often (not unlike some radio stations), I sailed away the hours while the sun gradually moved up from behind, over and across the sky to eventually descend into the sea, always off the port bow. It was compelling sailing. Hard-pressed under single-reefed main and jib, *Swirly World* reeled off the miles, surfing repetitively down waves ideally scaled for our waterline length.

Bands of clouds that had once carried water but still packed extra wind would catch us up and we'd race along from crest to trough, a fine sailing sight. Leaving a slightly reduced sail plan to keep the rig balanced for the self steering to cope, I'd retire below after a day's manual labour outdoors, complete the evening radio contact, then indulge in fried potatoes and an oily can of tuna. My compassion for underwater entities could never overcome the fact that tuna tastes like it's meant to be chewed.

After a couple more days we were through the psychological gate the 90-odd miles separating Lord Howe Island and Elizabeth Reef had become. It looked like Australia was indeed a possibility. Constantly sailing. More back-to-back moments than a beginner could possibly imagine. You just have to keep going.

Thirty miles south of Elizabeth Reef and clear of dangers, I set *Swirly World* on course for Mooloolaba, 400 miles to the northwest. Still blowing a good 25 knots and being a flat run, I decided to employ the rarely used twin-running headsails Mike Brien had made, especially for such fresh sailing conditions, to pole out from the mast. With sails hauled up and poled taut *Swirly World* rolled effectively along at almost a constant 6 knots, doing the self-steered miles without my assistance.

Lying strapped to the quarterberth, lee cloth stopping my body from rolling out of bed, I noticed the motion develop to an exaggerated degree. With too much wind power, a death roll was pending with no hand on the helm . . . a broach with the hull heeling far over and screwing around off course, sideways across the face of the following wind and wave; windward headsail viciously taken aback, backwinded with a vengeance.

Steeply inclined angles of heel were of little consequence, but extracting my dozy self from inside I looked up at the rig to see that one of the twin headsails had backwinded, forcing its pole aft against the capstay/sidestay.

Problem. It had snapped off the mast spreader halfway up, and the sidestay hung loose and ineffectual — a bad look given the circumstances. With no club patrol boat waiting in the wings to come and tow us back to the sanctuary of the yacht club for repairs, it appeared I was well and truly left to my own devices. Self-reliance it's called. It was getting dark in more ways than one, and what a dismal dusk it seemed.

Chapter 15

Warm beer at dawn

The other boats had all made it to Mooloolaba and I spoke to Jim and got a consortium of advice on how to best tackle the problem. It was going to require a spot of climbing, and while chewing through some glucose tablets, I pulled out all my containers of 'fix it' items. Things I might need in a serious moment.

I'd pulled the sails down and *Swirly World* continued to run slowly before the wind, her large Perspex dodger acting as a minuscule running sail for the self-steering. It was still blowing 25 knots from the southeast and a moderate sea was running over 3 to 4 metre swells. It was a lively and alive night. We were out there, alone with a slight problem. No view, no moon. All dark. One hundred per cent cloud cover.

I decided to cover the broken joint with plastic tubing, then wrap many different thicknesses of lashing about the spreader to stiffen it up. Jim Lowe suggested running lines from the outer end of the spreader forward and/or aft to brace the whole thing. With string and wire wrapped round my forearm, I loosened the sidestay sufficiently to force the spreader back in place then climbed up onto the boom and furled mainsail, to clamber upwards. Mast steps would have helped but I had to make do with my not overly developed upper body heaving me up to stand awkwardly on top of the twin poles fitting, both arms wrapped convincingly about the remaining spreader and mast. I wasn't very high but it seemed far enough.

The spreader light which illuminated the deck below me was a hindrance to the fit of the plastic sheathing, so I wrenched it off, shorting out the lights in the process and plunging my work space into total darkness. Bad move. Sliding back to the deck I returned indoors to find a miniature torch to hold between my teeth for the rest of the operation. Back halfway up the mast with the tiny pool of light barely illuminating the task at hand, I once again experienced the sensation of working in a virtual-reality chamber — most peculiar. Hanging on to the mast by wrapping legs, body and shoulder about it as *Swirly World* rolled diabolically sideways. A relatively light little boat, exaggerated motion. Beyond the immediate circle of torchlight, nothing.

Repeatedly I'd hear a lone breaking crest slowly catching us up from somewhere behind. As the larger than usual wave approached, I'd stop fiddling and cling on with both arms. They would disturb *Swirly World*'s precious equilibrium and lay us over further than usual. With large amounts of food and water still inside, she never succumbed to laying me in the water. The little cheapie torch in my involuntarily drooling mouth had a habit of regularly fading and I'd have to shake my head back and forth to brighten up its insipid beam. Primate on a sea tree with nothing to see.

I jammed the spreader back in place and began wrapping the lashings around it but the exertion from clinging on quickly drained my uncharged biological batteries. Many short journeys up and down the mast became the order of the evening. It was good that there were no impending dangers setting a time schedule for the repairs. Elizabeth Reef lay some 30 miles across the wind to starboard and nothing but Australia waited hundreds of miles to leeward.

Recovering, in the true sense of the word, inside after each climb and cling session, I hit the glucose and moithered on the competency of my bindings above. It was good lying there. Basic body recovery. Five hours later, shortly before midnight the repair was completed. Cautious satisfaction.

I carefully hoisted the genoa, poled it out and *Swirly World* picked up speed again, running flat off under self-steering. Bruised in previously unused quarters, I took to the embryonic sleeping bag and dozed between torchlight searches skyward to check the standard of my repair work. So far . . . . OK.

For four more days and nights we ran free before the wind, clocking off the miles in ideal, steady sailing conditions. A large slow-moving anticyclone south in the central Tasman Sea was conveniently responsible. By day the occasional rain squall converged on us but I was quick to reduce the load of the rig before the wind increased. Dolphins came and went in long processions, on course for somewhere known only to them, but otherwise that endless, uninterrupted circle of sea about *Swirly World* remained indistinguishable from all the other wet salty sea on the planet. There's a lot of empty, undefined miles of it out there. When you're in a plane the voyage is too fast and too high to truly relate to how far it really is between the land. Start sailing slowly over those wet miles and eventually you realise it's a long way.

The little GPS had unfailingly delivered our precise position twice daily every day so it came as no surprise to finally sight some high distant land where sky and cloud had previously monopolised the view.

Australia I presumed. The other side of the Tasman. The elevated lines of Moreton Island, sixteen days out from New Plymouth. The sighting failed to stir the reaction felt eight years previous, on spying Sunday Island for the first time, a confirmation of my elementary sextant skill. To a degree the GPS deprives you of that kind of satisfaction, but long-term peace of mind when faced with the uncertainty of reef locations compensates for the loss. There's a lot of elation in just seeing the land.

I had slowly been losing contact with New Plymouth on the SSB during the evenings, the Australian daylight affecting our signals. Jim on *Chinchilla* had continued to boom in as if he was permanently parked up next door, and as darkness fell that final evening it was evident a welcoming party was in progress aboard *Chinchilla*.

Neil Hodges had arrived in Mooloolaba for the prize giving and throughout the night we kept radio contact, updating my ETA at Point Cartwright. Various voices spoke to me and at me as the hours dragged on. Speeches became more drawn out and less defined, slurred even. It sounded like Queensland also had plenty of brown liquid. Pissed, more pissed, pissiest . . . The southeasterly obligingly became an easterly of moderate proportions, sliding Swirly World downhill towards the distant glow of Mooloolaba. Bright lights, human lights, a fond glow, it would be nice to see something else.

To counter the set of the strong southerly flowing current, I steered well north of Cape Moreton and Flinders Reef, paying careful attention to the numerous shrimp boats, floodlit and foraging beneath the sea. For a while I was surrounded. They'd come out for the night, back next day, their land never far away.

At 1.30 a.m. I sighted the sweeping beam of the Point Cartwright light and by 3 a.m. had only 14 miles left to run. Fourteen secure inshore miles. The incoming tide assisted us and just before 6 a.m. New Zealand time (4 a.m. in Aussie hours) I saw the red and green navigation lights of a boat heading straight for us. A little concerned at such impending close company, I got ready to round up and reach clear when the vessel circled round and the Mooloolaba Club rescue cat greeted us on the VHF radio. How exotic. 'Moo-loo-la-ba' my torch beam revealed along its side. A sloppy sea was running and they sped off ahead to guide us across the line.

More nav lights appeared and motoring well to leeward, rolling horribly without sail, was *Chinchilla*, adorned with most of my fellow competitors and their associates. Jim had won the race in nine days followed by Owen Stewart three days later in *Prospector*. Adam Lambert in *Gumblossom* made it an hour after, and Jim Williamson in *Miss Conduct* with Cole Butterworth's *Electric Blue* arriving later that night. Now it was my turn.

The wind refused to be ignored at that auspicious moment and suddenly dropped away, leaving us wallowing on a disorganised sea. A light rain squall blotted out the lights down the coast towards Caloundra. Sure enough, the air returned with rain on it blowing gusty from the southwest to set *Swirly World* hard on the wind for the finish line, just off the Mooloolaba river entrance.

With the genoa and full main heeling us over and driving *Swirly World* along, my port spreader repairs came under more stress than ever before. I silently encouraged the rig to stay put for just a few more crucial minutes. Back offshore in no-man's-land I would have changed down gears to the smaller jib, less pressure, no rescue tender waiting in the wings. Here with an audience so close to the end, the show must go on, running the gauntlet . . .

Crossing the line at 4.02 Australian time, the club boat fired a gun for us and our posse of enthusiasts hooted and hollered a special welcome for *Swirly World* and I. Mission completed. Seventeen days, 2 hours, 2 minutes and 2 seconds (motoring compensation included). Sails down, engine on and motoring up the tranquil river on the last of the incoming tide. The night lights of upmarket apartments and houses on the banks of the river made an outrageous change to the previous nights of seemingly endless black sea and sky.

We were ushered into the visitors' berth in front of the palatial glass windows of the Mooloolaba Yacht Club and the Solo Tasman Race banner (as long as the boat) was draped along the stanchions. Many hands were shaken. The customs man considered *Swirly World* too small for his formalities and we retired to the club custodian's brightly lit room, leaving the others gathered around *Swirly World* on the pontoon, looking slightly anticlimatic. Most seemed to be coming down a bit from their earlier brown liquid imbibing. I filled out the necessary forms, bracing myself against the mid-ocean motion of the room.

Back on the pontoon the Agriculture and Fisheries officer had failed to heed his late night call to duty so I stood around holding the crowds back from *Swirly World*. Not quite. Most of the other solo sailors had wandered off to sleep in their respective craft dotted along the flash marina. Jim Williamson from *Miss Conduct* hung in with a few cans of warm beer, he didn't want to stop, and we exchanged adventure stories while the sun came up and many exotic sounding local birds made their presence heard.

By 9 a.m. I had collapsed in a motion-free coma in *Swirly World*, only to be woken 20 minutes later by the Agricultural officer. He removed all my Australia-offending items termed garbage — garlic, onions, potatoes, peanut butter, honey . . . Then he left me to it. Down came the yellow inside-out sweatshirt doubling as the quarantine flag and up went the Australian courtesy flag. *Swirly World* was officially overseas.

The novelty of being able to step over the side and walk around was too much, so dismissing sleep for the time being wasn't hard. I wandered across the narrow isthmus to the surf beach on the other side and viewed the river entrance and the Point Cartwright coast by daylight. We'd made it. Land under legs a novelty worth sailing for.

Chapter 16

Evacuation by stool

The official prize giving was held the following evening (once *Swirly World* had arrived). I received a silver-plated tray for winning our division. There was no one else in it. Prize money was also forthcoming, along with a small black plastic miniature map of the Tasman with *Swirly World*'s elapsed time etched on it. It was similar to the one I had admired on *ROC* the year before on Waiheke and was to later see aboard *White Heron*. It was all I wanted. *Swirly World*'s waterproof certificate of achievement for posterity, proudly fixed aboard just inside the companionway.

The Mooloolaba Yacht Club is run as a commercial enterprise with full-time reception and catering staff, like many Australian sport clubs. Ablution facilities and organisation were impeccable but the sheer spirit of enthusiastic sailorising didn't seem as pronounced as the grass-roots style of the New Plymouth Yacht Club. 'You can't come in here in those, mate,' pointing to Jim Lowe's jandals. We were all granted a free week's berthage and *Swirly World* remained happily conspicuous in front of the bar. I'd lost weight on the way over, then gained a little in the last full-appetited week. On shore hunger turned to gluttony, with the variety of quick and easy nourishment available leading me to prolifically graze whenever the opportunity arose, which was often. Instant takeaway gratification.

I had my jobs to do and *Swirly World* soon shed her mast to deal to that spreader. Everything was toy scale compared to the others and there was much humour at *Swirly World*'s expense.

The eight-man life raft, GPS and myself had to return to Auckland and the plane option looked expensive. Weight and air freight are uneconomical flying companions. Jim Williamson on *Miss Conduct* from Whakatane was the only boat leaving straight after the race to return to New Zealand and he was more than willing to accommodate me and my baggage for the voyage back.

The band had some gigs booked for mid-May and *Swirly World* wouldn't have got back in time. I was ready to sail back, still in my sea mind, adjusted to aloneness, and Jim's offer was easier. The plan was to stash her somewhere safe, then hightail it back across the pond direct to Tauranga. I'd fly over at the end of winter to have a go at part two, the return voyage. Let's not think about that now . . . getting her back.

Australian customs pointed out that if I was leaving the boat unused I would have to deposit it within the Port of Brisbane area; Mooloolaba being just north of its outer limits. Jim recommended Scarborough, a suburb of north Brisbane; a man-made breakwater harbour, home of the Moreton Bay Boat Club and a clearance port for leaving Australia. *Miss Conduct* would be departing for Tauranga from there.

After a brief interlude of busy days in Mooloolaba removing mast, replacing spreader, and transferring the life raft to *Miss Conduct*, *Swirly World* set sail again. Ready, steady, sail.

The wind had remained virtually out of the southeast since our arrival, a trade wind pattern making the intended trip 30-odd miles south through the Moreton Bay shoals to Scarborough, almost directly on the nose the whole way. Leaving at first light, a good-sized sea was running out past Point Cartwright and *Swirly World* went to work reefed down and sailing well to windward, disappearing between the lumpy swells. Nice-sized swells. Plenty of windward boat speed, no stalling, beating up the coast to Caloundra, staying close hauled outside the breakers surfing in onto the long lee shore downwind.

Ominous white water seething over the Bray Rocks off Caloundra Head looked closer than before and it was time to tack further offshore, slim on sea room. Nearing the first of the Moreton Bay shoals and well-marked shipping lanes, it appeared we would have to bear away and lose valuable ground to windward if we were to follow the proper deep-water channel which began far to leeward, close in to the land. I didn't want to do that. There were miles to go. I couldn't even see where we were trying to get to, it was still over the horizon. The swells had eased in the lee of Moreton Island so we carried on to cross the North Banks further into the bay. It looked quite tame until, running down to intersect the channel, I saw patches of breaking waves to leeward. The patches of breaking waves started looking bigger. The closer we came the more I regretted my imprudent navigation.

Closing up the hatchboards I steered for a bit of normal sea between the white stretches and *Swirly World* slid through into the deeper channel over some very light blue, obviously shallow water; through into the reassuring darker tones of relatively secure deepness. The foaming bits on both sides looked impressive, considering the lack of real swell running. I wouldn't try that again.

Bribie Island stretches low for a long way up the coast and more and more of it kept appearing as we slowly sailed over the curve of the earth. When would it stop? It didn't look good. Our destination lay beyond Bribie. The wind veered to blow entirely parallel to the island and progress could hardly be called that. A full slog against wind and tide. Tedious stuff up the Skirmish Passage. Seriously considering that the island was being extended for our exclusive inconvenience, I resigned myself to a night arrival in Scarborough, using a chart that didn't have the harbour marked.

The tide finally turned in the early afternoon and *Miss Conduct* caught us (having left 4 hours later). I'd watched his boat growing larger to leeward, the inevitability of his overhauling us a foregone conclusion, yet I still sailed with an urgency that made me feel I may yet get away. Sailing to escape. The pensive sighting of another sail. A vessel to windward bearing down and slowly closing in on another. Rows of gunports, fighting men sponsored by 'gentle' men taking from foreign men whatever valuable items they happen to have on board at the time— legitimised wartime piracy.

Jim in *Miss Conduct* kept his gunports closed and passed close by to leeward, sails barely disturbed in our tiny wind shadow. We exchanged commiserations on the wind direction and he gave me the flashing details of the lights I was likely to encounter. My chart was the wrong scale for such crucial information. The tide turned and drew us like a magnet to windward, and it was getting dark before we reached the end of the island.

The last of the incoming flow pushed us through the narrow passage between Gilligan's Island (a low, dangerous-sounding sandbank in the dark) and the top of Bribie, then finally we were round, ceremoniously easing sheets to sail free on a beam reach in a light breeze, swept along slowly into Deception Bay.

The numerous clusters of shore lights were certainly deceptive and I missed the red flashing mark that showed the beginning of the clear passage into the bay. A quick reference on the GPS indicated we were well inshore of the last sandbanks so it was back to beating to windward on a compass bearing that led to Scarborough Harbour. In light rain we finally made the harbour leading lights and motored between the channel markers, 14 hours after setting out.

Fourteen hours to windward. No wonder some of the large racing craft we left at the Mooloolaba Marina thought we were ' bloody keen New Zealanders', not waiting for a favourable wind change before heading back to Brisbane.

The next day *Swirly World* was spied by the Moreton Bay Boat Club staff and ushered into the visitor's berth (in front of the bar) free of charge. The local press were summoned to experience the novelty of the tiny pea-green boat that had made it across the Tasman. Celebrity for a wholesome reason. A nice piece of endurance sailing. I enjoyed the attention. A female journalist insisted on interviewing me inside *Swirly World*. 'It's a lot smaller than I expected.' We received one or two favourable reviews in the local papers.

Jim had 'New Zeal' friends living on the Redcliffe Peninsula near the harbour and they kindly stored all the vital innards worth stealing from an unguarded boat. NZers in voluntary exile in Queensland. They'd left New Zealand in the late eighties, remembered me as a popstar on TV. It was a good start. We drove around the wide suburban streets, radials on a revving Holden. 'I like the subtropical climate better, cost of living's cheaper, more work.' The boys helped me store vital sails and stuff in a garage and a pile mooring was arranged for *Swirly World* to spend the next six months chained to, fore and aft.

Within a few days our responsibilities were dealt with and ex-pats and the customs man waved us off from the marina pontoon. Destination Tauranga by way of wind and sea, others for company. The 1400 miles still seemed a long way, even with a faster boat and friends to share them.

A southeast trade-wind pattern that had slipped south to guide *Swirly World* so smoothly from Lord Howe to Mooloolaba was still hanging around, making for a comparatively long 13-day passage back. Nearly on the nose all the way.

Fortunately, having not lost my sea legs, food figured highly in our lives. In the full stand-up galley I couldn't stop cooking and I couldn't stop eating. Toasted sandwiches were a speciality, along with pancakes and whatever else tasted chewable. The Elvis seal of approval.

In the quiet, dark hours the rustle of chocolate wrappers being feverishly torn open was a frequent accompaniment to the sound of wave slap and rushing water. Someone was thieving chocolate from the ship's stores in the late watches when others were asleep. I had a feeling it was me. I couldn't help myself, I had this problem, I was a sugar addict.

Bellies were always full, mine especially. More fuel than neces-sary for gentlemen of leisure, seated or prostrate most of the time. But appetite had grown to mean much. Too much. I also knew that while the pleasure of gluttony involved a lot entering at one end, very little seemed to be exiting from the other. I put this down to the amount of stodgy things consumed, but as the days passed and the volume within me grew, I feared that something was amiss. A blockage.

Once, long ago at a rock festival where sanitation arrangements had been quite public, I had gone without 'evacuation by stool' (as the ancient mariners used to call it) for five days. Upon returning home the hold-up cleared and systems functioned normally.

On *Miss Conduct* Jim preferred us not to use the on-board pump-out toilet, which was situated close to our accommodation area. He preferred us, and indeed led by example, to situate oneself over the transom of the boat, squatting down whilst clutching the aft side of the pushpit rail. With any kind of sea running this was demanding, holding on with both hands in a very physical way, to avoid being left squatting unceremoniously in *Miss Conduct*'s wake. Ard had no difficulty in remaining regular and would quite happily perch day or night, company or not, over the back corner of the boat and let drop. A bashful streak arose in me and I found my quick, virtually inconsequential efforts always, for some obvious reason, taking place during the less frequented late-night watches.

Once past Lord Howe Island a freshening rainy southeasterly roughed up an uncomfortable sea and we started using the indoor head (toilet). My first late-night encounter verged on disaster as I failed to open the necessary seacock to send the pumped goods out of the bowl. Water filled the bowl and as the boat lurched off the top of the waves to crash heavily in the troughs the unsavoury contents did their best to elevate and jump sideways to roam the cabin bilges. Jim tipped me off in the nick of time and they were banished to the ocean below without complications.

The next morning Ard, our fellow crewman, repeated the procedure only to find the exit pipe was blocked. *Miss Conduct* was in a lively mood, lifting high over the wave tops before crashing down. This time the faeces got the better of us and the full contents of the bowl elevated as *Miss Conduct* fell heavily into a trough. Once airborne they managed to somehow spill sideways and escaped into the bilges already awash with seawater. An unfortunate early morning moment. Ard tried to shoo them away out of sight like a sharemilker hosing the cows' business away, but in a watertight hull there was nowhere for them to go, only here and there, floating about, constant companions, lurking around under the floorboards. He did an admirable job cleaning up as best as possible, but discovering the odd bit of shredded globules of shit stuck all over the duty-free bags in the bilges tested vomit-susceptibility levels. It was almost a bit much but we had to live with it. As well as everything else, the boat was full of humour, which helped.

Ard was everything a keen forecastle man could be, never ceasing to volunteer for the wet, arduous headsail changing and reefing duties. Knew he wouldn't be out there forever, getting into it. I, on another hand, preferred to pull the damp sleeping bag further over my face and fake unconsciousness. Lethargically lying down, thinking quiet things. That wet world only thin wood away, noising it up, slappity wave flop, mile after mile, sailing us home. A larger boat certainly had greater boat speed and what was achieved in thirteen days would have taken *Swirly World* twenty.

Jim built *Miss Conduct* himself and had clocked thousands of miles sailing about the South Pacific. To build a boat, years of bothering. Jim was the essence of the Solo Tasman Race. Cabinetmaker from Whakatane, built his own boat, knew how to use it.

His high-powered SSB radio, borrowed in good faith to transmit our positions, had a dry joint inside and seemed intent on silencing us all the way across. Jim just thumped it. It worked enough times to let the world know about us . . .

Approaching the Wanganella Banks one night, I awoke to see someone craned over the chart table working out our position. Illuminated only by the dim chart lamp, the black eye sockets and fine bone lines looked unearthly. Another time and place. Some buccaneer, 1341, doing his chart work, the vaguer chart work of another time. Perhaps he was. It was the classic look of a swarthy ancient mariner. It was Jim.

The sea and sky stayed grey, low cloud and rain for days, too many days to call it a favourable crossing. A dreary, uninviting vista complete with accompanying headwinds from the southeast, then east, then south. Wherever we wanted to go, from there the wind would blow. But it never got dangerous. On finally being deposited off the east Northland coast to wallow becalmed, the overcast foreboding conditions lifted and the long-awaited contrast of blue sky and green land was certainly something worth looking at. Contrast and appreciation.

That night it was into the virtual-reality chamber again, the wind rushing back in from the west-norwest, surfing along on a broad reach through dense, dark rain squalls across the Colville Channel. Steering as you stared at the lit compass figures, braced against the cockpit seats, fighting the pressures on the helm, bearing away by numbers. Surreal and serious. Was there water out there . . . Surfing fast until we dropped the main, overpowered, stalling, then the undignified thrashing of the loud sailcloth overwhelmed by the squalls accelerating down off the blacked-out Coromandel Ranges.

Daylight brought it back to blue sky and green hills — the glory tones of land against water. Hoony Mount Maunganui grew larger, then arrived, slowly past the seaward shoals, through the channel close in, as close as can be under the tall Mount, leaving it to port, into the flat lagoon . . . What's for dinner?

Chapter 17

The Trance Fluid tour
The Trance Fluid tour

Back on land after a month at sea, born-again perspectives again. Everything smells new, poignant, for a while. The life refresher course. What do you want to do now? Better write some songs. Another CD. Another tour. Songs sourced and the lifeblood of the band circulated again. Nothing like a new song to make you keep trying. A national tour to wave ourselves about. 'Let's go round again. Someone's got to pay for it, I doubt if it's gonna be the audience.'

Playing the gigs that make a tour pay for itself. I should have known better but never did. Off we went again in the ambulance . . . Stolichnaya (the genuine Russian vodka) chose to sponsor our winter campaign, fuelling our economic and emotional rescue.

Driving through bleak snow squalls and cold sunshine, loaded up with musical black boxes and crates of Russian liquid. The Trance Fluid tour started in Oamaru. It appeared our popularity was not a foregone conclusion. In more remote regions the crowds, or rather clusters, were small if appreciative. We needed multitudes to make our expedition sustainable. For the moment the economics couldn't catch us. We had pushed south fast into winter and we were trancing forward where every band had been before. That wouldn't stop us. We were days ahead of fiscal considerations.

Accustomed to sleeping in small uncomfortable spaces, I chose to take my rest on the tattered couch in the ambulance, on watchdog duty after most performances. It was a bonus not having to wake up and check the compass course and trim sails every hour or two.

On a Nelson Saturday night, I lay in ambush on the couch behind the tinted windows of the ex-medication vehicle and did a survey of the passing humans prior to show time.

On the blackboard outside the venue it was clear who was on tonight. Groups of reasonably well-dressed youths and new adults out on the town sauntered past, all eager to see what was available for their amusement. As I lay there observing reactions it became obvious there was something wrong with the main attraction, who appeared to be me.

They all knew who he was and that we were part of a live band but many were reluctant to pay a cover charge to see him, not to mention me. The reason for their collective reticence was the shared opinion that 'Fagan is a faggot, mate.' I wasn't convinced myself. Groups of pressed trouser-wearing, clean-collared New Zealand males were without doubt and wholeheartedly dismissive of my misconstrued self. I felt sorry for him, then I remembered he was me. It was clear that all those early years of make-up adorned, un-orthodox dressing had stirred . . . a reaction. I'd succeeded in alien-ating all those blokes. Good job. Take no prisoners. That's showbiz. Back in the main centres we managed to find enough humans before us to constitute a crowd. Petrol (and CNG) were put in Amboland and the circus kept moving.

The last gig of the Trance Fluid tour ended on an anthropological high note in Wainuiomata. Having been bought to perform at a private 21st, we had a good night playing in a hired Red Cross hall opposite some rugby fields. In almost medical surroundings, we availed ourselves of the opportunity to give the retired ambulance a photo session.

The evening went appropriately with our new songs being well received with unselfconscious participation all round. Maybe not quite all round. In one semi-dark far corner a group of naughty-looking males clustered. Drawn by the loud sounds emanating through the thin walls to their still night outside in a nearby public place, they had entered the building as gate-crashers. Known to the birthday girl but generally ignored, they remained secluded and uninvolved, apart from making repetitive voyages across the hall to fill up their numerous plastic jugs with that infamous brown liquid that comes conveniently in kegs for functions of that kind.

Having witnessed a majority participating in the usual danceable manner, the seeds of their resentment may have been sewn. We would find out. There were more females jiggling about than males. Finally exiting the building in the customary early hours we did the load out, lugging the black boxes and instruments outside.

Nearly concluding our auspicious last pack out of the tour, it became apparent that the previously secluded lads felt their evening was coming to a premature end. Led by one intoxicated social adventurer, the group gradually circled closer to our mundane labours. It seemed their night didn't feel right unless it ended in a fight, and to that end two bold ones did their best to provoke our party into physical communication of an unpleasant kind. It looked that way or maybe I was reading too much into it. Having felt we'd already provided plenty of entertainment, and being self-preservationists, we tried to avoid confrontation.

Resisting feelings of compassion they circled closer like pack wolves round a dying campfire. One inebriated short, plump chap pushed forward and let out a howly noise directed at no one in particular yet delivered to impress. On receiving no response he withdrew his less than impressive presence. There was no cavalry to be seen on the horizon at that late hour and having made it inside our vehicles with one pack creature tokenly kicking at our door, we turned on the revolving light and roared off into the still Wainuiomata night. Once again accusations of being a 'girls' band' echoed round the valley and I wasn't sure but I think I might have heard the word 'faggot'. . .

'Mountain Rock' festival in the lower North Island. At night out amongst a crowd ensconced with stage activities, the way it usually is. Recognised as a performer from earlier on in the afternoon, I was introduced to Dave, the strapping brother of one of the far more compelling sisters close to hand. Dave proceeded to insist on my drinking bourbon with him from a bottle thrust in my direction. By his companions' interactions with him, it looked as if Dave was a bit of a loose cannon. Unpredictable. He was boozing. He was a bit overbearing. It started to rain. In the rain Dave had an argument with someone. Jan Hellriegel was playing on stage, too loud for me to hear. Dave turned ferocious and started flexing about and my new acquaintances began to resemble captors. After 20 minutes of Jan in the rain, Dave became distracted in another argument, with one of his sisters, at a distance further than before. I chose my moment to disappear into the crowd around. Having swallowed my forced rations of grog I thought I chose it well, plodding off wet through the bodies, back towards the sanctuary of the backstage area. Dave appeared suddenly like he'd been waiting for me to scarper. He was in a bad mood. I'd made a run for it. He didn't like me at all. 'I never liked you, I could destroy you . . . she only loves me because of my pecs.' I feigned vagueness but paid grave attention to his fighting talk. He bragged on and on, of fight after triumphant fight, the history of gangland Feilding carried on his shoulders. Gradually he ran out of hostile energy. It just petered out of him. Dave lost interest in me. This time I did it properly. The backstage security patrolled area had never felt so inviting.

In between songs, touring and avoiding the animosity of some of the audience, I received a letter from the current owner of *White Heron*, the 22-ft keeler that had done the Tasman solo in 1974 and 78. She was still moored on death row off Herne Bay.

Joe Davison had informed the current owner of my interest in reviving her, if only for the sake of her former glory. David Watts had been residing in Queenstown for four years and was happy for me to get *White Heron* back in sailable shape at his expense. Being temporarily without a vessel to care for I took up his offer. To many she is a heavy ugly duckling, but with a Tasman history, a wheel and centre cockpit, she is a boat of immense character, and besides, she was one of the tiny craft that sparked my imagination so often in those articles I had collected on the race. It was significant.

The Herne Bay moorings get roughed up a lot of the time. Any westerly quarter wind against tide makes rowing difficult. I picked an agreeable flat frosty morning to paddle out and inspect *White Heron* once more. Four years untouched and it looked like it. The aft galvanised self-steering and pushpit had severe rusting in places, and the heavy rust stains down the white stern and sides looked bad. Multiple seasons of rolling to wind and tide had carried the marine growth several inches up the topsides and mooring chain rust streaks adorned the bows. What looked like a millennium of birdshit covered the decks and cockpit. I climbed on the stern and immediately noticed the overly heavy displacement by comparison to *Swirly World*. She didn't heel at all to my weight. The mainsheet and headsail halyard had frayed away and the padlock keys were misplaced, so I hacksawed my way inside.

The two small cabins were neat and tidy and the sails and gear basic but functional. Orange sails. No winches on *White Heron*. She had the feel and robust sturdiness of a working fishing boat, not the dainty normal yacht. Sitting in a centre cockpit with a small spoked wheel was a novelty that appealed. How responsive? The internal steering blocks had come away inside and would need refastening. Joe had definitely built her like a tank. Triple-skinned and beams large and solid. No wonder she was heavy. The auxiliary stern-hung self-steering rudder was massive in its lay up and could double as a spare if need be. What a freakish boat — its unorthodox layout and proportions appealed. No engine or outboard. Every piece of hand-made fitting looked more appropriate for an old-time sailing ship. Four years of tugging on what was once new mooring chain had worn many links dangerously thin.

I rowed around her and had to admit the high cabin sides did look less than beautiful from some angles, but chunky and interesting from others. With all that marine life clinging on underneath it would be a demanding voyage across the harbour onto the piles at Little Shoal Bay.

A week later Frank came over from Waiheke and we picked the weather right. A light southerly gave us a short downhill ride through the Little Shoal Bay moorings under mainsail and worn old staysail, to round up on high tide at the piles in the corner of the tidal bay. The next exciting instalment was revealed when the tide went out, leaving six inches of seaweed and healthy mussels dangling beneath the hull. On the next day's high tide with the mainsheet and the headsail halyard replaced, plus new blue antifouling, we sailed *White Heron* off the piles and about the harbour — alive once more. In the breeze she felt underpowered but the wheel was responsive enough.

The next week I sailed her off the mooring in a fresh southwesterly and she performed well; slow to accelerate, but once moving, the momentum gave her a bigger boat feel. The long straight keel was something I hadn't experienced before. She would track in one direction well with the wheel pegged, a quality unobtainable on most fin-keeled, skeg-type hulls like *Swirly World*.

One vicious westerly morning I made my way down the Home Bay steps to crouch sheltered by the point and see how she was handling the gale-force squalls rushing across in a welter of rain and spray from Te Atatu. It was high tide and even though I'd put back pieces of chain over the dubious stretches, it was a demanding day for any hard-pressed mooring. There in the full fury of the steep little seas breaking over her bow, *White Heron* rode and rolled her way through the blinding spray. The lightly built boats careered up and down, veering about, but *White Heron*'s heavier hull rode with an air of composure. A different kind of roll and pitch. A wild, windy scene that brought her alive of her own accord. The potential was still there. Just got to use it.

We did the tour. Made it back to Auckland again, no casualties. Recorded more songs at Revolver in West Auckland, drove the ambulance late at night down very empty Remuera streets. Back to the cave before daylight. Six months were gone. I had to get *Swirly World* out of Australia. It had been inevitable, a sentence hanging over me. I had to get the boat back before the cyclone season.

This time I would be without the support and psychological security blanket the race and the New Plymouth Yacht Club had provided. It had been a good warm up and shake down for the return voyage. We were only halfway there. On making it back to New Zealand, *Swirly World* would become the smallest boat to have sailed both ways across the Tasman. That was a partial incentive. I wasn't sure I wanted to go, but it was obvious I had to.

The weather had changed, something I'd been counting on. Hard westerlies had been howling across the sea to New Zealand for the past couple of months, just the direction I was hoping for. The wind never sounds good at night. Blowing in the trees, hearing all that motion, the wind letting you know it's there.

Chapter 18

Three hours there, how many back?

The Tasman Sea beneath us was covered in cloud and kept from view. It didn't matter as I had no window seat and from that height there wasn't much to see. I arrived at Brisbane Airport with a limited budget (two hundred dollars Australian) and seven pieces of luggage. David Manzi from De Amalfi was true to his word and I was gratefully loaded down with the GPS, EPIRB etc. The life raft, and a pile of freeze-dried and boil-in-the-bag rations were to follow on later in the week. In packhorse mode I staggered from bus to train then to the Sandgate taxi rank and finally, just before another humid Queensland dusk, I was deposited at the Moreton Bay Boat Club.

Turning down past the tree-clad reserve next to the motor camp I spied *Swirly World*'s radar reflector on top of the mast. A mast high enough to need a hull floating on the surface. A good start. There were no other competitors about. No one I knew. The club was swinging into full action mode with lots of social members coming to the end of their 'happy hour', with a busy bar, food on tables, corner solo entertainer. Everyone having a reasonable time. The enormity of having to sail back to Auckland sullied my impression of things. I'd felt this way before.

John and Joy, from the steel replica of Slocum's Spray *Ada Jane*, had been aboard a few weeks earlier to mop out rainwater and I borrowed their dinghy to reach the pile mooring. Dave Walker, my Redcliffe-New Zealander storer of sails, sextant, SSB and folding dinghy turned up simultaneously and I ferried all the bits out to *Swirly World*.

Jim had warned me about cockroaches or 'cockies' as the locals fondly called them. Each item moved was intensely scrutinised but two still managed to make it onto *Swirly World*'s deck. They were more creatures than insects and equipped with wings. I expected a fight on my hands. They fought bravely, almost tactically, but somehow fell into the sea. Apart from the large pelicans having obviously enjoyed *Swirly World* as a defecation perch, all was as we had left it. Only the wind indicator was missing from the top of the mast. Pelicans . . .

I'd allowed seven days before leaving but it stretched to eleven while waiting for the life raft to arrive from Auckland. Each day the boat systems went back together, a new expensive carburettor for the engine, GPS wired in, secure stowage and plastic bags for everything and screwable bungs on the offending drainage holes in the main hatch. New antifouling, new log cable crimped in, weathercloths and self-steering, batteries charged on the marina. Sleeping aboard and slipping back into the rhythms of single narrow bunk living, one burner Primus — life in the *Swirly World* space capsule. The weather was unsettled, hard westerly one day, fresh sea breeze the next, light southeasterly, thunder and lightning storms. Each day more suitably subtropical than Auckland.

The Commodore gave me a temporary member's pass to use their clean and tidy facilities and to spend as much as I dared on Australian-made brown liquid. After the rapid loss of sunlight each evening I'd row back to get a weak portion of beer, empathise with the corner entertainment, and possibly do a conversation or two.

They were turning over forty thousand dollars a month in the bar. A lot of people are practised at standing around talking, interspersed with standing around drinking. Time goes by. Long periods of time. People enjoy it. I could have enjoyed it more, but something was worrying me. It had something to do with 1200 miles of sea to the southeast. In the company of others I didn't know, I felt left out and misplaced. 'New Zealand in what? How long? Have you thought about selling her?'

The party was over but I'd hung around too long. Now I was on my own. The only way home was *Swirly World*, the sooner the better. Stop hanging around. You'll envy them the security of their bar in a few day's time . . . I couldn't underestimate the mileage to come. Walking pace across the sea. We had to get out of Australia but what would the wind bring?

Dave Reid, another friend of Jim Williamson's, gave me rides about Brisbane, foraging for the overdue life raft and eventually retrieved it for me. A few days prior to leaving a Friday-night barbecue was held at his place in honour of *Swirly World*'s departure. We dined outdoors amongst the foreign chatter of exotic wild parakeets and caged canaries.

'So you're off then, can't say I envy you.' Someone mentioned Ross River fever, a localised neighbourhood thing.

'Which neighbourhood?'

'This one.' Mosquitos carried it. There had been a lot of little things flying around all evening. They should have said something earlier, I didn't want to go to sea with a subtropical disease on the boil.

Dave had wanted to hear some of my 'new stuff', so I brought a copy of the single 'Exciting' over for him. As the evening progressed Dave monopolised the sound system. 'Exciting' got its chance and quickly became anything but, as we all had many opportunities to hear it even louder next time. High on grog he invaded a teenage party next door. No one followed as reinforcements. Soon 'Exciting' was very audible across the back gardens. Dave was scouting for a fresh audience for me. Above and beyond the gardens, the ever-present wind waited patiently in the tall trees. No escaping it, soon we'd be with it.

In eleven brief days confined to the Redcliffe Peninsula, I locked in with shopkeeper faces and the rhythms of north suburban Brisbane. Sunny Queensland was rapidly running out of water and the farmers inland were feeling it bad. Parched earth and too much solar radiation, sunlight overload. A huge patch of the Indian Ocean, the size of Australia itself, had a surface sea temperature two degrees colder than usual and some believed it was responsible for the lack of precipitation.

Rain came by night, one particularly sticky, humid one. A fresh northeasterly and cloudless sky had given no warning of a cloud-bank rising out of the south. On the verge of sleep and thinking not particularly productive thoughts, I noticed the wind suddenly drop, cloud racing up through the starry sky then lightning and thunder tones, heavy rain driving horizontal on an instant southeasterly squall shift. The palms on Oyster Point bent to the onslaught and the thunderstorm raced through off to the north. I slept fitfully with nightmares of savage possibilities. Over as it began, a mere fifteen minutes, and the next day was dry and sunny once more.

The survival gear arrived on Friday afternoon but wasn't to be cleared by Customs until Monday. Weekend off. Monday afternoon it was aboard *Swirly World*, a gloriously compact four-man Beauport life raft tucked securely inside aft of the mast support post. Thunderbirds were definitely go. At nine-thirty on the Tuesday morning the pre-booked customs officer arrived at the Club pontoon and with a minimum of fuss gave us clearance. On his identifying form the customs officer who met us at Mooloolaba had described *Swirly World* as 'looking like half the boat's been cut off.'

I'd collected fresh onions, oranges, pineapples, lemons, bread and cheese earlier that morning when the shops had opened, and after a cursory peer inside from the slightly bewildered customs man, it was time to start the engine and glide out alone, the wind to be our everything once more.

Two hands were shaken and once again *Swirly World* moved away, leaving two mildly unsure people in her wake. She had a habit of it. It was a quiet, sunny, calm weekday morning and no crowds had gathered on the breakwater to wish us well. They were all at work. No expectations from others, nor any expected.

Departure. Motoring out through the breakwaters, a school of large dolphins swam near to let me know I won't be totally alone. The Customs man beeped the horn on his expensive government Holden parked out on the breakwater arm (making sure we left). Three hours there, how many back?

A light northerly on the nose (surprise) with the promise of a northeasterly sea breeze freshening in Moreton Bay had me motivated to get the most out of the outgoing tide and move up beside Bribie Island before all the elements opposed us. Before heading

southeast for New Zealand we had to go north round the top of
Moreton Island, 20 miles to windward. We motored up to Bonga-
ree on Bribie Island, giving the batteries a final decent charge until
the breeze began filling in and *Swirly World* could sail hard on the
wind on port tack for Gilligan's Island. A large motorised gin palace
roared past heading for the Caboolture River. Someone on the bridge-
deck bellowed the obvious question. 'New Zealand' sounded ambitious and probably wasn't heard.

Mathew Flinders would have approved. At the end of the eight-
eenth century he put in a lot of isolated miles around the coast of
Australia. He'd charted the Pumicestone Passage dividing Bribie Island from the mainland, by sails and oars in a little undecked boat.
He'd done many perilous coastal miles in the same vulnerable craft.
Swirly World's decked in, heavy-keeled, auxiliary-motored, GPS and
self-steering splendour would have impressed him. And the batteries were fully charged for all those future conversations with Penta
Comstat on the Australian coast and hopefully Kerikeri Radio in
the Bay of Islands. With the passage of time the mariner's lot has
undoubtedly improved.

Loaded down again with food and water for at least thirty-five
days, *Swirly World* ploughed enthusiastically along, full main and
genoa getting the best out of the breeze. The tide sucked us up to
windward through the gap between Gilligan's and Bribie, a shallow patch kicking up short, awkward, breaking wind against tide
wavelets. *Swirly World* was hindered more in such conditions than
in offshore-scaled waves. Water-line length has a lot to do with it.
Slam, crash, short slamming crash. Spray, spume, call it what you
like, wetness everywhere.

On the nose back up Skirmish Passage the other way this time,
the far distant skyline of the Caloundra buildings looked a daunt-
ingly long way. If we'd needed the depth of water the huge ships
racing past required, we would have been obliged to carry on all the
way up to windward and Caloundra before being free of the shoals
and able to head eastward. But as there was no significant swell or
sea running in the bay, I picked an early moment to hang a right on
to port again and tack out over the welcoming Wild Banks, setting
us on course for the northern tip of Moreton Island. The Wild Banks

were fortunately anything but, and the outgoing tide set us nicely to windward. We sailed over various shallow shades of blue suspicious sea and reached the less intimidating east channel exit to clear deeper water as the tide turned. Late thunderstorms had been forecast for Brisbane. The sea breeze eased to leave us wallowing maudlin with the prospect of seasickness and the reality of a long way to go, near the north end of Moreton.

Feeling unwell, I clung to the Perspex dodger on a lumpy swell. I watched the southerly cloud and associated thunder and lightning gradually work its way up the coast to eclipse Bribie, from where we had come, then Caloundra, and the distant peak of Mooloolaba's Point Cartwright, in violent black rain squalls. Ours was a parking spot with a view; the wind and wet stuff confined to the land behind. From there on the wind was going to be very important to me, and I didn't like the look of what it could bring.

I got our first GPS fix to check its accuracy before leaving land. The huge amount of application required in turning it on, holding it up and pressing a button was too much for me and I dry-retched my feeble self about the cockpit coaming. That windless sloppy sea had got the better of me. Grasping an immediate sense of purpose — progress, I resorted to motoring once more, direct for the Cape Morton light to pass close in near the cliffs under cover of darkness. The front hatch had to be open to cool the engine and a fair bit of wave toppings found their wet way inside. I was feeling too poorly to pay proper attention.

We rounded the corner in the company of a large motor sailer, spreader lights revealing its decks. It looked big, fast and comfortable inside. They turned south close in to the shore and followed the coast down. I steered *Swirly World* out further away from the immediate traffic lanes and onto the convenient conveyor belt known as the East Australian Current. The further out the better. Convenient if you want to go south at 3 knots without even trying. A few miles offshore I turned the engine off, resigned to a dark, windless night, feeling wretchedly ill and watching out for the lights of nearby shrimp boats. Setting the egg-timer alarm for the first of a series of deeply relaxing and refreshing (not) 20-minute mental disengagements. A catnap. Poor cat, never enough sleep.

On a confused sea *Swirly World* lurched and rolled vindictively. Leaving a headsail up and sheeted in hard steadied her a bit, but generally a despondent night was had by all. The current setting south revived my spirits when it became obvious we were being carried down to higher latitudes at wonderful speed. Without sailing or motoring, new shore lights were appearing on the coast, Stradbroke Island, old ones receding.

When it got light *Swirly World* was still becalmed and had done 20 miles south in seven effortless hours. Another sea-breezed afternoon arrived and with main and genoa poled out, we sledged south to reach Cape Byron by seven that evening. From being out of sight of land that morning, we'd edged back towards the coast all day to maintain maximum current thrust. With the even, rhythmic roll of running before the wind under self-steering my interest in existence picked up and I started functioning again.

The bright night-lights of the settlement cluster near Cape Byron glowed hospitable and secure. Let's go there, sell the boat, have a good time. The low flash of dim red ahead warned of lights unlisted on my large-scale chart so we gybed over to head offshore in a freshening northerly with a falling barometer, on course more or less for the top of New Zealand, 1100 miles southeast. Goodbye Australia. Offshore we must inevitably go.

Patches of fine drizzle set in and the barometer kept falling. Penta Comstat's morning weather forecast on 4483 confirmed that a depression was forming off the New South Wales coast. Coff's Harbour AM Radio began forecasting severe thunderstorms and strong to gale force northerlies. Great, just what I came for . . . what was I there for? Necessity. You've got to get the boat back, nowhere else to go. Don't remind me.

All day the wind increased as we reached away from the invisible land and south-setting current, under reefed main and working jib. Superb sailing was had by all, surfing down the growing seas at up to 9 knots. The low was going to bring the inevitable southerly change and southeasterly quarter blow right on the nose so the further southeast we tracked the better. Broad reaching in 35 knots I changed down gears to accommodate any further increases while I went below for a wind of the egg-timer alarm and a bit of a lie down. Going to bed before the gale . . .Warnings about huge hail-stones and getting your car under cover not to mention hiding humans indoors had me eyeing the horizon for improbable shelter. Australian radio was doing its best to unsettle me.

Clouds of malevolent intent had been gathering all day on the western horizon. Gradually they reached out to engulf *Swirly World* in a downpour of cold, fresh water accompanied by the dreaded sight of forked lightning darting, unpredictable and impressive, to the surface of the sea — all over the place. Places nearby. I'd already deposited a couple of metres of battery cable bolted to a copper plate over the stern — clipped to the uninsulated backstay, but held little faith in it conducting the electricity harmlessly away from us. I'd seen the full fury of the discharges up close.

Cowering like a wee doggie on the foam quarterberth mattress, careful to avoid touching anything metallic, I listened in awe to the tones of destruction zapping down outside with simultaneous thunder claps. How far away? I stopped looking. Fortunately all things come to pass and it did, taking much of the wind with it. No safe seat in the house — Australian thunderstorms. A couple of repeat performances, then the sky settled down. I elected to stay indoors for the evening, content to let the self-steering sail us gradually further southeast under working jib alone at 4 knots, 100 miles true east of Coff's Harbour, fatigued and disenchanted with the prospect of things to come.

While sleeping in the flash of the strobe light mounted on the cockpit dodger, the wind shifted to the southwest sometime near midnight and I awoke heading unhappily north. Going the wrong way for more than an hour without noticing a wind shift was tantamount to elemental deception. I would have to tune in more if we were going to get to New Zealand.

The sky was clear and cold, an audience of stars disinterested in our long overdue return to the right magnetic course. Sleepily re-aligned, we tight reached south as far as the wind would let us, before going hard on the wind against the inevitable southeasterly. Two reefs in the mainsail and the No.2 jib balanced well enough for the self-steering to cope with 30 knots.

Back indoors, strapped in the lee cloth and suspended in midair above the dirty dishes clanging about on the swinging Primus stove, it was life on an angle. The kind of conditions anticipated but not appreciated. A 4-metre swell built up quickly with a rough sea on top making progress for *Swirly World*'s water-line length slow — minimal even. Suffer the little children who grew into adults and wanted to go sailing on the deep, serious sea.

In the coming week *Swirly World*'s deck leaks were thoroughly detected. I knew where they were and the water knew how to get to where I was. The main offenders — air vents of course, keeping me mopping a bucket of water from the bouncing bilge every evening and morning, evening, morning . . . It was an uncomfortable start and my stomach agreed. Life in a lurching wet bed. Twice consumed by spasms of sicky expulsion when drawing up our position. Throwing up all remnants of application and enthusiasm into one small bucket. Appetite remained a distant memory. Plenty of food on board, but no one to put it in — yet.

Derek at Penta Comstat spoke of rough seas round Lord Howe Island and a heavy ground swell. The sky had begun to look friendly so things had to eventually ease. Rain squalls came and went, *Swirly World* ploughing faithfully on to windward over a very disorganised surface. The SSB roll calls made good listening with 'tremendous' being the most compelling adjective associated with one motor sailer's experiences off the coast. Appropriate that we'd got so far away from the wind versus current showdown before involuntarily hardening up onto the wind. The fresh southeasterly was there to stay due to a slow-moving high sitting south of us. We were destined to seven days on the wind slowly tracking east-northeast up and away, at a hearty 3 to 4 knots, away from beloved Aotearoa and towards Norfolk Island.

There was little to be done about it. The anticyclone was dawdling at 5 knots in the Tasman. To hang a right on to port tack and head south would have put us down into its windless centre, wallowing with only a suntan to show for our days becalmed. Any proper cruising monster yacht would have taken the 'aim straight for it' option, maintaining the psychological security of heading in the right direction with their diesel inboard maintaining an ETA. Not so for those of us small and fuelless enough to be confined to working the wind as the sea ancestors did. The reality of actually coming to a halt when the wind deems it so made *Swirly World* privileged in a purist way. But there was nothing privileged about being subjected to hours of perpetual unpredictable motion. The endless noise of wave-slapping sounds, water rushing, crashing, pouring, dripping all about. Patience, perseverance, endurance. Things to willingly manifest, I tried to convince myself. As Joe Davison said in a later letter, 'conditions sent to test a sailor's resolve.' A hard-work way to see it. Application was needed. Round-the-clock wind fluctuation called for sheets to be retrimmed, self-steering re-aligned. A constant sensitivity to balancing the wind's influence. And the rest of the time? Something's happening in your mind. Isolated environment immersion (IEI) makes you think differently. Or perhaps you think you're thinking differently? I'm not sure. Why aren't you sure? Haven't had enough sleep. Are you sure?

In the face of perpetual nonstimulus from outside distractions, emotions sift through memories. Encouraging or discouraging, made all the more poignant by sleep deprivation to an almost hallucinogenic degree. The things we've thunk about over the years.

The frequencies of sea colour and water movement sounds affect you physiologically. They tone up the etheric body and all the while you're immersed in one huge negative ion bath called salt water. All a bit natural.

As wind and sea moderated more sail came out until the deck was festooned with damp, smelly fabrics. *Swirly World* drifting becalmed 280 miles almost true west of Norfolk Island. There was nothing to see, hardly ever is, other than sea and sky. The anticyclone had decided to set us free and was heading slowly north over the top of us. *Swirly World*'s deck resembled a chemistry experiment. Salt crystals covered all, the residue of our wetness.

All alone here, but entertaining elsewhere, when I went into sleep consciousness I made contact with otherworldly entities. Called dreams on land, at sea they took on a greater significance. I'd meet with unidentified presences, most often encountered on rocks beside a still sea and twilight sky, and experience calm moments of conversation. My mind was keeping me occupied.

On a sloping, pastoral hillside, set in tall pockets of secondary manuka growth, a shantytown of scattered eccentric dwellings stretched down to mud flats in a sheltered tidal bay. A hard wind blew and handpainted flags with unorthodox motifs flew spectacularly from the ridges. Ancient vehicles, boats, watertanks and tent-like structures had been hauled up the hillside to provide accommodation of an unconventional kind. Perched in surrounding gullies, large hydroponic growing rooms soaked up sunlight. Large wind generators blurred energy-generating blades and solar panels absorbed the sun's silent radiation.

In a separate gully a large barn-like structure emanated live music and in smaller similar units it sounded like theatre groups and amateur bands were rehearsing. A network of flying foxes criss-crossed the slopes and gullies and people were travelling through the air.

Down on the mud flats a huge sailing catamaran — 75 metres long, sat high and dry, three tall masts devoid of sail. A large flying fox terminated beside it and people were loading bales of food. Not the kind of nourishment New Zealand is usually known for— mutton, beef and beer — it was concentrated protein, durable, long-lasting, just add water and you're in business. Beans. No refrigeration or rapid transit required. The hillsides were dedicated to legume production. On closer inspection even the odd dwellings were wrapped in the green tendrils of bean growth. Intensive horticulture and everything engineless. Winch and tackle, pulleys and hemp rope. Manual effort and a completely different concept of time replaced oil-based mechanical exertion.

Where was the dehydrated protein going? It sounded like a long-term Red Cross nutrition mission, transporting fresh water from isolated rivers, and grains and pulses from the growing regions to the overpopulated deprived zones. Wind-driven food and water carriers riding the timeless trade winds and Southern Ocean conveyor belts and currents of the globe to the under-resourced Old World. Only a drop in the ocean but not a bad sense of purpose.

Were they survivors of some human catastrophe or a voluntary branch of separated consciousness? A Spielberg post-meteorite thriller or parallel eco-universe? It was hard to tell. The sloping hillside looked good for launching a hang-glider, then I found myself running off the ridge and leaping faithfully out into empty air. The wind held me up and it was real, the sensation of flying unaided. With a few leg movements I could clumsily direct my airborne path and with a little effort I managed to lift up above the circle of hills to see the ocean stretching away up the coast. Down and out over the wave tops, using the breeze like a seabird, effortlessly controlling my elevation. The sound of the sea beneath became louder and the flight a little turbulent then I slowly seeped back into the all-consuming noise and motion. A sailing boat journeying on the surface of the ocean and I was in it. Alone again, hundreds of miles from land. For a moment I'd forgotten.

Then I remembered, it was my final segment of the Messiah World Championships. Your messianic vision of the future in less than 30 seconds. Keep it simple. The plan for the sons of man. The advertising agency's video representation of 'how your life could do more for you.' I needed a good night's sleep.

Technically asleep, I often had visitors. One lectured on the vitality of triangles and the triangular relevance of sails. I awoke with the name Vito Dumas in mind. An Argentinean solo sailor, since deceased, who circumnavigated the globe engineless in high latitudes in the 1940s.

Elderly, imposing entities were back the next night scrutinising my emotional attitudes and sorting out amongst themselves whether *Swirly World* should make it back to Cape Reinga. Penetrating and disconcerting, I can still remember their eyes. Otherworldly gatekeepers. Are you worth it? Did we deserve it? Pass on that one. A question of self-belief to a certain extent. Faith in oneself manifested in resolve. Mind was taking me where body could not. Most encounters would end with having to politely inform those in my company that I had to be elsewhere and would have to get back to my body hundreds of miles out to sea. Sensing the motion of the sea movement and sound of water noise returning, fully present in the *Swirly World* space capsule again.

Food finally resurfaced as a source of interest. Funny how a flat calm surface always did that. De Amalfi were the agents for the 'Freddy Chef' and 'Harvest Foodworks' brands of freeze-dried and boil-in-the-bag meals. Not quite what you'd seek out at the supermarket weekly shop but very convenient out at sea, when the only effort required was adding boiling water. An extra 'sauce' sachet gave more taste than expected; my one-pot extravaganzas became worth looking forward to.

Our pause, 600 miles short of New Zealand, was followed by a benevolent warm northerly blowing down from tropical latitudes and freshening to allow us the pleasure of pointing the bows finally towards the Promised Land.

For three days and nights *Swirly World* ran before the wind, clocking 115-mile runs in consecutive 24-hour periods. It appeared we weren't going to be out there forever so I took the opportunity to hand steer during the day as much as possible. Breakfast at dawn (muesli and water — dull but chewable) followed by the making of a packed lunch, then goodbye inside, hello outdoor living, hand on the stainless tiller instinctively keeping sails powered up with the thrust of forward motion, the invisible wind always urging us on. Steering away the day, the sun slowly moved through the sky, subtly changing the look of the seascape with its travels up, across and down. By dark the self-steering kept us going southeast, a slightly reduced sail maintaining the appropriate balance. Keep her moving, sliding southeast, home over the horizon . . . keep moving.

Typical low dark frontal cloud descended as we crossed the shallow Wanganella Banks and the agitated current induced a confused sea state. Bigger than before, gullies of water careered about. A shoal patch to be avoided in heavy weather. A serious place where freighters could founder. Not enough wind this time. Rain brought the southerly change and with two reefs and the No.2 jib, *Swirly World* hardened up onto another tight reach, on course more or less for North Cape, southeast and unseen. Successfully dodging cold harsh rain squalls on top of impolite seas, it was back to life on an uncomfortable angle, undoubtedly down in colder latitudes. It couldn't last and didn't, the gradual improvement in weather welcomed with more sail, an even sea and increased boat speed.

The shallow low responsible for our southerly wind direction paused over the upper North Island, kindly maintaining a convenient air flow compared with the impending southeasterly forecast. No more southeasterlies please. Not another contrary forecast.

Pointing where we wanted to go, even if the horizon ahead

remained endlessly empty, was a more fulfilling way of travelling. The wind spirits agreed with me and on the wind we stayed, heeled over for another few days and nights, pointing the right way.

To get the best out of *Swirly World* and maintain concentration over long periods of time I stuck Chris Dickson, and when he got tired, Russell Coutts, down to leeward in an identical boat to *Swirly World*. Hour after hour I kept a loose cover on them, *SWI* keeping *SWII* and her furious champions pinned down to leeward. Maybe if we got Kevlar sails and changed the keel shape we'd get a bit more out of her . . .

Inner Dunedin Harbour is shaped a lot like Evans Bay. Wind blowing up or down it. Coutts stood behind me in the queue at the P Class nationals while we waited to have our centreboards measured. It was what competitive teenage males did in their weekends. Even Russell had to stand in line at the Nationals. 'I remember you.'

'I remember you too.' That's because I beat you. I beat him twice again in similar conditions in the Tauranga Cup. Sixty-something little boats behind us . . . If the wind picked up I usually ended up further back in the fleet, crossing tacks with an also-ran from Nelson or Bucklands Beach, heroically battling it out for the honour of ourselves primarily, and our sailing clubs sometimes. I didn't know that would be the pinnacle of my fleet competitiveness.

On our sixteenth day out from Scarborough the horizon renewed my interest with the Three Kings appearing ahead to starboard at dawn, just as the GPS predicted. Land ho. It looked great, all grey and permanent. A distant solid something. All day watching the shape of Great Island gradually close and change as we sailed slowly past towards the top of the North Island. After another tireless circuit of the sky the sun plunged down to silhouette Cape Reinga and Spirits Bay where it's said the released souls of Maori dead soar north. I didn't see any in the daylight but I kept looking. *Swirly World* was close in under North Cape, having tight reached at 6 knots for 12 hours, relatively secure with the proximity of land.

Being so close to New Zealand that I could see it was a pleasure. I was too pleased, and at 3 a.m. a close encounter with a steel ship got me rethinking my application to lookout duties. We saw each other. They looked close enough to disturb my sleepy startled self.

Close to the coast on the route from the rest of New Zealand to North Cape there are lots of those things motoring around. Big steel mobile islands. In 20 minutes one can come over an empty horizon and be on top of you. Out in the Tasman the chances are slight, but you never know, they might. I only saw one coming back. How many saw me?

While sleeping in the more frequented areas I enlisted the support of a strobe light designed 'for when you need to be seen', a description appropriate for on-stage performances. It ended up seeing more indoor activity than out. But there in the watery darkness it flashed with reassuring conspicuousness. Egg-timer catnaps were brief. No one's going to run us over now we're this close. Just stay awake, go on, it's fun.

Next day the wind left us to savour the primary scent, colour and contrast of land close at hand off the Cavalli Islands. Eighteen hours worth. I did a little becalmed battery charging, motoring towards a hazy, distant Cape Brett but it seemed hardly worth it at 3 uneconomical knots. Too much noise, vibration and heat. Let's wait for the wind.

There was an old Cavallis chart on board, all brown and heavily stained, more like a treasure map. When I first found it years previous, the Cavallis looked a very long way from Auckland. At that time I hadn't sailed alone past Waiheke. Having done 1100 miles to get there, the way I viewed distances had changed considerably.

An obliging northerly crept up unseen by dark and sent us on our way gurgling downwind once more. Whales off Whangarei checked us out in a big way. Lots of them at rest and play, launching thin chins and bluff profiles lackadaisically skyward. It was their gig. I'd write the review if they let me off the stage. Large smooth pools of disturbed sea water, where coy monsters had recently surfaced then sunk, all around us. We were outnumbered and outsized. While waiting for the wind we stayed surrounded. They weren't that interested in us. I couldn't say the same and I had no choice. The wind eventually allowed an escape, running flat off with the spinnaker drawing us south for the gap between Leigh and Little Barrier Island. None of them bothered to follow.

The spinnaker. Nasty little spinnaker that had humiliated me at the start of the Tasman race. I'd left it sodden and twisted into a disgusting snarly ball in its sail bag for some time after that. Now near the end of the voyage I retrieved it from exile and gave it another chance. Without an audience the kite filled out with an air of redemption. I let it off. Could it really have been my fault? Not enough practice.

Swirly World tracked past familiar landmarks and into the outer Hauraki Gulf at her maximum 6 to 7 knots, surging to 9 on the right piece of liquid slope. Moonless, the phosphorescence made its presence known in no uncertain terms and dolphins joined us as *Swirly World* surfed into the Hauraki Gulf, their phosphorescence-lit bodies looking like benign torpedoes. For 2 hours we shared the closing miles of our voyage with an entourage of streamlined naturals. Apart from them, I was the only one watching.

A 12-metre American cruising yacht identified on the Kerikeri roll call was a couple of miles east of *Swirly World* and motoring for Auckland, giving an ETA of around 3 a.m. Overhearing them on the radio, they only had a 5-knot following northerly, hence their motoring. *Swirly World* on the same piece of sea most definitely had 15 glorious knots behind her and it was obvious by the respective progress of navigation lights that we were holding our own against them.

Precarious but successful, the kite was gybed under self-steering off Flat Rock light, then we ran down against a swiftly departing spring tide to Tiri Island. There they were again, opening up from behind the Whangaparaoa Peninsula, the bright lights of Auckland's East Coast Bays. After nineteen days and nights of sailing I'd come a long way to see Auckland with a more appreciative gaze.

Onto a broad reach that tightened all the way, we were finally aiming for the lit-up Auckland City buildings suspended over the Takapuna skyline. I'd done this run many late nights before. This time we were coming in out of the darkness beyond New Zealand without having stopped since being sick in the company of Moreton Island, almost three weeks before.

Now that we had become a part of the dark, the lights of the city looked spectacular. Free from the mid-sea worries of windworld it should be a pleasure to readjust to the land. At this point in my life it was hard to feel glum in paradise.

The motoring yacht had gradually pulled ahead of us but *Swirly World* had done admirably, holding 6 to 7 knots by wind alone. At 3 a.m. on 5 November, the spinnaker came down on top of me, all over the foredeck, and we gybed off North Head to ghost up the flat harbour on the beginning of the incoming tide. The batteries went flat in the handheld VHF as I was talking to the customs representative so I was left guessing where, and if, a welcoming committee of officialdom would greet us.

Johnny Wray in the *Ngataki* had always returned to Admiralty Steps but that had been in the 1930s. I aimed there, and discovered the American had already parked up. He was conspicuous, big and seaworthy. No sign of life on deck. There was no welcoming party, no finishing gun. I rafted *Swirly World* up to the pilot boat and paused to fill in a final log entry. Three hours there, 432 back. We'd doubled the Tasman. Good morning Auckland.

At 6 a.m. with the seeping of dawn into a sky of many office buildings above the open hatchway, Customs and MAF personnel arrived, camera clicking lest their colleagues didn't believe such a tiny craft had actually come in direct from Brisbane. 'You've been living in here for how long?'

'Long enough to want to get out now.'

After swift and friendly formalities I pulled down the inside-out yellow sweatshirt that had once again doubled as the quarantine flag, then motored round to Hobson Wharf and the Rangitoto Sailing Centre. There wasn't much traffic on the Waitemata at that hour.

I intended to take David Ingram by surprise, placing *Swirly World* in beside the Soling moorings. With the sun, the wind had picked up from the north sending a sloppy little sea onto the exposed pontoons. It was a man-made leeshore of exceedingly minor proportions. My sleep-deprived mind made a lot of it and I became apprehensive about stopping. I didn't stop for another reason. No matter how grand a voyage I conjured up for *Swirly World* to have sailed, the security man on the pontoon with a walkie talkie in his hand wasn't buying any of it. 'You have to have permission to berth here.' I'd seen his grim face before. He knew me, and I knew him, sailing Solings in and out, we'd seen each other. 'You can't stay here.'

While I was being made to feel unwelcome in no uncertain way, the wind picked up and set a little sea jostling *Swirly World* against the pontoon. It was time to clear out. I didn't hold it personally against him, although I suppose I did.

We motored under the Harbour Bridge against a swiftly exiting spring tide, revving hard. 'Don't stop now little engine, can't be bothered sailing anymore, lost interest.' *Swirly World* found her way to a neglected-looking mooring, our own, all weedy and marooned without boat. Secure once more to the harbour floor it seemed like all those miles had never really happened. Had they?

Back on land, it's all over. The anticlimax after the long tour. Coming down from 'road fever', the continual movement, late-night lifestyle. Reimmersing into the normal rhythms of the day. What's the wind doing? For the moment it doesn't matter. There's some air moving out there. A tree is scribbling fluid graphic shadows over the writing paper. The sun is low and travelling the roofline of the neighbour's house. There's no view, except the well-painted weatherboards of the very comfortable zone next door. But the view doesn't matter all the time. Paradise taken for granted. I know it's out there — that sea with no walls, but you can't stay on it forever, self-funded, running the gauntlet between weather systems . . .

The hyena needs running, and swimming to expend its urban pet energies — a good excuse to frequent the edge of the land. Some evenings, tide coming or going, on the reclaimed rocks facing Watchman's Island, I give a silent moment to that liquid thing called sea. It joins up the land interludes, no doubt about that. The water neutral, the wind unpredictable, an inciter of liquid malevolence or calm surface soother — away from the land you take your chance, run the meteorological gauntlet. Never can tell. *The wind, the wind, the invisible wonderful wind . . .*

Tonight all the lights are on along the Herne Bay cliffs. Auckland windows lit up with televisions glowing, meals pending. A freshening northeasterly front gusting it down the North Shore gullies and off the Harbour Bridge to Te Atatu, the Waitakeres. Another low-pressure system on the way, barometer dropping. Some things don't change.

A few hundred miles west the Tasman heaves again with the disturbed leftovers of colliding cross swells. No moon tonight to light the black surface. It's still there, and others are out on it now, the wind their master, between the land until they make it back to the edge of somewhere. In between voyages until they are compelled to do it all over again. It's bound to happen.

Glossary of sailor-type terms

Aft: Back.

Antifouling: Paint on underwater parts of boats, which retards the growth of marine life.

Backing wind: Moves anticlockwise in the Southern Hemisphere.

Barometer: An air pressure indicator to help diagnose meteorological dangers.

Beat: To sail one's way against the wind.

Bilge keels: Little stubby protrusions on the boat's underbelly (complete with ballast) which enable her to stand upright on the sand.

Boom: The horizontal head-knocker that swings about above the deck attached to the mast and mainsail.

Bear away: Turn the boat away from the wind; to sail with the wind blowing from behind.

Bow: The front bit.

Breastwork: A place to tie up at the wharf.

Broad reaching: Sailing with the wind on the quarter.

Bulkhead: A boat wall.

Centreboard sailing: Sailing a boat that has a board (instead of a keel) that slots down to stick out underneath, reducing the sideways motion.

Coaming: A raised border round the cockpit or hatch of a yacht, to keep out water.

Cockpit: Where one sits to steer, trim sails and generally have a barley sugar-chewing time.

Companionway: Equivalent of a doorway.

Coracle: A small, round boat made of wickerwork covered with a watertight material.

Cross-sea: The result of a wind shift that leaves the old wind-driven waves to collide with the new wind-driven waves. Very unpleasant and sometimes perturbing.

Dory: A small flat-bottomed rowing boat.

Downhill sailing: Sailing with the wind coming from behind the boat.

DSB radio: Old-fashioned radio transmitter, now obsolete.

Ebbing tide: Outgoing waters.

EPIRB: Emergency Position Indicating Radio Beacon. Once activated it transmits on two frequencies, which planes, ships and satellites can use to trace the signal's source.

Fathom: 6 feet or 1.82 metres.

Fin-keeled vessel: Similar to an upside-down shark. The fin stops the boat going sideways or fatally falling over.

Flooding tide: Ingoing waters.

Flush-decked: A deck without vulnerable protrusions such as cabin roofs or glasshouses.

Forepeak locker: Place for stowage in the very front of the boat.

Genny pole: An extra stick for poking out the spinnaker sheets when on a tight reach.

Genoa: The largest of all the sails that set in front of the mast.

Ghosting in: Imperceptible progress by sail.

Grinders: Big fast winches on large racing yachts.

Halyards: Ropes that pull up the sails.

Handbearing compass: Held in the hand for quick bearings on awkwardly placed objects.

Hank on: To attach the frontsails to the frontstays via a multitude of time-consuming little clips.

Hard on the wind: Sailing to windward.

Headsail: A sail set in front of the mast.

Heavy displacement craft: A heavy boat which takes the brunt of breaking waves without flinching — unlike *Swirly World* who prefers to skip sideways.

Hove to: Shuffling over the sea with the sails backed.

Lee: The downward side of the boat.

Lee cloth: Strong cloth rigged to leeward of the bunk to stop one being hurled out and impaled on the foghorn.

Lee shore: Where the wind and waves arrive after travelling the sea — not a nice place for a small boat to be.

Lying ahull: Lurching and leaping about with all sails down, usually offshore.

Mare's-tails: Clouds that foretell an impending gale.

Port: Left.

Quarter: The corners of the boat (port quarter and starboard quarter).

Quarterberth: A bunk in the back corner of the boat.

Reach: Sailing with the breeze blowing side-on to the direction one steers.

Reefing the main: Reducing the size of the mainsail by tying a slab of it down onto the horizontal head knocker.

Rhumb line: An imaginary line on the earth's surface cutting all meridians at the same angle.

Rigging: Loose ropes that control the sailing (running rigging) and fixed wires that keep the mast in place (standard rigging).

Samson post: A sturdy short post sticking up on the bow to tie mooring lines to.

Self-steering wind vane: The breeze-sensitive mechanism which steers the boat relative to the wind direction.

Servo-tab: The underwater part of the self-steering, which corrects the course relative to the wind direction.

Sextant: The instigating instrument of celestial navigation.

Sheets: Ropes that control the sails.

Shoal: A shallow piece of sea.

Squab: My inadequate mattress.

Submerged containers: As opposed to the type that prefer to stay on the deck of cargo ships, these choose to fall off and float, waiting for the unsuspecting mariner with treacherous intent.

Sumlog: Like the speedometer in your car, tells you how fast you are going and how far you have travelled.

Sunsights: The work of a sextant.

SSB radio: Single sideband radio. A modern marine transceiver.

Stalling: The sails spill their quota of wind to the detriment of progress.

Stanchion: Stainless steel upright through which the guardrail lifelines are threaded.

Starboard: Right.

Tiller: Connected to the rudder, useful for steering.

Transom: Back of the boat.

Trysail: Tiny triangle of gale-proof fabric hoisted when the mainsail must be suspended from active service lest it sustain physical damage, or the boom has been broken.

Twin-running headsails: Two sails used especially for sailing with the wind directly behind the boat.

Veer: Wind moving north to east in the Southern Hemisphere.

Warp: A rope used for moving a vessel.

Weathercloths: Fabric around cockpit suspended from the stanchions. Gives the helmsperson more shelter.

Willie-waw: Towering sheets of spray lifted from the surface of the sea, often travelling at 50 knots plus.

Zephyrs: Disgusting little puffs of wind designed to work the sailor into a state of mouth-frothing madness.